Henry C Lockwood

The Abolition of the Presidency

Henry C Lockwood

The Abolition of the Presidency

ISBN/EAN: 9783743324770

Manufactured in Europe, USA, Canada, Australia, Japa

Cover: Foto ©ninafisch / pixelio.de

Manufactured and distributed by brebook publishing software (www.brebook.com)

Henry C Lockwood

The Abolition of the Presidency

THE ABOLITION

OF THE PRESIDENCY.

BY

HENRY C. LOCKWOOD,

OF THE NEW YORK BAR.

NEW YORK:
R. WORTHINGTON, 770 BROADWAY.
1884.

Copyright, 1884,
BY
JOHN W. LOVELL COMPANY.

TO
EVERY AMERICAN CITIZEN,
WHO BELIEVES IN A
REPRESENTATIVE GOVERNMENT,
WITH AN EXECUTIVE RESPONSIVE TO THE
WILL OF THE PEOPLE,
AND EFFECTIVE IN THE
EXECUTION OF THE LAW,
THIS WORK
IS
DEDICATED.

"Unsettled questions have no pity for the repose of nations."
JAMES A. GARFIELD.

"A patriot cannot serve his country better than to do his best to purge it of error, and to make its influence an unmixed benefit to mankind."
M. D. CONWAY.

"Your President may easily become a King."
PATRICK HENRY.

"I am fond enough of Kings, as soon as they have a canopy of stone over them."
HORACE WALPOLE.

"Under the shell there was an animal and behind the document there was a man."
TAINE.

"Under no form of government is it so dangerous to erect a political idol, as in a democratic republic, for once erected it is the political sin against the Holy Spirit to lay hands upon it."
VON HOLST.

"And I confess that I feel humiliated at the truth, which cannot be disguised, that though we live under the form of a republic, we are in fact under the rule of a single man."
Life and Letters of J. STORY.

"The evil has gone on until the Chief Magistrate has come to regard constitutional opposition to any scheme of his own in the light of a rebellion or a crime which the executive must punish. This is at present, in my opinion, our most serious national danger."
CHARLES SUMNER.

"If such a President has, in addition, large privileges in virtue of his office, he easily degenerates into what, among German Republicans, is called 'ein König im Frack'—a king in a dress coat."
KARL BLIND.

"The dragon of despotism is not slain by decapitation, for where one head, called by the name of a King, has been cut off, another, in the form of a President or First Consul, has often grown out in its place."   G. HARWOOD.

"It was called a Democracy, but it was in reality the rule of one man."   THUCYDIDES ON PERICLES.

"Si une république a toujours été dans les dissensions, je ne veux pas pour cela qu'on détruise la republique. On peut réformer ses lois."   VOLTAIRE.

PREFATORY NOTE.

The design of the author in the following pages is to suggest not only a theory of our fundamental law, but to present the historic facts which illustrate the working of our governmental system.

Whenever he has found it necessary to refer to party actions it has been done for the purpose of demonstrating in the concrete what he has asserted in the abstract.

The writer, it will be observed, has made use of the words "democratic" and "republican" interchangeably. These terms are properly applicable to a government in which the power ultimately resides in the whole people, who conduct it by a system of equal representation and delegation of powers. When, therefore, reference is made to the two great political parties, it must always be borne in mind that these terms are employed in a strictly party sense. The historical student will, doubtless, remember that up to the period of the Jackson administration, what is now known as the Democratic was then called the Republican party, while the present Republican party bears a close resemblance to the Federal, National Republican, and Whig parties of our earlier history.

As the book goes to press the writer observes that two Bills have passed the Senate, one of which provides for the counting of the Electoral Vote, the other designs to settle the question of the Presidential succession. The settlement of these and other questions, in regard to the mode of choosing the President, although deemed by the writer temporary expedients, are considered vital to the peace and prosperity of the country.

If instrumental in drawing attention to the subject matter of this book, and successful in convincing his readers of his earnest interest in the burning questions which he has discussed, the writer's object will have been accomplished.

NEW YORK: *February 1, 1884.*

CONTENTS.

CHAP.		PAGE.
I.	INTRODUCTION.	9
II.	POWERS AND DUTIES OF THE PRESIDENT.	17
III.	SYSTEM OF CHOOSING THE PRESIDENT.	23
IV.	TERM OF OFFICE.	34
V.	COMMANDER-IN-CHIEF.	44
VI.	REPRIEVES, PARDONS, AND TREATIES.	63
VII.	APPOINTMENT AND REMOVAL FROM OFFICE.	72
VIII.	VETO.	83
IX.	IMPEACHMENT.	103
X.	THE CABINET.	109
XI.	EXECUTIVE POLICY.	119
XII.	CAUCUS.	125
XIII.	REMARKS UPON THE CONSTITUTION OF THE "CONFEDERATE" STATES.	131
XIV.	THE ADMINISTRATION OF ANDREW JACKSON.	136
XV.	ADMINISTRATIONS OF VAN BUREN, TYLER, AND POLK.	148
XVI.	ADMINISTRATIONS OF TAYLOR, FILLMORE, AND BUCHANAN	155

CONTENTS.

CHAP.		PAGE
XVII.	ADMINISTRATION OF ABRAHAM LINCOLN.	162
XVIII.	ADMINISTRATION OF ANDREW JOHNSON.	181
XIX.	ADMINISTRATION OF ULYSSES S. GRANT.	188
XX.	ADMINISTRATION OF RUTHERFORD B. HAYES.	196
XXI.	ADMINISTRATION OF GARFIELD AND ARTHUR.	204
XXII.	THEORIES OF O'CONOR, LAWRENCE, SMITH, AND BARTLEY.	221
XXIII.	VIEWS OF THE FOUNDERS	234
XXIV.	SUPREME POWER UNDER THE BRITISH CONSTITUTION PRIOR TO 1688.	252
XXV.	THE PRESENT WORKING OF THE BRITISH CONSTITUTION.	262
XXVI.	REPRESENTATIVE GOVERNMENT.	279
XXVII.	CONCLUSION.	301

THE ABOLITION OF THE PRESIDENCY

CHAPTER I.

INTRODUCTION.

In the early stages of existence every man was hunter and warrior. The most powerful became the chieftain. This first ruler made his own weapons and built his own tent. The distinction between subject and ruler gradually became more pronounced. Hereditary power asserted itself. The chieftain then attended to the duties of directing only. Religion took its rise by the side of the state. The ruler was the head of the church. At this point in the development of the Science of Government he arrived at the acme of his power. He controlled the state and the church by his mere will.

At this time, too, there existed a most pernicious belief that absolute power conferred upon a good man would be the best form of government. The next question was how to devise a means of assuring such qualities in the monarch as would enable him always to act in the interest of the people. This would be impossible, for to be qualified and fit for such an undertaking, he must be all-wise, as well as all-good. He must also be all-powerful. He must be versed in the law relating to the rights of persons; the law of property, of taxation, of finance, of jurisprudence, of procedure, of evidence, of penal legislation, of commercial polity, of corporations, of the rights of capital and labor,—each of these subjects being a science of itself. It need hardly be remarked that a man with all these qualifications has never lived.

Centuries rolled on, and a highly complex system of kings, ministers, commons, lords, courts of justice, and departments was developed. The commonwealth became differentiated into the country, the town and the municipal government. The church, with its priests, colleges, monasteries, and convents grew apace. While there existed a complicated aggregation of customs and habits regulated by law, the masses had been segregated into minute divisions. Communities were classified into special workers, and different sections produced distinctive manufactures.

All these various steps undoubtedly tended to a progressive and an economical aggregation of the human race. But let no one assert that perfection in government has been reached in any system. Let us rather hold to the theory that, while many nations show a continuous growth, they have travelled the same causeway of humanity. The landmarks of the different faiths and conquests, the reformation with its individuality of thought, the commonwealth with its military power, the American and French revolutions with their new forms, were successive degrees of development in the evolution of government.

Take England from her early conquests, continental extension, the rise of the people, the development of parliament, the Great Charter, the conflict with the Italian ecclesiastics, the struggle against absolute monarchy, and the final settlement into the crowned republic, and you have an illustration of the same dominating principle.

In the course of this argument it will be our aim to show that many incongruities and imperfections exist in our system of government; that while we claim to be republican in form, we are monarchical in respect to the powers conferred upon the Senate and President. We must remedy these grave defects if we would preserve the essence and spirit of American liberty.

INTRODUCTION.

The colonies rebelled more against the unwarranted acts of the reigning King, than against his constitutional prerogatives, more against the laws specially affecting them, than against the English system, as that system should have been interpreted. "Even in August and September, 1775, that is, half a year after the battle of Lexington, so strong was the Anglo-Saxon spirit of conservatism and loyalty among the colonists, that the extremists who dared to speak of violent disruption of all bonds, entailed chastisement upon themselves and were universally censured."* "It is true, indeed, that in the beginning we aimed not at independence."† "It is an immense misfortune to the whole empire to have a king of such a description at such a time." ‡

The system of checks, and balances of the American Constitution, is an attempt to create a sovereignty without having it apparent, by the formation of three co-ordinate and co-equal powers in the same government.§ It has often occurred since our existence as a nation, that the executive has thrown down these divisions and virtually achieved his own sovereignty. And at the times he exercised these extraordinary powers, it has often been claimed that he was acting within the limitations of the law. The better opinion seems to be, as far

---

* Works of John Adams, 394; cited by Von Holst, Vol. 1, p. 2. American Archives, III., 21, 196, 644. Works of J. Adams, II., 423. Writings of John Jay, II., 420. Brownson's American Republic, 208, 209. Gibb's Administrations of Washington and J. Adams, 1, 2, 3.

† Webster's Speeches and Arguments, Boston, 1843. Vol. 1, p 85.

‡ Jefferson, by Morse, 31.

§ It should be carefully borne in mind that the President is an independent, co-ordinate department of the government. The grand theory of the Constitution makes him a co-equal in the tri-partite organization. He draws his power from the same source as the national legislature and judiciary; he is answerable to neither; his discretion is as absolute as that of any legislator, and more so than that of any judge; no other branch of the government may rightfully interfere with him in the exercise of that discretion; he can only be reached by an impeachment, when he has used his discretion not merely in a mistaken or even arbitrary manner, but in a corrupt or criminal manner.—[An Introduction to the Constitutional Law of the United States by John Norton Pomeroy, 417.]

as the fundamental law is concerned, that the executive power is in organized conflict with the other two branches, and the surprise of many has been that the people have been able to work this bad polity as well as they have done.

There has always existed a class of men in this country who have believed that a general government and state governments exist within the same territorial limit, and are endowed with separate and distinct powers of sovereignty; that the separate states are like foreign governments, independent of each other and of the general government. They speak on all occasions against what they term centralization of power in Congress, and deny the right to perfect the Nation. They look with distrust upon any powers exercised by Congress although it is the only central representative body that exists, barring always the abnormity of the organization of the Senate. This class of men when in power, or expectation of power, have nothing to say against the monarchical powers of the President. * The reason is that they would rather enter upon a presidential campaign with the hope of controlling the result, with its immense patronage, by means of the skilful manipulation of these so-called state sovereignties, than appeal even indirectly to the voice of the people. But what are the extraordinary powers of the President against which these people speak no word of condemnation? It is the object of this essay to awaken the solicitude of thinking men concerning this great question. On examination it will be found that in defining the powers of the Executive many of the ancient prerogatives of the King were incorporated into the Constitution. Many of our prominent men desired to adopt the English Constitu-

---

* In these days when superstitious horror of what is regularly termed centralization, has to a large extent blinded public men to the fact that the good or the evil of it chiefly depends upon the kind of centre in which power is organized, it seems to me sufficient attention has not been given to the illustration of the danger of extreme decentralization, to a republic, furnished by the history of the United States.—[Republican **Superstitions**, by M. D. Conway, 10.]

tion as a whole. If tradition is correct, it remained with Washington to say whether it should be taken as our form of government. "Jay did not wish to have a king, while other expedients remained untried, and the Ministry of England harbored the thought of a constitutional monarchy with a son of George III. as king, and they were not without alarm lest gratitude to France should place on an American throne a prince of the house of Bourbon."* The people thought that, the office of president was created for Washington. This fact is fully deducible from the language of Adams, who said that "The establishment of justice in the intercourse between the nation and foreign powers was thus pre-eminently committed to the custody of one man, but that man was George Washinton," † In any event we borrowed boldly and bodily from the ancient powers of European kings; and to-day Congress may pass laws, but the President commands. Members of Congress are compelled to go to the President to procure appointments for their friends, and when they go out of office for appointments for themselves. During the recess of Congress, the inmate of the White House has little to restrain him from the performance of any unconstitutional act. If Mr. Lincoln had been ambitious, he could have easily made himself Dictator. "One of the greatest objections to the office, as now constituted, is, that it presents too great a prize to the ambition of an individual; that it is utterly removed, as was the imperial power of the Napoleons, from the entire people, without anything to fill the space between the sovereign and the citizens at large."‡ Mr. Lincoln was repeatedly requested to assume such powers, but he had the utmost respect for Congress, and if he had lived a few weeks longer, he would have convened that body to decide the great questions

---

* Sparks, IX., 510. Adams, VIII., 420.
† Cited by William B. Lawrence, *North American Review*, Nov. 1880
‡ Ibid.

then before the country. His death brought his opposite into power. An extraordinary crisis demanded the convening of Congress, but President Johnson defiantly assumed the responsibility of settling all questions himself. His audacity overawed the people—they were paralyzed.

The cry, "to the victors belong the spoils," had already been heard at the presidential mansion above the clanking of the spurs of a military president. More than once in our political history have the American people been forced to the consideration of the words of Mr. Williamson, spoken in the Convention which gave us the Constitution: "Another objection," he said, "to a single magistrate is, that he will be an elective king, and will feel the spirit of one. He will spare no pains to keep himself in for life, and will then lay a train for the succession of his children." It was pretty certain, he thought, that we should at some time or other have a king; but he wished no precaution omitted that might postpone the event as long as possible.*

Taking the warnings of the past into consideration, let the present generation omit no precaution to guard against a form of government which may place a king at its head. And, if on investigation of our system, we find all the tendencies to such a consummation, and conclude that the presidential form is not the correct one, then let us abolish it. Even in the England of to-day, the real use of the Queen seems to be that of a figurehead. The reasoning is that the mass of mankind can understand that they are governed by a monarch, but would fail to comprehend the complex machinery which actually rules them. Any one may understand the action of a single will, but few can the workings of a Constitution. The idea of a government by a queen is simple, but the rules by which she governs may be almost incomprehensible. So it occurs

* "Mason said Sept., 1787, that the Government, as established by the Constitution, will surely end either in monarchy or a tyrannical aristocracy." Gilpin, 1594., Elliot, 359, 552, 553.

that a constitutional monarchy is now upheld because it is fitted to all minds—the ignorant have the central figure to look up to, and the intelligent the complex laws of the nation to investigate. These laws are ever changing and new issues forming, new forces working. Such arguments may be very plausible for those who wish to apologize for that system, but they have little application to a truly representative government, where the people are supposed to have outgrown the almost primitive idea of being governed by a ruler—a king, or even a president.

Notwithstanding the English support the principle of a crowned head, by numerous plausible arguments, still in many other respects, and in the actual working of their plan, it is claimed that they are more representative than we. They are abandoning many effete ideas to which we, in America, are giving unqualified adherence.

It is thought that no one can read the Federalist, without coming to the conclusion that the framers intended to found, form, and establish a government with a strong executive at its head; * and that the reader of the historic pages of later times will perceive, that while the presidential powers have been increased, † the prerogatives of the king have nearly all been stricken from the law, in the uninterrupted march of England towards a Republic.

General Hamilton argues in favor of the unity of his model Executive, whose proceedings were to be characterized by " decision, activity, secrecy, and despatch." For the purposes of illustration, he goes to the history of the Consuls of Rome. He enlarges upon the dissensions which arose between them. There seems to be, at least, an inference that he believed there

---

* Mason and the Pinckneys desired that the Executive should have a qualification of landed property. Gilpin 1211-1213.

† " We have now at last seen the Legislature of a State thanking the President in the name of its people for appointing one of its citizens to a place in his Cabinet." David Dudley Field in *North American Review*, May, 1881.

was a similarity between the powers of the President and these Consuls. The fact is, that these Consuls were kings, robed in royal purple, attended by body guards, and preceded by lictors. At first, they were chosen by the patrician families, but at last the plebeians had the right to elect one. Is it any wonder that conflicts should have grown up between these two classes? The Consular Government was simply an attempt to place the sovereign power in two persons, both reigning at the same time. Corruption, intrigue, and dissension were certain to attend it.

If General Hamilton believed that our Government should be an absolute monarchy, then we agree with him that it would be better to have all authority centred in one single will. Thus would the sovereign power be distinct and pronounced. One king could be found and held responsible by the people, who could at least, by their right of revolution, strike him down; while if there were two kings, the people might be arrayed against each other in the interest of the contending potentates. Let us ask ourselves how history may aid us in the establishment of a representative government. The Government of Rome never was a Republic. Have we one in America?

In the Declaration of Independence may be found the following words: "All experience hath shown that mankind are more disposed to suffer, while evils are sufferable, than to right themselves by abolishing the forms to which they are accustomed." The evils of the presidential system are already widely acknowledged to have within them the potency of danger to the public weal, and it seems to us that the time has arrived for the people to act directly and bravely, and by intelligent, sustained, and peaceful opposition, put an end to this department of our Government.

CHAPTER II.

POWERS AND DUTIES OF THE PRESIDENT.

The executive power of the United States is vested in a President who is elected for the term of four years. Before entering on the execution of his office, he takes the following oath or affirmation :

"I do solemnly swear (or affirm), that I will faithfully execute the office of President of the United States, and will, to the best of my ability, preserve, protect, and defend the Constitution of the United States."

It is desired particularly to draw attention to a very ominous omission. There is nothing direct and specific which makes it the duty of the President, that he shall execute the laws of congress. His conscience is not bound so far as the obligation of an oath may go to do the will of congress. Nor is the defect remedied by the subsequent section of the Constitution which provides that the President shall take care, that the laws be faithfully executed, for this is an obligation standing outside of the oath, and leaves the matter of executing the law too much to the discretion of the executive. If the framers believed that an oath was efficacious in binding the conscience of the chief officer of the government, then they should have inserted in it the requirement that he execute the laws of congress—what they did do was to require the President faithfully to execute the office of president.

The oath of office of the president is in strange contrast with the coronation oath of the King of England, which is "that he will govern his kingdom according to the statutes in parliament agreed on, and the laws and customs of the same." It is an interesting fact to note, that so long ago as the time when Henry III. was trampling on the Magna Charta, Henry Bracton claimed that the King should rule his people according to the laws, as they were the birthright of the people. During the reign of the Henrys there may have been some palliation for the tyranny they exercised, for the law controlling the executive had not then been well settled and defined, but the usurpations of George III. in the face of the struggles against monarchy in the civil war were simply unjustifiable and wrong.

It can hardly be disputed that the framers intended to vest extraordinary powers in the President, and to make him the actual depositary of executive power, independent to a great extent of the will of congress. The executive was to be a co-ordinate power, acting within his own sphere. He was not to be regarded in any way the creature of congress. His duties and powers were to be defined, and in their exercise he was to be supreme.*

The following are the powers particularly conferred: the

---

*" As the President is an independent, co-ordinate branch of the government and as the Constitution contains some express affirmative grants of power to him alone, there are and must be certain attributes and functions which have no connection with proper legislation; which are completely conferred by the terms of the organic law; which do not depend upon any prior statutes for the opportunities or occasions for their exercise, nor for their number and scope: which would still exist and might still be carried into operation, if congress should blot out all its laws, or should attempt to restrain and limit the President, in his official proceedings, from calling them into action." * * * * * " In respect to the executive powers which fall within this class, the President is clothed with an absolute, unlimited discretion. The acts done by virtue of these powers are completely political. The subjects themselves, over which the power extend, do not fall within the province of congressional legislation; and that body cannot by any laws enlarge or diminish the President's capacity; it can do nothing more than pass such laws, if it thinks proper, as shall aid the Chief Magistrate in the execution of these powers, nor may the Courts interfere and assume to regulate the President's conduct." An Introduction to the Constitutional law of the United States by John Norton Pomeroy 420, 421.

President shall be the commander-in-chief of the army and navy of the United States, and of the militia of the several states, when called into the service of the United States. He may require the opinion, in writing, of the principal officer in each of the executive departments, upon any subject relating to the duties of their respective offices; he shall have power to grant reprieves, and pardons for offences against the United States, except in cases of impeachment; he shall have power by and with the advice and consent of the senate to make treaties, provided two-thirds of the senators present concur; he shall nominate, and by and with the advice and consent of the senate, shall appoint ambassadors, other public ministers, consuls, judges of the Supreme Court, and all other officers of the United States, whose appointments are not therein otherwise provided for, and which shall be established by law; he shall have power to fill all vacancies that may happen during the recess of the senate, by granting commissions which shall expire at the end of their next session: he may on extraordinary occasions, convene both Houses, or either of them, and in case of disagreement between them, with respect to the time of adjournment, he may adjourn them to such time as he shall think proper: he shall receive ambassadors and other public ministers, and shall commission all the officers of the United States.

"Under the implied powers which the President of the United States has received by general investiture of power as the chief executive officer of the United States, may be enumerated the following:

As Commander-in-Chief of the army and navy of the United States, he has power to engage in hostilities, to institute a blockade, and to authorize captures and condemnations on the high seas. He has power to recognize a state government, in so far as to recognize whether the government organized in a state, is the duly constituted government of that state. He has power to protect aliens, as the care of our foreign relations is committed to him; to remit forfeitures under his pardoning powers; to order a *nolle prosequi* to be entered at any stage in a criminal proceeding in the name of the United States; to order a new trial on the sentence of a Court Martial, and in time of war to suspend the writ of *habeas corpus* in any district where for the time being the civil authorities are powerless. He is authorized by the Constitution to appoint heads of departments in his official household * * * * this official household constitutes the cabinet."*

All these various powers belong to the monarch, not to the executive officer of a representative government, who should merely execute the will of the people, as manifested by the laws of the legislature †—these belong to the "one man power," of which we have heard so much.

* The Constitution of the United States, by Simon Sterne, 83.

† Upshur, in his work on "The Nature and character of our Federal Government," says: "The most defective part of the Federal Constitution, beyond all question is that which relates to the executive department. It is impossible to read that instrument without being forcibly struck with the loose and unguarded terms in which the powers and duties of the President are pointed out. So far as the Legislature is concerned, the limitations of the Constitution are, perhaps, as precise and strict as they could safely have been made; but, in regard to the executive, the convention appear to have studiously selected such loose and general expressions as would enable the President, by implication and construction, either to neglect his duties, or to enlarge his powers. We have heard it gravely asserted in congress, that whatever power is neither legislative nor judiciary, is of course executive, and as such belongs to the President under the Constitution! Be this as it may, it is a reproach to the Constitution that the executive trust is so ill defined as to leave any plausible pretense, even to the insane zeal of party devotion, for attributing to the President of the United States the powers of a despot, powers which are wholly unknown in any limited monarchy in the world." John Quincy Adams, in his discourse on "The Jubilee of the Constitution," says: "It has perhaps never been duly remarked that, under the Constitution of the United States, the powers of the executive department, explicitly and emphatically concentrated in one person, are vastly more extensive and complicated than those of the legislative. The language of the instrument in conferring legislative authority is, "All legislative powers herein granted shall be vested in a Congress of the United States, which shall consist of a Senate and

If the framers had not had in their mind as a model the ancient British constitution, they would not have given these kingly prerogatives to any one person, even if he had the honor of being selected through that wonderfully complicated piece of machinery, (which embraces so many compromises of republicanism with monarchy) known as the Electoral college. It may be urged that these very compromises made the American union possible. Admit that this is true, and still these very compromises have always stood in the way of liberty in this country. They have constituted the great barrier to progress and advancement. They have been an incubus upon the dream of representative government. Many of them have been swept from the Constitution by the last amendments. They, together with the declaration contained in the preamble to the Constitution, which provides that the people have established the government, form larger guarantees for liberty than all the rest of the fundamental law.

At different periods in the history of this country, the President has been rightfully charged with unlawful assumptions of power to such a degree as to impress the minds of the people with the danger of impending tyranny. Constitutional expounders have excused those acts in long and learned dissertations upon the powers of the executive, holding that some of them are potential, and others mandatory. Endless distinctions have been raised as to which are powers and which are duties. They are all strictly technical arguments, enveloping and obscuring the rights of the people in the mists and shadows of metaphysics, which, when dispelled exhibit plainly to our view the stubborn fact that the Constitution has established not only an elective monarch, but "the most delicate and the most artificial political system ever devised by man."*

House of Representatives." But the executive authority is committed in unreserved terms. "The executive power shall be vested in a President of the United States of America.'"—[Cited by William Beach Lawrence, in North American Review, Nov. 1880.]

* Tibbits' Reform in Federal Executive, 10.

Nearly every important word found in the fundamental law expresses some abstract idea upon which is reared a fabric of political casuistry. The luminous minds that gave us our government were bent upon the formation of political dogmas. These postulates not only attempted to determine what the condition of man should have been from his creation, but to prescribe his course of conduct for all time to come. They were the articles of faith in which we were to believe, or be politically lost. If those most respectable and conservative persons had been able to forecast the inferences which have been drawn from premises so solemnly laid down, and to anticipate the disputes which have taken place over their doctrines, they would have been filled " with horror and dismay."

"It was nearly impossible," says Mr. G. T. Curtis, "for many Englishmen to understand the legal and constitutional theory which gave the Federal Government a moral and constitutional right to resist the secession of States from the Union." And Mr. Hurd, in his Theory of our National Existence, speaking of the multiplicity of constructions which has been placed upon every clause of the law, says: "Such statements," referring to Curtis, "of our position might suggest to foreigners the inquiry, if the Americans themselves could not know until they had fought it out, what their own Constitution was; was it not expecting a good deal to demand of strangers, in 1861, that they should understand it in advance." *

Thus the American people are led into the tortuous paths of discussion as to the effect and meaning of the words, "shall, will, and may," occurring in the text of the Constitutional provisions which confer these extraordinary powers upon the President. The question to which they should direct their efforts is, how to reform the whole system which tolerates the continuance of such an anomaly as an elective king in a republic.

* Hurd, 299.

CHAPTER III.

SYSTEM OF CHOOSING THE PRESIDENT.

The low mutterings of Civil War, which threatened this country during the unhappy presidential contest in 1876, have died away. The uncertainties of presidential succession of 1881, have been temporarily settled. In 1884, we shall attempt to elect another President. The constitutional powers and duties of the President are the same. The law of the machinery of election is the same. As far as the human mind can divine, the next contest will be as acrimonious and revolutionary as those which have preceded it. The Democrats still speak of the decision of the Electoral Commission as an outrage and a wrong. They assume they were defrauded of their right to seat Mr. Tilden in the Presidential chair.

From the writers of the Federalist, down through successive administrations of the National Government, to the present day, the press, the writers on constitutional law, and the judiciary, have all discussed the mode of the election of the President. Although a century has shed its bright light upon the subject, the question of the proper system is still unsettled and unsolved. Party zeal, engendered by the continuous contest for monarchical power, has infused into the discussion an element not calculated to effect a clear judicial solution of the problem. It remains true that one of the greatest defects in our system is the mode of choosing the President, although no provision of the Constitution received a more thorough examination and debate. Guided by historic facts, the framers saw that the choosing of the Executive was the weakest point in the proposed Republic. All plans which the imagination could suggest were projected. In the first scheme submitted to the Convention, by Edmund Randolph, the electoral system had no place; but it suggested that a National Executive be instituted, to be chosen by the National Legislature for a term of years. James Wilson declared in favor of an election by the people; Roger Sherman was for the appointment of the President by the Legislature, that he should be absolutely dependant on that body, as it should be their will that was to be executed. Mr Wilson then submitted the first proposition for an electoral system (*). Mr. Gerry thought the people ought not to act directly, even in the choice of electors. Mr. Williamson urged that the electors chosen as proposed would bear the same relation to the people that the State Legislatures did. Mr. Wilson's proposition was then voted upon and lost. It was then agreed that the Executive should be elected by the National Legislature, for the term of seven years. This action was reconsidered. Mr. Gerry moved that he should be elected by the Executives of the States. Mr. Randolph opposed Mr. Gerry's mode of selecting the President, and it was defeated. Alexander Hamilton advocated the election of the Executive for life; the election to be made by electors chosen by the people in electoral districts. Again, a committee reported that he should be chosen by the National Legislature. Gouverneur Morris thought he should be elected by the people at large. The question again recurred on the election by the people, and was lost; the words, "To be chosen by the National Legislature," being inserted; the motion was again carried. The next day this was reconsidered, and it was agreed that he should be chosen "by electors appointed by

---

* To the electoral system Caleb Strong, of Massachusetts, made this objection: "A new set of men, like the electors, will make the Government too complex."

the Legislatures of the States." This was reconsidered. Once more it was agreed that the Congress should elect, and once more reconsidered. Then Mr. Wilson moved that the Executive be chosen by lot from Congress. Mr. King said we should be controlled by reason, not by chance. Mr. Gerry then moved, that the Executive be "appointed by the Governors and residents of the States, with the advice of the Councils." Mr. Madison spoke in favor of electors chosen by the people. He said, "As the electors would be chosen for the occasion, would meet at once, and proceed immediately to an appointment, there would be very little opportunity for cabal or corruption." After many other propositions and long discussions, Mr. Brearly, of New Jersey, reported the present electoral system, which was carried in the stead of the mode so often adopted by the Convention for electing the Executive by Congress.

The Constitution, as amended, provides that each State shall appoint a number of electors, "equal to the whole number of senators and representatives to which the State may be entitled in the Congress."* It will be perceived that, in addition to the representatives, who are apportioned according to population, each State shall be entitled to two members in each Electoral College. In other words, the great State of New York has the same representation based upon the Senate, as the State of Delaware, and the objectionable features of the Senate are embodied in the system of electing the President. The people are not equally represented in the choice of the President. As the electoral colleges do not represent the people, it follows the President does not. The electors meet in their respective States, sign, certify, and transmit, sealed, the lists of all persons voted for, to the seat of the Government; the person having the greatest number of votes for president, shall be president, if such number be a majority of the whole number of electors appointed; if no

* Art. II., Sec. 2. Cons.

person have such majority, then from the persons having the highest numbers, not exceeding three, the House of Representatives shall chose by ballot the President—the votes to be taken by States, each State having one vote, irrespective of its population. If the Vice-President does not receive a majority of the electoral votes, then from the two highest numbers on the list, the Senate shall choose the Vice-President. Under these conditions, the States in the House and Senate have the naming of the President and Vice-President, and the people are virtually disfranchised.* General Hamilton says, in the sixty-seventh number of the Federalist, that the mode of appointment of the Chief Magistrate of the United States is almost the only part of the system, of any consequence, which has escaped without censure, or which has received the slightest mark of approbation from its opponents. He says that it was desirable "that the immediate election should be made by men most capable of analyzing the qualities adapted to the station, and acting under circumstances favorable to deliberation, and to a judicious combination of all the reasons and inducements which were proper to govern their choice. A small number of persons, selected by their fellow-citizens from the general mass, will be most likely to possess the information and discernment requisite to such complicated investigations.†" This is certainly a rose-colored view of the anticipated working of the plan, but what are the historic facts? Those who had devised this complicated piece of machinery, had only to wait until 1800, to find that it was defective and out of joint. It was then that one of the most dramatic incidents in our history took place in the undecided Presidential election of that year. In the following February the electoral votes were counted and found to be, for Jefferson 73, Burr 73, for Adams 65, for Pinckney 64, and for Jay 1. No name was highest, therefore there was no

* Article XII., Amendment Constitution.
† Gilpin, 767-787; Elliott, 143-154.

choice; the equality of votes cast the election into the House of Representatives, which was restricted to a choice between two Republicans. The Republicans could not control the choice, while the Federalists could prevent any election. The balloting disclosed eight States for Jefferson, six for Burr, and two were without votes because of equal division among their numbers. There was no election. Six days were consumed without result, and the Federalists threatened to prolong the balloting until the 4th of March, for the avowed purpose of making Chief Justice Jay provisional President. Widespread anxiety was manifested throughout the land. Party spirit ran high. The position of the "high-flying Federalists" was prompted by embittered vindictiveness. They were bent upon naming a President by what they called simply a "stretch of the Constitution." They preferred anarchy to Jefferson. December 31, 1880, Jefferson wrote: "We do not see what is to be the end of the present difficulty. The Federalists propose to prevent an election in Congress and transfer the Government by Act to the Chief Justice, or Secretary of State, or to let it devolve on the Secretary *pro tem.* of the Senate till next December. The Republicans propose to press forward to an election. If they fail in this, a concert between the two higher candidates may prevent the dissolution of the Government and danger of anarchy, by an operation bungling indeed and imperfect, but better than letting the Legislature take the nomination of the Executive entirely from the people."* Jefferson said that the non-election of a President would have placed the Government in the situation of a "clock or watch run down." The truth is, that the Republicans "would hardly have succeeded in such an extra-constitutional process of national watch-winding in the teeth of the daring and vindictive men who led the powerful Federal minority." Jefferson wrote: "But we thought it best to de-

---

* Jefferson by Morse, 201

clare openly and firmly, once for all, that the day such an Act passed (transferring the Government to Jay), the Middle States would arm, and that no such usurpation, even for a single day, should be submitted to." At last the strange paradox occurred, by which Hamilton used his influence to make Thomas Jefferson President of the United States. Upon the seventh day of the balloting the Federalist representative from Vermont, absented himself; the two Federalists from Maryland put in blank ballots, and thus ten States, a sufficient number, voted for Jefferson for President. This brief recital demonstrates how soon the people of the United States found the most important part of the machinery of the Government "watch" both defective and out of repair. Civil war and chaos were threatened as the result of this law from its inception, and the vision of internecine strife resulting therefrom has never been absent from the American people. Astonishing as it may appear, no successful effort to repair the "watch" has ever been made, and we are to-day in the same position with a Presidential election coming on, with a good prospect of seeing the Constitution once more put to the same strain to which it has so often been subjected.

When the opponents to the Constitution gave their assent to the system of choosing the President, it is fair to suppose that they believed the selected persons would be more likely to possess the discernment requisite to a wise choice, and that they would analyze the qualities of the person receiving their appointment. It is equally fair to presume that if they had thought the persons to be selected would become the blind and unreasoning agents of party conventions, that they would have withheld their approbation. For it is a well-known fact that, since the establishment of the national caucus, the electors afterwards chosen by the States, are mere registering machines to cast the party votes for the choice of the Convention. We believe that no elector ever acted independently in his choice for the President of the United States.

If, for example, they could have looked into the future and beheld that insensate struggle of 1876, called a Presidential election, would not these same opponents have, beyond all peradventure, visited their severest censure upon this very provision of the Constitution? Whatever may be the merits of the plan, it has signally failed.* It is certainly instructive to compare the actual workings referred to, with the almost Utopian ideas of General Hamilton. He says: "As the electors chosen in each State are to assemble and vote in the State in which they are chosen, this detached and divided situation will expose them much less to heats and ferments, which might be communicated from them to the people, than if they were all to be convened at one time, in one place. Nothing was more to be desired than that every practicable obstacle should be opposed to cabal, intrigue and corruption. * * * * Thus, without corrupting the body of the people, the immediate agents in the election will, at least, enter upon the task free from any sinister bias." He then speaks of the duties of these electors, and of the law which requires them to vote for a fit person for President.

This confidence in the perfection of the system is expressed in the following words: "The process of election affords a moral certainty that, the office of President will never fall to the lot of any man who is not in an eminent degree endowed with the requisite qualifications."

The framers were the wisest of their day and generation, but still they were but human, and liable to err. It remained for us of this later day, to contemplate the great weakness and imperfection of this portion of our fundamental law. Even if the Presidential system were correct in other respects, the machinery by which he is chosen, if not already broken down, is so rickety and out of joint, that a complete collapse is to

---

*Tibbits' Reform in Federal Executive, 14.

be anticipated whenever it is put in motion.* It is a remarkable fact that, the Federal Convention voted three times to elect the President by both Houses of Congress, once by the State Legislatures, and finally by the electors. The proposition to elect by direct vote of the people found little favor. The undoubted purpose was to remove the election as far from the people as possible, and to create a select body of men to deliberate and choose the President.† We all know that the whole system has failed. We now have a medium for the States to express themselves through. The largest States have the decision of the momentous question. They hold the balance of power. Although there seems to be no one foolhardy enough to defend this electoral system, still there is the same difficulty of agreeing upon a substitute as existed in the Convention which framed the Constitution. If, for the sake of the argument, we admit that the government of an elective king is the proper one, yet if it be proven that no effective mode can be devised for his election, we submit that the latter fact is, of itself, a substantial reason why the office should be abolished. Should the sword of civil war be forever suspended over the head of the nation? Devise any law we may for the election of President, so long as he has his present monarchical power, the country will stand in imminent peril of civil war.‡ If it were more generally un-

* Mr. George Mason, in the Virginia debates, in unmeasured terms, denounced the mode of electing a President as "a mere deception—an *ignis fatuus* on the American people, thrown out to make the people believe they were to elect him."

† "As a matter of historical curiosity, I would direct attention to the circuitous ways and multiplied elections by which it was frequently attempted in the middle ages to insure an impartial or pure election. The master of the Knights of Malta was elected by no less than seventeen consecutive elections of electors, each election connected with oaths; and the Doge of Venice was elected by nine different acts, namely, five elections alternating with four acts of drawing lots, with the addition of collateral votings.—Vertal Hist. of Malta, cited by Lieber on Civil Government, 178.

‡ This makes the election enlist all the feelings, excite all the passions, and involve all the dangers usually accompanying the choice of an elective king;

derstood that the electoral colleges do not ensure the election of the President, either by the choice of the people, or, strange to say, by a majority of States, we think that the present system would not be so strenuously adhered to. The united vote of the Democratic candidates in 1860, was 2,787,780, while Mr. Lincoln's was only 1,857,660. Mr. Lincoln had one hundred and eighty electoral votes, while the total Democratic vote was but one hundred and twenty-three.* After the day of election had passed in 1876, the country realized that duplicate sets of returns would be forwarded by contending colleges. It was apparent that we were not far distant from a condition of strife and anarchy. The law did not provide any escape. The temporary measure of the Commission was created, and its decisions were promulgated, as has been described, to avert a civil war, likely to arise from the present system of electing the President. The plans which have been submitted since the inauguration of President Hayes, have been very numerous, too numerous to be mentioned here. Senator Edmunds introduced a bill to regulate the count of the votes for President and Vice-President;

two parties divide the nation, who not only contend over the policy that shall govern the state, but over the personal advantages and disadvantages that the result involves; every ambitious man sees his personal interest involved in the struggle and every unscrupulous man who is also ambitious feels the temptation to employ unfair means to accomplish the desired result when honest means are inadequate. And unfortunately the machinery of elections with the possibility of perverting it, for defeating the will of the people, is largely in the hands of those who are deeply interested in the result." [Method of Electing the President, by Thomas W. Cooley, International Review, June, 1878.]

* Thus, suppose Ohio, Virginia and Maryland, have between them to select A or B to be President and cast votes as follows :—

   Ohio, A, 250,001.   B, 250,000.
   Virginia, A, 240,000.   B, 230,000.
   Maryland, A, 220,000.   B, 250,000.

B has a majority of 19,999 and is defeated. Ohio and Virginia have returned A's electors. As a matter of fact there have been several minority Presidents in the history of the United States."—[Republican Superstitions, M. D. Conway, 16, 17.]

which proposed, among other things, that each State may provide by law for the appointment of electors, and for the trial and determination of any controversy concerning their appointment, before the time fixed for their meeting. Mr. Bayard, of Delaware, was among the three Democrats who supported the bill. He said there was an urgent need that the question should be settled; that the present time was propitious; the nation needed peace and rest; that the bill would restore confidence to the public mind; it met his approval because it reaffirmed, in clear and explicit terms, the power of the State over the subject of appointing electors; that it wiped out all pretext of Federal supervision over the selection of electors, and confided everything to the State itself; that the State had the sole power to execute that act, and the voice of the State should be conclusive. This is substantially the position taken by him. If anything was necessary to condemn the whole measure, this praise bestowed upon it by the Senator is all sufficient. The bill, in the first place, is clearly unconstitutional; in the second place, it is absolutely wrong to place such power in the State organizations. The enigma is that the Democrats, who are so much in love with their theories of State sovereignty, did not support it. "The importance of timely legislation, with respect to the ascertainment and declaration of the vote for President electors, was sharply called to the attention of the people more than four years ago. It is to be hoped that some well defined measure may be devised before another National election, which will render unnecessary a resort to any expedient of a temporary character for the determination of questions upon contested returns."* The only explanation of this paradox, of the Democrats refusing to support the Edmunds Bill, which we can make, is this: The Presidency, with its monarchical power, is the great prize in the coming desperate struggle. The Democratic politicians know that they have greater chances

* Message of Chester A. Arthur, December 6, 1881.

of success if the whole question be left open. They wish to be governed by the circumstances which may surround the count. They do not desire to be circumscribed by law. Justice will play an unimportant role in this great drama. Whatever misgivings we may have, it is to be hoped that the curtain will be rung down upon a tableau of liberty and peace.

CHAPTER IV.

TERM OF OFFICE.

UNDER the system of absolute monarchy, the king once enthroned, becomes the Government for a definite period—at least, as definite as the life of the incumbent. His will is law as long as he reigns. He may ride roughshod over the liberties of the people. He may involve the nation in war on a mere fancy, or unsheath the sword to revenge an insult to a courtesan. He may oppress his people by taxation. In fine, he may be a tyrant; still nothing short of revolution can remove him. There is no lawful and peaceful remedy to depose him. Anomalous as it may seem, we in America have adopted the fixed period to the extent of four years. This applies to the President and Vice-President. They may both prove to be tyrants or imbeciles, good or bad. There they are, inflexible and unyielding. "What," inquired Gunning Bedford, of Delaware, "will be the situation of the country should the first magistrate elected for seven years be discovered immediately on trial to be incompetent."[*] They may use the vast power against the very people who placed them in office. They may form combinations against Congress. They may organize many conflicts with the legislative branch. Antagonism and conflict may follow, but the four years must elapse before a change can be had. General Hamilton, in the Federalist, not only discloses that he was in

[*] Gilpin, 767. Elliot, 143.

favor of a strong Executive, but of his long duration in office.*
He thought that a short period would destroy his personal
firmness in the execution of his constitutional powers; that
his fortitude would be debased. This learned gentleman
acknowledged that the Constitution did not intend a pure
Republic, but provided for a mixed and complicated one, of
what he terms federal and national powers. He naturally
promulgates the doctrine that subserviency to the people was
not desirable in the Executive. He thinks that the President
should be independent of the people. The stubbornness of
King George does not seem to have furnished a warning for
that class of thinkers, who insisted upon closing their eyes to
the many reforms which had occurred, and were then taking
place in England, and upon clothing our President with the
ancient prerogatives of the king. The President, they insisted,
must be surrounded, if at all, with an irresponsible body of
advisers, like those of the Privy Council. He must be installed
in office for a fixed period. It was said the President would
lose interest in his position, if the period of his office was not
long, and his independence would be seriously affected.
When we remember the lively interest Presidents take in the
office from the day of their election, even forbidding the incumbent from acting after that date, this remark seems rather
amusing.

General Hamilton submitted a plan to the Federal Con-

* There was a great diversity of opinion in the Convention as to the period;
and different terms of service were proposed. "From ten to twelve," said Williamson, Elliot, 366 "Fifteen," said Gerry; and King facetiously proposed,
"twenty years, the medium life of princes," Elliot, 360. Mason replied: "An
Executive during good behavior is only a softer name for an Executive for life ;
the next easy step will be to hereditary monarchy. Should the motion succeed,
I may myself live to see such a revolution." Elliott, 326. After explanations
by McClurg, four States, New Jersey, Pennsylvania, Delaware and Virginia,
Madison voting with McClurg, expressed their preference for the term of good
behavior to the tenure of seven years, with perpetual re-eligibility by the National
Legislature.—[Bancroft's History of the Formation of the United States.] Gilpin, 1129. Elliott, 327.

vention, which provided that the supreme executive authority of the United States **be vested in** a Governor, to be elected to serve during good behavior. He said: "And let me observe that an executive **is** less dangerous to the liberties of the people, when in office during **life** than for seven years." Mr. Luther Martin said, in his letter on the Federal Convention, that there was a party which attempted to have the President appointed during good behavior, without limitation of time. When we bear in mind that this same elective king was to have the same powers which the President now possesses, it is not a little remarkable that there ever existed a party among the framers that was in favor of going so far in the direction **of absolutism.** It is certainly food for reflection. Mr. Bedford, in the Federal Convention, begged the Committee to consider what the situation of the country would be, in case the first magistrate **should** be saddled on it for such a period, (seven years was then under discussion), and it should be found on trial **that he** did **not** possess the qualifications ascribed to him.

Mr. Gladstone, in comparing **the two** systems, uses this language: "Do not they in England part with their power and **make it** over to the House of Commons, as completely as **the American** people **part** with it **to the** President? They give it over for four years, we for a **period** which on the average is somewhat more; they to resume it at a fixed time; **we, on an unfixed contingency,** and **at a** time which will finally be determined, **not** according **to** the popular will, but according to the views which a ministry may entertain of its duty or convenience. **All** this **is true,** but it is not the whole truth. * * * * * But mediately, though not immediately, they gain the end, for they **can work** upon that which works upon the Ministry, namely, the House of Commons. Firstly, they **have not** renounced, like the American people, the exercise of their **power for** a given time; and they are at all times free by **speech, petition,** public meetings, to en-

deavor to get it back in full by bringing about a dissolution.
* * * * * So we may say, then, that in the American Union the Federal Executive is independent for each four years, both of the Congress and of the people. But the British Ministry is largely dependent on the people, whenever the people firmly will it; and is always dependent on the House of Commons, except when it can safely and effectually appeal to the people."

These words of the English statesman show how much more republican the British Constitution is, under the present workings of its actual executive branch, than ours,* how much nearer the Ministry are to the people than our executive, how elastic is their law, how unyielding ours. Our Vice-Presidents, (who are presumed to be less capable men than our Presidents), on their accession to the Presidency have generally opposed the party which elected them.† Continued strife with Congress has ensued. Andrew Johnson served nearly the whole term for which Abraham Lincoln was re-elected. During that time he battled with the loyal people of the North and with Congress; but as the Constitution provided that the powers and duties of the office of President should devolve on the Vice-President, for the unexpired term, the time was fixed and the people had to endure.

Look at the absurdity of the position. Profound peace exists. The National caucus meets. They nominate a man who, if he be at all fit for the office, has qualifications which would make him efficient in times of peace. He is elected—inaugurated. A month passes and a war breaks out. The nation demands a man at the head of the Government who has the accomplishments of a war executive. The Constitution says no. The term of office of President is four years. The incumbent may be totally incompetent and inexperienced.

* "English institutions have the smooth, steady, frictionless action which is in strongest contrast with our harsh and grinding system." Prof. William G. Sumner, in The Princeton Review, January, 1881.
†President Arthur is an exception to this rule.

There he must remain an incubus and a barrier. It is organizing a Government before the occasion occurs for it to act. It is an attempt to provide for an emergency which is not known. It may be claimed that Mr. Lincoln did well, although selected in time of peace. Admit this to be true, does it prove anything? Certainly not, except that he did well. By all the rules of reason and experience he should have objected to all salutary and vigorous measures for war. He should have vetoed appropriations of money for carrying on the war for the suppression of the rebellion. A system which selects a War President in time of peace, and a Peace President, in time of war, is one of an "unknown quantity." Would it be too harsh a term to call it an immense gambling operation—a lottery? Its peculiar features cannot exist a moment on the basis of reason or experience.

A very interesting discussion has arisen in connection with the question as to whether the President should be eligible for re-election. Of course the position of this essay is, that there should be no President in a true republic; but if he be retained, that there should not be any fixed period for his term of office. The first position carries the second out of the inquiry. But, as a matter of speculation, it may be remarked that the question of presidential re-election is one of great importance. It is vexed and complex. Nothing can be more capable of demonstration than that the system of two or three terms places it in the power of the President to use unfair and unrepublican means to re-elect himself, and that some of the worst phases of the Presidential plan has been developed in this respect. From the earliest period of our Government this tendency appeared. "Electioneering for the Presidency has spread its contagion to the President himself, to his now only competitor, to his immediate predecessor, to one at least of his Cabinet councillors, the Secretary of War, to the ex-candidates, Henry Clay and Daniel Webster, and to many of

the most distinguished members of both Houses of Congress.*
Webster and Clay, N. C. Rives, Silas Wright and James
Buchanan are among the first and foremost in this canvassing
oratory; while Andrew Jackson and Martin Van Buren, with
his heads of department, are harping upon another string of
the political accordeon by writing controversial electioneering
letters." † ‡

One of the effects of the fixed period is to force an election
of President when there is no real issue to be decided, as was
the case in 1880. It seemed at first that the campaign would
be carried on upon the personal character of the candidates.
The Republicans discovered, however, that the Democratic
platform provided for a tariff for revenue only. The Republicans were not slow in making the point that their party was
the only one in favor of protecting American industries.
There was no issue in point of fact, for both parties differed
in Congress upon the question of the tariff. Even as it was,
severe personal attacks were made upon General Garfield,
and he was nearly defeated by a forged letter, the contents of
which had no reference to any issue as framed by the party
platforms. The object was to divert the attention from party
issues, so far as the people were led to believe they existed, to
questions of personal integrity of the candidates. The Americans pay too much attention to names and too little to issues.§

---

* Memoirs of J. Q. Adams, X 352-353.   † Ibid, 356.

‡ One of the first principles which should be carried into effect in a republican government, if not in all elective ones, is that the temporary power-holder or trustee of the people, constituting the existing administration, should keep his hands off the machinery of elections. The Duke of Polignac was tried for his life, after the revolution of 1830, for having allowed or induced Charles X. to influence certain electors to elect government candidates. We wonder how many of our Executives would have gone unscathed if this rule had been applied to them. We apprehend most all of them would have met untimely ends if their lives had been thus at stake upon such an issue. No threat, violence, or inducement must be used by the person in office to assist his friends to office.

§ The New York Times sent a circular letter to the newspapers of the country asking their opinion as to the preferences of their particular neighbor-

We proceed to an election because a certain date has arrived. Who can give any good reason to-day (May, 1883) why the

hoods upon the question of presidential candidates in the coming campaign and received many hundred answers, which were published July 16, 1883. The following are a few extracts from the published letters.

"Mr. Arthur * * * is not regarded as available, and there is no boom for him."—*Denison, Texas.*

"Lincoln * * * comes from the right section of the country; his name would fire the popular heart; he has not been identified with any of the factions."—*Scranton, Penn.*

"The President's 'Southern policy' * * * will enable the President's variety party to appoint whatever kind of delegates he may desire."—*Rome, Ga.*

"Neither men nor measures will weigh a feather in the balance with expediency in the estimate of the Virginia Democracy."—*Shenandoah Valley, Va.*

"Arthur's * * * course toward Mississippi River improvements and liberality toward her citizens has given the President strength largely in advance of his party."—*Jackson, Miss.*

"The Grant wing rises up and says with unanimity, 'Let Blaine remain on the shelf.'"—*Decatur, Ill.*

"The general expression of opinion is that the next nominee should be a Western man."—*Tuskegee, Ala.*

"Bayard went out of sight at the same time the duty on matches was removed."—*Mobile, Ala.*

"It is only necessary * * * to mention the name of Grant to put the wildest enthusiasm in the negro ranks, and even those who vote with the Democrats in local elections would vote for Grant as a unit."—*Lynchburg, Va.*

"Benjamin F. Butler looms up with no uncertain silhouette."—*South Norwalk, Conn.*

"The name of Secretary Lincoln seems to be the most favorably canvassed as an available candidate."—*Milan, Mo.*

"Edmunds' * * * nomination would tend greatly to heal the differences between the two factions."—*Johnstown, N. Y.*

"The Mahoneites, to a man, are 'for Arthur, because Arthur is for us.'"—*Norfolk, Va.*

"The Republicans will vote for Arthur or any man he may suggest."—*Greensboro, N. C.*

"The popular theory * * * is for some younger man, and the sound and statesmanlike views expressed by R. P. Flower * * * have directed attention to him."—*Lyons, N. Y.*

"Logan * * * controls the Post Office machinery in this city, is strong in the Internal Revenue Department, is the favorite of Gov. Hamilton, and is heartily supported by officials in all the State institutions."—*Chicago, Ill.*

"It is universally conceded that Blaine is the profoundest statesman in the

Executive should be changed in 1884. Governmental affairs are going on fairly and well. The President has not put himself in antagonism to his party or to the people. No real question in the shape of an issue has been framed in Congress; but the election must take place, and probably the whole matter of getting up questions will be submitted to the tricky platform-maker at the National caucus or convention. In the meantime we hear much about the persons who are going to run. Every country newspaper has put up its favorite man as a Presidential candidate. Who is the coming man? But there are two to be elected, a Vice-President as well as a President. Therefore, geography enters into the subject. The selected men must not only be available, but they must come from the proper section to give strength to the ticket. Fit-

Nation to-day, but would not make as available a candidate as Lincoln "—*Somerset, Ky.*

"The party here is quite prepared to accept Tilden with his 'bar'l'—especially the 'bar'l.'"—*Hudson, N. Y.*

"The Federal official class * * * are now beginning to ask each other whether Mr. Arthur does not really wish a second term."—*Philadelphia, Penn.*

"With him (Hewitt) the Democrats believe that New York State would be secure and New Jersey a walk-over."—*Newton, N. J.*

"McDonald's * * * views on the tariff are satisfactory, and he has a powerful supporter in Senator Butler."—*Charleston, S. C.*

"Many Democrats are in favor of Gov. Butler. As they put it, they think 'Butler would raise h—l.'"—*Danville, Ill.*

"The name of the 'Great Defrauded' is tenderly mentioned as his bar'l is brought to mind."—*Riverhead, N. Y.*

"R. P. Flower * * * has the support of Tilden's friends and the followers of John Kelly."—*Watertown, N. Y.*

"It is thought by some that Tilden and Watterson would make a strong ticket, and that the clever Kentuckian had this in his mind's eye."—*Scranton, Penn.*

"Bayard * * * could not be elected, owing to his integrity of character and the fact that he is from so small a State."—*Jamestown, N. Y.*

"In regard to Ben Butler there is no doubt the Democrats would 'go' him if * * * through him they could obtain the spoils."—*Oswego, N. Y.*

"One prominent Democrat, who is very extreme in his views, declared that if he had the power to make the ticket for 1884 he would put up Jeff Davis and Bob Toombs."—*Winchester, Ky.*

ness has little to do with the question. The candidates are talked about very much as men speak of matching horses for a race.* While the politicians are plotting to put forward some local favorite—generally because he has served in the army, or been a party manager in some State,—the people have visions of the coming struggle, and wonder why it should take place at all. In the meantime the economical, commercial and industrial issues of the country must suffer. Is there any statistician who can estimate the cost of the coming senseless and foolish contest? †

The growth and prosperity of this country is saddled with a system which constitutes an elective monarchy, or something very like one. As long as that Government continues, a President must be elected. In exercising our duties as citizens we must do the best we may. We cannot remove, at once, the Presidency from our laws. As a concrete proposi-

---

* "We have here," says an Englishman, writing from Washington, "persons who tell you that the republican experiment * * * * is a failure; that prejudice, ignorance, or fraud determine the result; and they are ready to give you reasons why the whole system should be discarded. But even if they could by possibility prove all they allege, there is something too exciting and attractive in the choice of a President for the Americans ever to give up that great national sport. It is to them what the Derby is to you over the water—a great race, in which now one, and now the other competitor seems to be ahead."—[Republican Superstitions, 114.] If this foreigner had been in the city of New York during the last Presidential campaign and visited the pool rooms, usually devoted to the race track, and had seen the machinery of the French combination pools, as well as the bookmakers and all other known gambling systems in full operation, selling the chances of the candidates and their majorities, he would have had an additional evidence to substantiate his statement. These immense pool rooms were crowded with every manner of men, from the welsher of the race track to the prominent local politician. It is an admitted fact that Americans have a great penchant for betting in the Presidential campaign.

† "There is now noticeable, I think, in the public mind a growing terror of presidential elections. * * * * The presidential elections throws an artificial and injurious excitement athwart all the industrial and other permanent interests of the country. This must be more and more the case as time goes on, and as our society is bound together, by the finer fibres which only grow as a nation gets older and more settled."—Prof. William G. Sumner, in Princeton Review, January, 1881.

tion we are forced to advocate the election of some one whom we believe will honestly execute the laws of the land. As an abstract problem we ask for the abolition of the system. Jules Grevy, the present President of France, advocated the abolition of the Presidency in that country. That was before personal government there had been so thoroughly overthrown. It would be entirely consistent for President Grevy still to advocate the abolition of the very office he fills. So let us Americans, while urging the abolition of the system which we believe to be wrong and harmful, at the same time temporarily turn the present law to the best interest of the liberties of the people.

The theory that a person once elected to office might govern for a fixed period of time without regard to his competency or honesty, is only equalled in absurdity by the assertion that such officer should not be allowed to serve the nation longer than such term, however wisely and ably he had administered the law.

CHAPTER V.

COMMANDER-IN-CHIEF.

The Constitution of the United States provides that the President shall be commander-in-chief of the army and navy of the United States, and of the militia of the several States, when called into the actual service of the United States. This is truly a kingly power. It is difficult to conceive of a greater one. The right of naming the commander-in-chief, was not conferred upon Congress. The Constitution designates the officer who shall exercise this prerogative. He may be inimical to Congress; he may be a traitor; still he is at the head of the army and navy. Impeachment is too cumbersome a method to be effectual in staying the hand of a President who might destroy the usefulness of the army and navy. In the event of a civil war he could employ the army to assist his adherents at home, and scatter the navy "in distant seas, leaving but a very small part of it within the immediate reach of the Government."

At the time the Constitution of the United States was before the States for ratification, the opposition press claimed that it provided for standing armies in time of peace, and that it "vested in the Executive the whole power of levying troops, without subjecting his discretion, in any shape, to the control of the Legislature." This assertion is not based upon sound grounds. However, it shows the feeling that existed against giving such large powers to the Executive. General Hamilton also thought it of enough importance to reply in the 24th number of the Federalist. The opposition returned to the attack, declaring that the "provision which limits the appropriation of money for the support of an army to the period of two years would be unavailing (against the President if he desired to keep up a standing army), because the Executive when once possessed of a force large enough to awe the people into submission, would find resources in that very force sufficient to enable him to dispense with supplies from the acts of the Legislature." General Hamilton answers this in this wise: "Few persons will be so visionary as seriously to contend that military forces ought not to be raised to quell a rebellion or resist an invasion, and if the defense of the community, under such circumstances, should make it necessary to have an army so numerous as to hazard its liberties, this is one of those calamities for which there is neither preventive nor cure." The idea was that an assumption of military power could not be guarded against. This is undoubtedly true, but the idea of having the army commanded by a responsible War Minister, completely amenable to the Legislature, does not seem to have been entertained. The question may be propounded: "Why could not a War Minister become an usurper?" Very true, he could, but not nearly so easily as a President, who is placed at the very head of the nation, endowed with many of the attributes of absolutism. The existence of the War Minister under the present form of the British Constitution is that of responsibility to, and dependence upon, the House of Commons; but the President of the United States is Sovereign within his constitutional limits. It is only a step from the Presidency to Monarchy, while it would be rank treason for a minister to assume powers not specifically conferred. After the close of the great rebellion in 1865, President Johnson was seriously advised to march the immense army, over which he found himself the commander, into Mexico, to make conquest and annex territory. It was thought that it would be a good means of healing the animosities of the war. We verily believe that if the President had invaded the domains of that neighboring country, that the American people being so inured to the exercise of extraordinary power by our President, would have quietly submitted.

Although in the early councils of the nation there were those who favored giving the extraordinary power to the President to command in person the army, navy and militia of the country, yet there was a strong minority who opposed such a course in the Federal Convention.

Mr. George Mason animadverted upon the magnitude of the powers of the President, and was alarmed at the additional power of commanding the army in person.

Mr. Patterson was opposed to a single Executive having the command over the army, and submitted a plan for a number of persons to be the Executive, with power to direct all military operations, provided that none of the persons composing the Federal Executive shall on any occasion take command of any troops, so as personally to conduct troops, as a general, or in other capacity.

Notwithstanding strenuous objection, the power was actually conferred upon the President, and is now universally acknowledged.

It was clearly and almost unanimously admitted in a debate which occurred in the House in the first session, forty-sixth Congress, that the President had the undoubted right to send or order the troops of the United States from any one section to another. This would give him the power, in case of another civil war, to send arms and ammunition to the section with which he might be friendly, and to order detached bodies of troops into positions where they could easily be captured. Mr. Robeson said (the question being the repeal of the law directing the President to use the army to preserve peace at the polls): "You cannot take from the President the power to send the army even to put down domestic violence at the polls." Mr. Haskell asked " whether, in spite of this proposed repeal, the President could not, on the application of the Governor of New York, order troops to protect the peace at the polls in the city of New York." Mr. Frye said: "Does the gentleman know that Mr. Cushing, when he was Attorney-General of the United States, gave an opinion that the marshals and deputy-marshals can call upon the United States soldiers as a *posse comitatus* in the enforcement of the law." * * * * Mr. Robeson replied: "What I claimed was simply this, that if these words 'to keep the peace at the polls' were stricken out, that would not be any restriction whatever on the power of the commander-in-chief of the army to transport the army from barrack to barrack, and from State to State, as he saw fit. That is all I claim, and does not the gentleman admit that?" Mr. Carlisle said: "I agree to that." Then Mr. Robeson asked: "If that be so, and if it does not take away the President's power, and if that contingency shall happen, as it possibly may, and if officers of the army are sworn to obey the lawful orders of the President, then what becomes of the officer who is ordered by the President to suppress a riot and to quiet domestic violence at a place where a general election takes place?" It was evident that great power was claimed for the President, and as every officer of the army is subject to the direct orders of the President, he becomes actual commander and director of these forces for good or evil. In the same debate Mr. Stevens said that Congress had the right to raise armies and to designate the purposes for which they should be used; that the President's right to control and direct their movements was clearly an Executive one, with which Congress held no power to interfere. These gentlemen seemed to think that while Congress has power to raise armies, the President actually commands.

Mr. Williams, of Wisconsin, contended that there was no place where the President had not the right to send troops, whether to the polls or to the church of Christ.

Mr. Davis, of North Carolina, asked if he claimed that,

under the constitutional duty to see that the laws were enforced, the President had the right to send troops into States.

Mr. Robeson replied, that when there is on the statute-book a law passed by Congress and authorized by the Constitution, it is the duty of the President to see that the law is enforced and executed against every obstacle and despite every resistance, and he believed that when that time came, there would be at the call of the Executive, on either section, a million of men rising in arms (if need be) to maintain the supremacy of the laws of the United States. He believed that his friends on the other side, many of whom had entered into a resistance of the laws before, would be found ranging themselves on the side of constitutional government, and of the power of the national authority. He cited with commendation the course of President Jackson, in putting down the threatened resistance in South Carolina, and quoted, as a direct answer to Mr. Davis, the law passed by Congress on that occasion, authorizing the President to issue his proclamation, and, if not obeyed, to use the whole force of the United States to enforce the laws of the United States.

When Mr. Garfield said, during the great debate, that he was in favor of the repeal, if brought up separately, upon being accused of inconsistency, he said, that he always believed that the President had such powers directly from the provision of the Constitution and he had voted against the law when passed in the first instance as an act of legislative supererogation, and now for the same reason was in favor of entirely striking the law from the statute book. If Mr. Garfield be right in his view of the fundamental law, and we are inclined to the opinion that he is, then it is clear that the President has most extraordinary power over the exercise of the elective franchise and (if he were a blind partisan, or tyrannous despot) could completely overturn the liberties of the country, and at the same time act under the color of law. Every protection should be thrown about the elective franchise : upon it the whole fabric of our government rests; but the power of supreme command of the army, (even to keep the peace at the polls) should not be given to any single man. In times of peace, at least, the regular army is quite small, numbering but about twenty-five thousand men. However, the great military power of the President lies in his being the commander of the militia when called into service.

There was a prevailing opinion at the time of the adoption of the Constitution " to apprehend danger from the militia itself, in the hands of the Federal Government. It is observed, that select corps may be formed, composed of the young and ardent, who may be rendered subservient to the views of arbitrary power." Those who referred to the "Federal Government," and to "arbitrary power" in this connection, meant that authority vested in the President of the United States. It was he who had the actual power to call upon the militia and to command them. It has become true that the militia of Massachusetts have been transported "to subdue the refractory haughtiness of the aristocratic Virginians." General Hamilton, in the thirty-fifth number of the *Federalist*, rather immoderately discusses this subject, but we think he fails to meet the many objections that were made to giving the President the command of the militia forces.

The Constitution recognizes a well regulated militia, and article I, section 8, confers upon Congress " the power to provide for organizing, arming, and disciplining the militia, and for governing such part of them as may be employed in the service of the United States, reserving to the States respectively the appointment of the officers and the authority of training the militia, according to the discipline prescribed by Congress." The various acts in pursuance of this provision were embodied in sections 1625 to 1661 of the Revised Statutes of the United States. They require the enrolment of every able-bodied male citizen between the ages of eighteen and forty-five. They shall be armed and accoutred, and be arranged in divisions, brigades, regiments, battalions, and companies; the adjutant-general of each State shall annually make return of the condition of the militia of the State to the President of the United States, and it shall be the duty of the secretary of war, from time to time, to give such directions to the adjutants-general of the militia, as may, in his opinion, be necessary to produce a uniformity in such returns. This system of discipline and field exercise, which is ordered to be observed in the different corps of the regular army, shall be observed in such corps, respectively, of the militia; and the militia when called into actual service shall be subject to the same rules and articles of war as the regular troops; and shall be entitled to the same pay, rations, and clothing. Every officer who refuses to obey the orders of the President of the United States shall be punished as prescribed.

It must be borne in mind that these are the laws of the United States. They create a perfect system under the control and direction of the President of the United States. It would almost seem that the organization is intended to be the same as the regular army. It is very true that the President does not directly command the militia in time of peace; still they are always subject to his will as appears by section 1642, which provides that "whenever the United States are invaded or are in imminent danger of invasion from any foreign nation or Indian tribe, or of rebellion against the authority of the Government of the United States, it shall be lawful for the President to call forth such number of the militia of the State or States most convenient to the place of danger, or scene of action, as he may deem necessary to repel such invasion, or to suppress such rebellion, and to issue his orders for that purpose to such officers of the militia as he may think proper."

The language of the above act originated in a statute

passed May 2, 1792, was re-enacted in Febuary 1795, and at last embodied in the Revised Statutes of the United States. The fact is mentioned, to show that it has always been the settled policy of the Government to centre in the President great power and control over the militia of the country. This was never so thoroughly understood as during the great rebellion. Citizen soldiers who had thought they were only enlisted to serve within their own State, were ordered to march to distant ones, to protect the Central Government. Each proclamation of the President, as he called for six hundred thousand more men, was a fresh proof of the power vested in one man, under the law. These immense powers have not gone unchallenged in the Courts, and many interesting questions have arisen under this law. In the case of Houston v. Moore, argued in 1820, before the February term of the United States Supreme Court the full powers of the President were upheld. The Statute which formed the grounds of controversy in the State Court provided that every commissioned officer or private of the militia who shall neglect or refuse to serve when called into actual service, in pursuance of any order or requisition of the President of the United States, shall be liable to penalties defined by the act of Congress, passed February, 1795. The Supreme Court of the United States in the case of Martin v. Mott 1827, decided: "we are all of opinion that the authority to decide whether the exigency (of calling forth the militia) has arisen belongs exclusively to the President, and that his decision is conclusive upon all other persons." * The State Court-martial was to furnish a list of delinquents who refused to

---

* Wheaton, Reports, XII, p. 39; Curtis, Decisions of the Supreme Court VII, p. 12; See also Kent, Comm. I, pp. 278, 279; Story, Comm. §§, 1210,1215; Compare also Act of Congress of March 3, 1863; Statutes at Large, XII, p. 731 etc; See Paschal, Constitution of the United States, p. 136; American State Papers, VIII, p. 317: Statesman's Manual, I, p. 300; Cited by Von Holst, Vol. I, pp. 241,242.

march, or were absent without leave, to the Comptroller of the Treasury of the United States, that further proceedings might be had according to the laws of the United States. Mr. Justice Washington, who delivered the opinion of the Court, said, that the question was whether the above Act was repugnant to the Constitution. There seemed to be no doubt that the President had the power to issue his orders, either to the executive magistrate, or to any inferior officer of the State. This exact question has never been directly passed upon, except in an *obiter* manner. It is asserted that President Grant stood ready to issue his orders to the commanding officers of militia, in the event of any State executive refusing to obey requisitions for troops to enforce the inauguration of President Hayes. If the threat of open resistance had ripened into civil war, no State magistrate would have long interfered with the resistless will of President Grant. In that particular instance he may have served the best interests of the nation. The existing law made the President the only competent officer to command the army, navy, and militia. If resistance to the inauguration had taken place, the President would undoubtedly have crushed it. But civil war or anarchy itself threatened, and he seemed to be the only officer who had the power to make use of the army and navy.

This is no reason why the great power to command should be concentrated in one man. The law places it in the power of a single will to defeat the very objects of the law itself; for the President is in a position to assist either claimant where there is a disputed election. If the Presidency is to be continued, let Congress reserve to itself the power to enforce and superintend the inauguration of the incoming President.

Mr. Justice Washington proceeds to discuss the question as to the exact time when the militia should be considered in the service of the United States, and whether State courts have concurrent jurisdiction to punish delinquencies prior to the militia being actually mustered into the United States service. The learned justice held that the offence of disobedience to the President's call upon the militia was cognizable by a court-martial of the United States; but an exclusive cognizance was not conferred; that after the militia was mustered into the United States service, the jurisdiction of the government was complete. It was also held that the act of the State of Pennsylvania punishing an officer, or private, for refusing to obey the call of the President, was not repugnant to the Constitution. In another case occurring in the United States Supreme Court, in Martin v. Mott, in 1817, the President was held to be the exclusive judge, whether the exigencies had arisen upon which he is authorized to call forth the militia of the Union. "It was left to the Supreme Court of the United States to decide finally that, when the militia were called out to repel invasion, it belonged to the President alone to determine when the exigency existed." *

Mr. Justice Story said: "The power thus confided by Congress to the President is undoubtedly of a very high and delicate nature. A free people are naturally jealous of the exercise of military power, and the power to call the militia into actual service is certainly felt to be one of no ordinary magnitude. * * * * The power itself is confided to the Executive of the Union; to him who is by the Constitution the commander-in-chief of the militia when called into the actual service of the United States. * * * * The law does not provide for an appeal from the judgment of the President, or for any right in subordinate officers to review his decision and in effect defeat it." That the President is made by the Constitution the absolute autocrat of the army, navy, and militia, is established by the unmistakable language of the law beyond a scintilla of a doubt. How long can a nation remain free which places the sword in the hand of a single

---

* William B. Lawrence, *North American Review*, Nov., 1880.

man? Sooner or later, it will be used to destroy our liberties. Once already in the history of our country, the Congressional branch has been compelled to invade the established limits of the Executive and forcibly deprive the President of this power. Andrew Johnson had instituted a policy opposed to the will of the people, and particularly to the views of those who elected him. He was about to re-construct the South to suit himself, and to use the army to enforce his orders. Congress, in effect, deprived him of his functions as commander-in chief, and assigned it to the Commander-General of the army, who at that time was General Grant, and who could not be removed, suspended, or relieved from command, or assigned to duty elsewhere than at headquarters, except at his own request, without the approval of the Senate; and any officer who obeyed the orders of the President, except such orders as were issued through the General of the army, was to be imprisoned. Under our present form of government, this law was of a revolutionary character. If the President had had a sufficient following, this conflict would have caused a civil war. No more glaring illustration could be offered of the great defect in the presidential system, which attempts to place the sovereign power in co-ordinate branches of government, and to prescribe their limits in such a manner that there shall never be a conflict.

After the light of a century shed upon our boasted Constitution, there is not a settled, defined, and accepted theory of the limits of the various branches of the government. And upon this very subject there is pending (1879) in the army bill a contemplated addition to the power of the Commander-General. Two-thirds of the speech of Senator Burnside was occupied in explaining this topic. It is asserted that the bill undertakes to restrict the power of the President in a manner not contemplated by the Constitution. The General is to be empowered with the appointment, assignment and detail of officers, both in line and staff; to make reports, to issue orders, to have the supervision of staff departments, arsenals, and the engineer and ordnance corps, and the signal service. It is claimed that the only purpose is to give to the army a fixed head, not varying with the fortunes of politics. How this can be accomplished while the President has the power of removal is not clear. We claim that the bill is an admission of the fact that the provision of the Constitution giving the President autocratic power over the army is wrong.*

We now wish to call attention to the working of the English Constitution in relation to the prerogative of declaring war and making peace, and to the right of commanding the army and navy. It is necessary in the furtherance of our point to show the manner in which the supreme power of the State is vested, as a matter of fact, in parliament, and how with us it is distributed in the different departments of the government; to demonstrate the extraordinary power conferred on our executive, and the mere fictions of authority that remain in the Sovereign of Great Britain.

If certain writers upon constitutional law were consulted, it would appear that the English Constitution vests the exclusive right of making war in the Crown.

"But this, like all other prerogatives, must be exercised by the advice, and upon the responsibility of ministers who are accountable to Parliament, and are liable to parliamentary

---

* Clay, in his speech of the 10th of July, 1840, at Taylorsville, said: "Accordingly, the process of converting them (the army and navy) into exclusive instruments has commenced in a court-martial assembled at Baltimore. Two officers of the army of the United States have been there put upon their solemn trial on the charge of prejudicing the Democratic party by making purchases for the supply of the army from members of the Whig party. * * * * But the charge was that to purchase at all from the opponents, instead of the friends of the administration, was an injury to the Democratic party, which required that the offenders should be put upon their trial before a court-martial." Von Holst, Vol. I., 346.

censure or impeachment for the improper commencement, conduct, or **conclusion of war.*** Parliament must grant supplies, and pass the **annual** Mutiny **Act,** and this fact, taken with the ministerial responsibility, as a matter of substance, vests the **power of** declaring **war** and making **peace** in the Legislature. The **Bill of** Rights, in the reign of **William and Mary, forbids** the king **to** raise an army, or any part of **it,** without the consent of parliament. The guards of Charles II. were anti-constitutional, and **the army** of James II. regarded **as** such a violation of law **as to amount** to abdication.

The most interesting **instance to** Americans of war being brought to a close **by** the **House of** Commons was when, on **the 4**th of March, 1782, it resolved that "**All** those who should advise the continuance of the American **war were to** be considered as enemies **to the** king and country." This brought **the war to an end,** despite the wishes and intentions of George III.† **Subsequent to** this, in **1791, Mr. Pitt** was compelled to abandon an intended war with Russia because **the** House **of** Commons was opposed to it. In March, 1857, **the House** condemned the policy of **war** with China. Many other illustrations could be given **of** this actual power being **vested in the people, as** represented **in the** popular branch of the **Legislature.**

On the subject **of locating the power of** command of the army **and navy under the British** Constitution, we have consulted that very valuable **work on** Parliamentary Government **by** Alpheus Todd, **and we shall** (so far **as our** limited space will allow) substantially employ his language in this connection. The army **has always been regarded with** greater constitutional jealousy **in England than the navy,** and the **command of the army** has, by uninterrupted usage—until a comparatively recent period—been more immediately in the hands

---

* Cox, Inst. Eng. Govt., 596; Bowyer, Const. Law, 160.
† See May, Const. Hist., vol. 1, page 458.

and under the control of the Crown than of its responsible advisers. As respects the navy, the responsibility for the administration thereof has, from the epoch of the revolution, been considered as resting upon the First Lord of the Admiralty. It is now fully conceded that the control of the army must be exercised by the Crown, through the medium of a responsible minister. Until recently, the direction and responsibility in military affairs, although formally centred in the administration for the time being, was practically divided between a number of officers of the war department, of the government, and of the colonies. "On the declaration of war against Russia, in 1854, the opinion which had for some time prevailed, that a more direct and efficient control should be exercised by the government in military affairs, led to the separation of the duties of war minister from those of Colonial Secretary, and the appointment of a Secretary of State for War, in whose hands should be concentrated the supreme and responsible authority over the whole military business of the country, heretofore transacted by various independent departments." On account of the grievous mismanagement attending the conduct of the Crimean campaigns, it was suggested that the Duke of Newcastle should be removed from office and be replaced by Lord Palmerston, who, it was contended, was the only member of the government properly qualified to prosecute the war with success, and also because he was a member of the House. Lord John Russell insisted that it was necessary that the Secretary of State for War, like the Chancellor of the Exchequer, should always be in the House of Commons, and that the adoption of such a rule was open to no constitutional objection. The office of the Secretary of War was abolished, and now the war minister himself moves the estimates, and represents his department in the popular assembly. This latter arrangement has since been carried out, with but one exception, in the case of Lord Panmure. " In proof of the necessity for a concentration of power in the

direction of military affairs in the hands of one man, at all events during the continuance of hostilities with a foreign power, Lord John Russell makes the following remarks:—
'In the prosecution of a war it is clear either that the Prime Minister must be himself the active, moving spirit of the whole machine, or else the War Minister must have ample authority to control other departments. A Cabinet is a cumbrous and unwieldy instrument for carrying on war; it can furnish suggestions or make a decision upon a measure submitted to it, but cannot administer. To do this effectually, you must have a war minister of vigor and authority.' Elsewhere he says: 'In order to carry on the war with efficiency, either the Prime Minister must be constantly urging, hastening, completing the military preparations, or the Minister of War must be strong enough to control other departments. Every objection of other ministers, the plea of foreign interests to be attended to, of naval preparations not yet complete, and a thousand others, must be forced to yield to the paramount necessity of carrying on the war with efficiency of each service and completeness of means to the end in view. This great duty may be performed either by the Prime Minister himself, or by a separate War Minister. We have examples of both. Lord Godolphin, on the one hand, as first minister, superintended the campaigns of Marlborough; Lord Chatham, when Secretary of State, guided the operations of the Seven Years War. Again, the glorious termination of the war against Napoleon was directed by the secretaries Castlereagh and Bathurst, under the premiership of Lord Liverpool.'" In point of fact, during the Crimean war, the War Secretary, while he had the responsible direction and control of everything, yet the Cabinet were largely consulted, and exercised considerable influence. The selections of the commanding generals were submitted to the Cabinet for their approval. "During active service the Secretary of State for War must have entire control over the operations as bear-

ing upon the conduct of the Commander-in-chief, of the Admiralty (notwithstanding that department is presided over by another cabinet minister), of the Commissariat, of the Transport Board, and even of the Treasury itself. All these must be, to a certain extent, superintended by him; and it is his duty to combine and concert together the various powers and authorities of all those different departments, in such a manner as to conduce to the proper management of the military operations of the country. Considerable alterations take place in the relative position of the departments of state upon the breaking out of a war. The admiralty is a totally independent office in time of peace; no secretary of state interferes or controls it in any way whatever; but, the instant war is declared, the whole thing is changed, and the Board of Admiralty comes under the immediate and entire control of the Secretary of State for War. Thenceforward, as long as the war continues, the operation of the war office, and of the admiralty, and the direction of the movements, both of the army and navy, become a part of the special duty of the Secretary for War." This, however, does not limit the responsibility of the admiralty "in regard to the details of the naval service, which continue to be transacted, as in time of peace, without reference to any other department. The Secretary for War gives his instructions to the admiralty, and it is the duty of the board to see these instructions properly carried out."

The commander-in-chief, who has control of the routine, military command, and discipline, is appointed by a letter from the Secretary of State for War. The commander-in-chief has frankly and fully acknowledged the supremacy of the war minister, and his own subordinate position. With regard to the disposition of the forces at home and abroad, the Secretary for War is cognizant of every movement. "A schedule is sent to him, containing the scheme of new distributions, which he approves or not, as he may think fit, and the movements take place under his previous sanction. A Secretary of State has, indeed, the power of ordering the commander-in-chief to move the army, without assigning any reason to him.

This doctrine of keeping the military administration subordinate to the civil government is not new. It was asserted by Lords Grey and Granville, during the Regency in 1812, and was fully recognized by Lord Hill, and by the Duke of Wellington, when they held the office of commander-in-chief, before the consolidation of the civil and military departments of the army. Lord Wellington, in 1836, publicly declared that the commander-in-chief cannot at the moment move a corporal's guard from London to Windsor without going to the civil department for authority; he must get " a route."

Lord Grey, upon being asked whether certain changes he had recommended would not bring the army more under the influence of the House of Commons than in times past, replied: "The truth is, that the House of Commons has always exercised, and always ought to exercise, a great control over the administration of the army; it cannot be called on to provide for the expense of the army without inquiring in what manner the money so granted is applied. Moreover, the very existence of a standing army depends on the annual mutiny act. The army would be disbanded *de facto* at the end of a year if the mutiny act were not renewed. The conclusion of the matter is this, that, notwithstanding any reservations heretofore contained in his patent, the Secretary of State for War has supreme authority and responsibility in all matters affecting the administration of the army; that he may act either directly himself, or through the commander-in-chief, who is his military adviser, and subordinate to him; and that there is no act of the commander-in-chief, however small or great, that does not constitutionally come within the revision of the Secretary for War, and for which he is not therefore responsible."

The prerogative of the king, which gave him all military

authority and command, without qualification, was, at the Revolution of 1688, subject to such constitutional restraints that it is impossible to exercise this power to the detriment of English liberty. It was declared "that the raising or keeping a standing army within the kingdom, in the time of peace, unless it be with consent of Parliament, is against law."

According to our system, each State organizes its militia, over which the President has absolute control (in effect), without any permission granted to him by Congress.

While under our presidential system the President is the commander of the militia when called into actual service, and has at the same time power to call them into such service, thus making him the virtual commander of all military forces, for he is the commander-in-chief of the regular army and navy, the English people in 1859 and 1862 (when the volunteer movement assumed such great importance) devised means by which the actual command and control of the movement should not be subject to the will of the sovereign, and commissioners laid down the rule to be that "the duty and responsibility of deciding that question (the limit of the total number of the force) must rest exclusively with the responsible advisers of the crown."

The Secretary of State for War shortly afterwards issued a circular forbidding the enrolment of volunteer corps. There were those who contended "that the command of the army and navy should be left to the control of the Crown; but it was decided that no distinction should exist between the exercise of the royal authority over the army and navy and the other departments of the government."

We have quoted thus fully from this authority on English Law, in order to show how much more in accordance with true representative government is its manner of controlling and commanding its army and navy than our law, which places the supreme command in the hands of a President, who holds his office for a fixed period, and who cannot be removed except by a long, cumbrous, unyielding process known as impeachment. In England, the people control the army through a responsible minister; in America, the President's will is the law. In England, if a war minister offend the Commons, he may immediately be removed; in this country, it would probably cost us a revolution to depose the President. Already has the President, in two instances, declared war without the sanction of Congress. Behold the precedents which may be used to overthrow our liberties!

CHAPTER VI.

REPRIEVES, PARDONS, AND TREATIES.

The power of the President to grant reprieves and pardons places his wish, his will, his favor above all law and justice. As a matter of reason, it should rest with the power which prescribes the penalty, the legislative branch. The power conferred by the Constitution embraces all penalties from the forfeiture of life to the smallest fine. An Attorney-General has given it as his opinion that it includes fines imposed by the Courts for contempt and on defaulting jurors. It has been exercised before conviction and even before indictment. It has also been held to include conditional pardons. So high an authority as Lord Coke has expressed the opinion that this prerogative should not be exercised except in such cases which "the law itself may be presumed willing to have excepted out of its general rules, which the wisdom of man cannot possibly make so perfect as to suit every case." This principle has been repeatedly and almost continuously violated by our elective kings, who seem to exercise the power more improperly than those holding office by heredity. President Taylor unconditionally pardoned a man who had been convicted of counterfeiting while assuming to be a religious zealot. President Johnson indiscriminately pardoned persons convicted of similar crimes. He thrust pardons upon traitors before they could doff the Confederate gray. It was particularly the province of Congress to grant pardons for treason, but the President blindly and recklessly used it. General Hamilton thus expresses himself upon the subject of pardons:—" The expediency of vesting the power of pardons in the President has, if I mistake not, been contested only in relation to the crime of treason. This, it has been urged, ought to have depended upon the assent of the one or both branches of the legislative bodies. I shall not deny that there are strong reasons to be assigned for requesting in this particular the concurrence of that body, or a part of it. As treason is a crime levelled at the immediate being of the society, when the laws have once ascertained the guilt of the offender, there seems a fitness in referring the expediency of an act of mercy towards him to the judgment of the Legislature. And this ought the rather to be the case as the supposition of the connivance of the chief magistrate ought not to be entirely excluded." George Mason wrote on this subject as follows: " The President of the United States has the unrestrained power of granting pardons for treason, which may be sometimes exercised to screen from punishment those whom he had secretly instigated to commit the crime, and thereby prevent a discovery of his own guilt.* " Randolph and Madison disliked leaving the pardon for treason to the President alone.† There is no page in American history more startling than that which describes the manner in which President Jefferson exercised the prerogative of pardon. Under the Adams administration, one Callender was tried for a violation of the alien and sedition laws, found guilty, and imprisoned. As soon as Jefferson came into office, he hastened to remit the remainder of the term of imprisonment, and caused the fine to be repaid. The President knew the man had been tried by a court, but he said—in his capacity as an executive officer—that the law was " a nullity, as absolute and as palpable as if Congress had ordered us to fall down and worship a golden image," and " that it was as much his

* Vide Elliot's Debate, vol. I., 494.
† Bancroft's Constitution, vol. II., 215. Elliot, 549.

duty to arrest its execution in every stage as it would have been to rescue from the fiery furnace those who should have been cast into it for refusing to worship the image." * It remained for Jefferson to assert a new theory of the executive power, namely, that the office was not instituted for the execution, but the obstruction, of the law. He was a man of many brilliant though Utopian ideas of government, but this was the most pronounced in its suggestion. It was evidently due to the subjective operation of his mind—purely *a priori*—for no such theory can be found in the writings of any other statesman. He evolved his duty to violate law from his own inner consciousness.† The pardoning power has been

---

* Jefferson by Morse, 227.

† Although not in strict logical connection with the particular subject under consideration, we desire to cite the following as evidence of presidential absolutism : " Let us consider another instance. The right of an accused person in a criminal prosecution to have the assistance of counsel for his defence has always in this country been allowed to be essentially necessary for securing the liberty of the citizen. And so important was it deemed by the founders of our government, that even in the Constitution of the United States it is secured by special clause, though it was not in ordinary times, or at the hands of ordinary men, thought to be in danger. On the trial of Burr for high treason, Mr. Luther Martin, one of the lights of the American bar, was one of the counsel for the prisoner. And during that trial Mr. Jefferson, then President of the United States, wrote to his friend Mr. Hay, who was concerned in the prosecution:— "Shall we move to commit Luther Martin as *particeps criminis* with Burr ? Graybill will fix upon him misprision of treason at least, and, at any rate, his evidence will put down this unprincipled and impudent Federal bulldog, and add another proof that the most clamorous defenders of Burr are all his accomplices." " In later years we have seen the President of the United States ostentatiously welcome a prisoner in the dock, at a state dinner in the executive mansion. It has, however, seldom been the case that the chief magistrate of this country has used the influence and power of his position to hinder the conviction and punishment of criminals, or to interfere with the administration of justice. For executive action of this class, Mr. Jefferson gives us the earliest precedent, and it needs high authority." " Now Mr. Jefferson was a conscientious man. Nor was he a man who seriously intended to violate his oath of office. But he was the first high official in the government who set the example to the people of the United States of deliberately defying the law. From his teachings of resistance to what he called illegal laws came the whole theory of nullification, and the whole fact of the rebellion. Would he have ever done the things here mentioned except

abused in this country from its earliest history. It can hardly be expected that the President, as the average President goes, can resist the tendency to abuse this power, as he stands preeminently at the head of his party dispensing favor and exercising revenge. He naturally falls into the use of subjective views and succumbs to individual feeling. Arbitrariness, vindictiveness, revenge, and favor, too often characterize his action. A board of pardon should be instituted consisting of several members to be appointed by the legislature.

Treaties.

The Constitution confers power upon the President to make treaties with the consent of the Senate. At first glance this might seem to be a wise provision, but when the workings of this law are more particularly inquired into, it will be perceived that the President can overcome the difficulty of getting the concurrence of the Senate. Secretly prepared treaties may be forced upon the Senate. It is claimed that this was done in the San Domingo affair. The principal objection to this power being conferred upon the President, is

for the presence of party and party ends?" The practice instituted by Mr. Jefferson of making appointments to, and removals from, office for mere party reasons, grew until Mr. Van Buren established it in all its fulness. From his time it was the regular system, acted on by both parties, that public offices were the spoils belonging to the victors in the party contests. And from that time down to the present the ordinary practice has been, on the coming in of a new party, to remove every official belonging to the old party, and use his place as a reward for party service, except that some experienced men who were needed to carry on the ordinary department business have generally been continued from one administration to another.'—*Stickney's* "*True Republic*," 1873. We do not agree with Mr. Stickney that this presidential action was brought about by the abuse of the demands of party. We believe that it grew out of the fact that the Constitution placed it in the power of the President to exercise this authority. This was the cause; abuse of party power was the effect.

that he may covertly communicate and negotiate with foreign countries, and in this way embarrass the nation. During certain early administrations of the Republic, the President not only consulted with the Senate upon the ratification, but in the inception, of treaties. The Senate and President, after full communion, also agreed as to what instructions ministers should receive. The President now makes all treaties secretly and then submits them to the Senate. The President pledges, the Senate submits. These are startling considerations which the people of this country are called upon to contemplate. When President Polk first assumed his duties, it was thought he was a man of no nerve and defective in will. It was soon discovered he was no manikin. It was not long before he declared that the claim of the United States to Oregon was "clear and unquestionable," and pledged himself to support this position. This language Lord John Russell, in the House of Commons, characterized as a "blustering announcement."* The President threw down the wage of battle before he learned the will of the people. Correspondence with the British Government ensued. Congress strenuously insisted that the President should disclose what was going on, and the friends of the Executive resisted, and claimed that the President should first be allowed to determine what the treaty should be, and then submit it to the Senate. Questions like the Oregon one are too important to leave to the decision of a small conclave of men. The matter of a boundary line should be submitted to the people; they are the best judges of their rights. It is a subject of such general interest that the whole people should discuss it, in order to insist at the same time upon an equitable decision, and that the government shall not be involved in a useless war. One half of the wars of the past have been caused by disagreement between single men in their endeavor to settle disputed questions existing

* Niles' Register. LXVIII., 114.

between nations. An insult is given, a council broken up, a shot is fired, and war is upon the country. The one-man power appeals to the patriotism of the masses, who are ever too ready to support those in authority, and horrid war devastates the fair fields of agriculture, and destroys the workshops of manufacture. It is an error that a treaty can only be negotiated by means of the ancient kingly rules of diplomacy.* It is difficult to conceive of a case where the open, frank, ingenuous method of submitting the whole subject to the people, should not be preferable to the means of the miserable legerdemain of those who make it a profession to so word their thoughts as to disguise their meaning. The people of these later times want to know as much as they may of the peculiar morals and conscience of the man who is the temporary power-holder. For instance, the people as soon as they found out what Grant was about in the West Indies, they overthrew the whole scheme of annexation, and even in the Oregon affair, the President was compelled to abandon his boastful position, after the subject was debated before the masses. An officer clothed with authority like that conferred on our chief executive always has friends, and in this controversy they gave out a battle cry of "fifty-four, forty or fight," but it is now known that the line was determined at 49° north latitude. The President thus receded from a position he should never have assumed. We do not refer entirely to the later period of our history. It is true that these practices have grown with the country, but as early as the 24th of January, 1842, Mr. Clay said in support of his resolutions for

* "If the Republic has anything to transact with a foreign nation, let its messenger start with the spirit of his country still fresh upon him. Let him not be trained to smoothness of tongue and ingenuity in indirection in the atmosphere of aristocracies. Let the Republic select its wise and sufficient man for each such task, as it may arise; let him go to the foreign capital as the voice and seal of his country; let him drive to the door of cabinet or palace in his cab, transact his affair, and then return home."—[Republican Superstitions, by M. D. Conway, 129.]

the amendment of the Constitution, that "while there had been no such thing in practice as an encroachment by the Federal upon the State government, there had been, within the Federal government itself, a constant encroachment by the executive upon the legislative department." "First, it attacked the treaty-making power. None could now read the language of the Constitution, without at once coming to the conclusion that the intention of the authors of that instrument was, that the Senate should be consulted by the President, not merely in the ratification, but in the inception, of all treaties; that, in the commencement of the negotiations, the instructions of the ministers appointed to treat, the character and provisions of the treaty, the Senate should first be consulted, and should first yield its assent. And such had, in fact, been the interpretation put upon the treaty-making power in the first and purest years of our government. Every one must recollect the early history of the exercise of this power, and the high sanction for such a usage. The first President had been wont to come to the Senate, there to propose a foreign mission, and to consult with his constitutional advisers, the members of the Senate, on the instructions to be given to the minister who should be sent. But this practice has been abandoned. The President now, without a word of consultation with the Senate, on his own mere personal sense of propriety, concluded a treaty, and promised to the foreign powers its ratification; and then after all this had been done, and the terms of the treaty agreed upon, he for the first time submitted it to the Senate for ratification. Now every one must see that there was a great difference between rejecting what had been already actually done, and refusing to do that thing if asked beforehand. All must feel that they often gave their official assent to what they never would have sanctioned but for the consideration that the treaty was already concluded, and that the faith of the nation was in some sort pledged for its ratification."* These constitutional or assumed powers are essentially dangerous to our liberties, for the reason that the President has power to involve the nation in foreign complications. Washington said in his farewell address, that we should have " as little political connection as possible " with foreign nations ; that it would "be unwise in us to implicate ourselves " * * * * * in "the ordinary combinations and collisions of her (Europe's) friendships and enmities " * * * " by interweaving our destiny with that of any part of Europe." If it was regarded as impolitic for us, as a nation, to form foreign alliances, how much more so is it to give power to the man who may live at the White House " to entangle our peace and prosperity in the toils of European ambition, rivalship, interest, humor or caprice ? "

We must bear in mind that all treaties made under authority of the United States became the supreme law of the land. In addition to this power conferred upon the President, " he shall receive ambassadors and other public ministers " accredited from foreign governments. " He shall nominate, and with the advice and consent of the Senate, shall appoint ambassadors, other public ministers, and consuls. Thus the President, in connection with the Senate, is placed in charge of all foreign relations. We have only to reflect for a moment to comprehend the transcendent importance of these powers conferred upon the Executive. It is he who is alone authorized to hold communication with other governments. After our ministers have been appointed by the President, they are compelled to communicate with, and receive instructions from,

---

* Mr. George Mason foresaw, in the early history of the country, the condition of things which afterwards took place, and to which Mr. Clay refers. He wrote that the Constitution, " By declaring all treaties supreme laws of the land, the Executive and the Senate have in many cases an exclusive power of legislation, which might have been avoided by proper distinctions with respect to treaties, and requiring the assent of the House of Representatives, where it could be done with safety."

that magistrate. Congress has absolutely no control over their proceedings. The practice is to conduct all negotiations secretly. The great danger to the peace and welfare of this government is, that the President has it in his power to plunge this country into a war at any time. A hasty note written to the British Government in the negotiations of the Trent affair, would have brought a fleet of English ironclads in uncomfortable proximity to every seaport city of the United States, or the President could have produced a similar condition of things by unfriendly demands upon the French Government in regard to its occupation of Mexico. The President thus holds in his keeping "the safety, welfare, and even permanence of our internal and domestic institutions; and in wielding the power he is untrammelled by any other department of the government; no other influence than a moral one can control or curb it; its acts are political, and its responsibility is only political."* Be it remembered that in the exercise of all these powers the President is absolute. Congress has no power to abrogate or modify any action of the Executive. No Tudor king could have exercised greater power, for these powers are simply absolutism in themselves.

* An Introduction to the Constitutional Law, by John Norton Pomeroy, 447, 448.

CHAPTER VII.

APPOINTMENT AND REMOVAL FROM OFFICE.

The Constitution is silent as to the powers of removal from office, if we except the filling of vacancies that may happen during the recess of the Senate. In the discussion of the powers of the Senate, General Hamilton championed those powers in the *Federalist*, and seemed to think that its consent would be necessary to displace as well as to appoint. He regarded it as a joint power. He said that "where a man in any station had given satisfactory evidence of his fitness for it, a new President would be restrained from attempting a change in favor of a person more agreeable to him by the apprehension that the discountenance of the Senate might frustrate the attempt, and bring some discredit upon himself." Judge Story, in his Commentaries on the Constitution, says, referring to the necessary consent of the Senate, that it had a most material tendency to quiet the just alarms of the overwhelming influence and arbitrary exercise of this prerogative of the Executive, which might prove fatal to the independence and freedom of opinion of public officers, as well as of the public liberties of the country. During the first session of Congress, in 1789, a bill was introduced to establish a Department of State, and it was provided that whenever the Secretary shall be removed from office by the President, that he shall designate the person who shall have charge of the records. This was accomplishing by indirection what was not conferred specifically. This construction was placed upon the Constitution by Congress, after a thorough discussion of the subject. It is evident that the giving of this immense power to the Executive was wrong, and contrary to the letter, if not to the intent, of the Constitution.* Beyond all doubt, it was antagonistic to the spirit of liberty as expressed in the Declaration. The fact that such legislation was ever deemed necessary is one of the best arguments against the whole presidential system. The fault lay in the fundamental law, for by it the system of an elective king was established, and there were many who were willing to claim that the prerogative of removal resulted from the character of the powers conferred, and the necessity of their being exercised; that it was a part of the Executive authority. Washington was one of the purest, greatest, and best of men. He was at the head of our government. Men were willing to trust him with almost any power. Unfortunately, the people who were in authority in the early days of the Republic failed to foresee that the Presidents who were to follow might not have the virtues of Washington. On the formation of the government it was thought that if a President should attempt to make a removal from office, from personal motives, that he would imme-

---

* Nay, sir, if Warren himself had been among the living, and had possessed any office under the government, high or low, he would not have been suffered to hold it a single hour, unless he could show that he had strictly complied with the party statutes, and had put a well-marked party collar round his own neck. * * * * * Mr. President, so far as I know, there is no civilized country on earth in which, on a change of rulers, there is such an inquisition for spoil, as we have witnessed in this free Republic. The inaugural address of 1829 spoke of a searching operation of government. The most searching operation, sir, of the present administration has been its search for office and place. Whenever, sir, did any English minister, Whig or Tory, take such an inquest? When did he ever go down to low water mark to make an ousting of tide-waiters? When did he ever take away the daily bread of weighers and gaugers and measurers? Or when did he ever go into the villages to disturb the little post offices, the mail contracts, and anything else in the remotest degree connected with the government? Sir, a British minister who should do this, and should afterwards show his head in a British House of Commons, would be received by a universal hiss."—[Webster's Speeches, 145.]

diately be impeached.* Those who were in favor of granting the kingly power, continually urged it upon the ground of the necessity of the President's having the power to remove an unfaithful officer during the recess of the Senate. Pending this discussion, Mr. Madison said, "for I contend that the wanton removal of meritorious officers would subject him (the President) to impeachment and removal from his high trust." But there was a difference of opinion, for in the House there were 34 votes for the power of removal and 20 against it. In the Senate, the Vice-President gave the casting vote. This legislative action was afterwards modified, enlarged, or curtailed, according as Congress was friendly or hostile to the President. The Tenure of Office Acts show this. Chancellor Kent upheld the legislative construction of the Constitution against its specific provisions, on the old ground that the power was a part of the Executive authority wholly vested in the President, and the Senate should not have the right of interfering. In other words, the proper construction was that these powers did vest in the President under the Constitution. The time has arrived when the people ought carefully to study the tendency of our Constitution, and the drift of the thought of those who control its destinies. An elective Executive is created by the Constitution—no power of removal is specific-

---

* "During Washington's administration nine persons were removed from office, during John Adams' ten, during Jefferson's thirty-nine, during Madison's five, during Monroe's nine, during John Quincy Adams' ten, and in the first year of Jackson's administration two hundred and thirty officials of higher rank, and seven hundred and sixty postmasters and subordinate officials.'"—[Works of Calhoun, II., p. 428; Niles, Reg., XLIII., p. 9.] Benton admits that during the first year six hundred and ninety officials were dismissed. [Thirty Years' View, I., p. 60.] Clay writes March 12th, 1829, that is eight years after the inauguration: "Among the official corps here, there is the greatest solicitude and apprehension. The members of it feel something like the inhabitants of Cairo when the plague breaks out. No one knows who is the next to encounter the stroke of death, or which with many of them is the same thing, to be dismissed from office. You have no conception of the moral tyranny which prevails here over those in employment."—[Priv. Corresp. of H. Clay, p. 225.]

ally given. But Congress declares its opinion to be that this power is incidental to the office. Among those who approved of this kingly prerogative was Mr. Webster. While he denied to the President all powers save those specified, still he thought that the power of removal belonged to the power of appointment, and as the one vested in the President and Senate, so should the other. Washington, Adams, Madison, and Monroe had occupied the chair. These were great and good men. But they were not to live always. Would the successors of Madison and Monroe abuse these powers? Jefferson as the successor of Washington did. It is generally thought that Andrew Jackson was the initiator of the system of removals for political reasons, but it was, in point of fact, the great Republican leader, Thomas Jefferson, who first used this kingly power which he found conferred upon him as President of the United States. What he really did can be best understood by reading what he himself says in his writings.* "All appointments to civil offices during pleasure, made after the event of the election was certainly known to Mr. Adams, are considered as nullities. I do not view the persons appointed as even candidates for the office, but make others without noticing or even notifying them. * * * * The Courts being so decidedly Federal and irremovable, it is believed that Republican attorneys and marshals, being the doors of entrance into the Courts, are indispensably necessary as a shield to the Republican part of our fellow-citizens, which, I believe, is the main body of the people."

These words exhibit a singular idea of the purity of the Courts, and of the powers of the President. Is it possible that Jefferson thought it was his duty to invade the Courts presided over by Chief Justice Marshall, in the interest of his particular friends ? What better evidence can there be that the framers of the Constitution intended to confer kingly power upon

* Vol. III., 464.

the Executive than this confession of so early a President as Jefferson, that he had the right of removal of all United States marshals and attorneys, for the purpose of opening the doors into the Courts in order to shield the members of his own party. The naivete displayed by this letter is truly refreshing. It simply means that he wished to use the Courts and its officers in the interest of his party friends. It may be commendable for an elective officer to act within the law for the furtherance of the objects of his party; but this President violated the law. Subsequent Presidents did not only use the high prerogative of their office to "shield" their friends, but exercised it to crush the very people who had elevated them to power.

In March, 1829, a victor, crowned with the laurels of success, proclaimed from the Presidential chair of this Republic that he would distribute the spoils of office to his army of faithful followers. Andrew Jackson was well qualified for the task. He was a soldier, illiterate, passionate and revengeful. Unacquainted with the law, and having no sympathy with it, except so far as it might serve his own preconceived notions of it, and looking chiefly to the power of will and force, he violated the trust he had been called upon to execute. Until the accession of Jackson our fortunes had kept an upward course, if we except Jefferson's administration. Now they were on the wane; neither intelligence nor honesty was potent enough to save the incumbent, if this tyrant desired the office for some blind personal partisan. Nearly all the old governments of the world have had a Civil Service from time immemorial. It is doubtful whether this soldier king had ever heard of that fact, and if he had he would probably have characterized such laws as barbarous, and as unfit for a government by the people. England and other European, and even Asiatic governments, put such restrictions upon their sovereigns, but Jackson argued, by some *non sequitur*, that the President of a free people should be allowed to act as a satrap.

APPOINTMENT AND REMOVAL FROM OFFICE.

Incomprehensible as it may seem, it was accorded to the President that he might create vacancies by the mere act of appointment. The removal was effected by the operation of law. This error marks our first downward course, which, if not checked, will lead to a complete destruction of the Republic. The public offices were treated as if they were instituted for the use of those temporarily occupying them. The officeholders came to think themselves the servants of the appointing power. Mr. Clay said of President Jackson that " to understand how he obtained such a stronghold, so as to be able for many years, as President, to do as he pleased, and make the people believe he was seeking their good, when he was doing them the greatest possible injury; as to make them satisfied with measures and acts, which, but for their idolatrous regard would have shocked them, and driven them forever from the support of him; as still to maintain his popularity when he was revolutionizing the government and its institutions, disturbing and disregarding the commercial habits of the nation, and bringing upon the people calamity and distress like a whirlwind;—to solve this problem requires to look somewhere else." The post office, the land office, the army and navy, were regarded as the personal property of this elected monarch. On the 9th of February, 1835, a committee which had been appointed by the Senate to investigate the subject of Executive patronage, reported the increasing expenditures of the government and showed that at that early date the number of persons who held office at the will of the President, was over 60,000; they conclude their report as follows :—" It is easy to see that the certain, direct, and inevitable tendency (of the practice) is to convert the entire body of those in office into corrupt and supple instruments of power, and to raise up a host of hungry, greedy and subservient partisans, ready for every service, however base and corrupt. Were a premium offered for the best means of extending to the utmost the power of patronage; to destroy the love of country, and substitute a spirit of subserviency and man-worship; to encourage vice and discourage virtue; and, in a word, to prepare for the subversion of liberty and the establishment of despotism, no scheme more perfect could be devised." " The disease is daily becoming more aggravated and dangerous, and if it be permitted to progress for a few years longer, with the rapidity with which it has of late advanced, it will soon pass beyond the reach of remedy. This is no party question. Every lover of his country and her institutions, be his party affiliation what it may, must see and deplore the rapid growth of patronage, with all its attending evils, and the certain catastrophe which awaits its further progress, if not timely arrested. The question now is, not how, or where, or with whom the danger originated, but how it is to be arrested; not the cause, but the remedy; not how our institutions and liberty have been endangered, but how they are to be restored."

In the debate which followed this report, Mr. Webster said:—" Sir, we cannot disregard our experience. We cannot shut our eyes upon what is around us and upon us. No candid man can deny that a great, a very great change has taken place within a few years, in the practice of the Executive Government, which has produced a correspondent change in our political condition. No one can deny that office of every kind is now sought with extraordinary avidity, and that the condition, well understood to be attached to every office, high or low, is indiscriminate support of Executive measures, and implicit obedience to Executive will." These are eloquent words of warning.

The great impending and overshadowing danger of a change of administration in 1880 was averted. What imagination can picture the result which at that time would have followed the election of a Democratic President? Confederate soldiers impoverished by the rebellion would have rushed upon the Government to seize the offices, with a desperation never before equalled. The old war cry, "to the victor belongs the spoils," would have resounded throughout the length and breadth of the land. The efficient and honest would have been displaced by the venal and corrupt. It would soon have been clear that it was not Lee, but Grant, who surrendered at Appomatox. Every office in the gift of the Government would have been attacked by the serried ranks of grey, and the President elect would have led the advance.

If the American people could have foreseen all the demoralizing effects of the course pursued by President Jackson, they would have hurled him from power. Possibly they would have experienced difficulties, for since that time the process of impeachment has proven, for some inexplicable reason, both unyielding and impracticable.

The exercise of executive will continued through various administrations, but was, at last, prominently brought before the people. When Andrew Johnson became President, the astounding spectacle was presented of the reckless, dishonorable and relentless exercise of the one-man power to elevate his own political enemies, and to destroy, if possible, the very party which conferred upon him his office. To all the characteristics of the use of the monarchical will was added that of ingratitude and thanklessness. From April, 1865, to March, 1869, this single man brandished his sceptre in the face of the nation. The cry went out, "how can we depose him?" The answer came back, "he is but exercising the prerogative of his office." He pretended to love the Constitution which he violated. He enunciated the dictum, that he was the depositary of executive power, and then made war upon the liberties of his country. It was a humiliating sight to witness this great nation of freemen, or rather of men claiming to be free, at the feet of such a conqueror, surrounded as he was by "his partisans, dependents, favorites, sycophants, and man-worshippers."

In March, 1869, Congress put a check upon the wanton

exercise of this power by the passing of an act regulating the tenure of office. Of course this bill was passed over the veto of President Johnson. It provided that every person holding any civil office with the consent of the Senate, shall be entitled to hold such office until a successor is appointed in like manner. The secretaries of the various departments were to hold office for the term of the President by whom they were appointed, and until one month thereafter, subject to removal with consent of the Senate. The last section was intended to prevent Mr. Johnson from turning Mr. Lincoln's appointees out of office. And it was further enacted, that when any officer (except the Judges of the Supreme Court) is shown by evidence satisfactory to the President to be guilty of misconduct or crime, he shall become disqualified to perform his duties; in such case, and in no other, the President may suspend such officer and designate some suitable person to perform the duties until the next meeting of the Senate, and until the case shall be acted on by the Senate; the President was to report such case to the Senate, with the evidence for his action, and the name of the person designated in his place. If the Senate concur, then the President might remove; and such officer resume his duties. Before the passage of this act an army of officeholders was displaced by the political followers of the President. What humiliation! As a nation, we proved to be strong enough to suppress a stupendous civil war, but paradoxical as it is, we were weak enough quietly to submit to the arbitrary acts of the "depositary" of the kingly power. One day he would threaten to recognize a few of his adherents and certain Confederate soldiers claiming seats in Congress, as the Congress of the United States; the next, he would issue a military edict giving political rights to a rebel State. The loyal representatives had a hard struggle to save the Government from the tyrannical acts of this man. These were troublous times and not less dangerous to our liberties than the conflict of the battlefield. Let us profit by our experience,—if we do not we may as well bid farewell to the Republic. The impeachment of Andrew Johnson should have followed quickly after his assumption of power, and ought not to have disturbed the American people more than the removal of a justice of the peace.

On General Grant's becoming President, the Act passed during the administration of Andrew Johnson was very much modified and remains so until this day. During the recess of the Senate the President is authorized to suspend any civil officer appointed with the consent of the Senate (except Judges of the United States), and to designate some suitable person to perform the duties of such suspended officer in the meanwhile. The President shall, within thirty days after the commencement of each session of the Senate, nominate persons to fill the vacancies, and if the Senate, during such session, shall refuse to consent to an appointment in the place of the suspended officer, then, and not otherwise, he shall nominate another person to the same session of the Senate. It is by virtue of this last law that President Hayes suspended the collector of the port of New York. If the person who was designated to fill his place had been rejected, the President could have designated another. Thus he has virtually the power of removal. This is the operation of the law, notwithstanding that the only specific provision for removal in the Constitution is that of impeachment. The powers of the President are set forth, and by a familiar rule of construction, it would seem, that he is forbidden all exercise of power not enumerated. On this subject of authority to remove public officers, one salient fact remains, and that is, that the President claims to derive such power from some source ; and while the dispute goes on as to whether it is the Constitution or the law, or implication, he continues to act.

Among the extraordinary powers granted to the President by the Constitution is that of appointment of the Judges of the Supreme Court of the United States. Under our system, issues of immense importance to the welfare of the people come before this tribunal for adjudication, for instance, the question of the constitutionality of the legal tender act. President Grant has been openly charged with packing that Court in the interest of the large corporations of the country. Another strange anomaly is that the President appoints the very judge who may preside at his trial upon impeachment.*

* "If the official patronage of the President, when the United States had scarcely three million of inhabitants, was deemed excessive, how may it now be regarded when we have fifty million; it is not the augmented number of officials, to which the patronage applies, and which possibly is susceptible of some modification under a well regulated "civil service system," which alone invite Presidential intervention, but it is the projects to which the action of the Executive is continually invoked, with the hundreds of millions of capital involved, to legalize monopolies in railroads and other enterprises, that we have to take into account when considering the powers of an American President and the possible danger of their misapplication."—[William Beach Lawrence, (*North American Review*) Nov. 1880.]

CHAPTER VIII.

VETO.

THE proposition of conferring upon the President the power of negativing the proposed laws of Congress, was thoroughly discussed by the framers. Mr. Luther Martin, in his letter on the Federal Convention of 1787, says that there was objection to that section which relates to the negative of the President. There were some who thought no good reason could be assigned for giving the President a negative of any kind; that it was unnecessary: that the President was not likely to have more wisdom or integrity than the senators, or any of them, or better to know or consult the interest of the States than a member of the Senate.

Dr. Franklin seconded the motion of Mr. Butler in the convention, that the national Executive have a power to suspend any legislative act for a given time, not an absolute veto.

On the other hand, General Hamilton defended the veto power upon the ground that there is a propensity of the legislature to intrude upon the rights of the other branches, and of the necessity of furnishing each with constitutional arms for its defence. The natural conflict between the different branches was here foreseen. "This author deprecates the idea that the Legislative and Executive powers might speedily come to be blended in the same hands." This is virtually what the present British Constitution is, and what the constitutional writers believe to be its glory and power. Hamilton took the opposite position, and urged that the primary inducement to conferring the power of the veto upon the Executive was to enable him to defend himself.

Wilson and Hamilton desired to trust the Executive with an absolute negative on acts of legislation, but this was opposed, although from widely different motives, by Gerry, Franklin, Sherman, Madison, Butler, Bedford, and Mason, and was unanimously negatived.*

Wilson urged upon the Convention the Virginia plan of vesting a limited veto on legislation in a council of revision, composed of the Executive and a convenient number of the Judiciary.†

That which stands out more prominently than anything in American history is the great similarity of our fundamental law with the ancient and obsolete theories of the Constitution of Great Britain.‡ The veto power of the President is no exception to this rule.

The power of the two Houses of Parliament to frame laws was presumed to be held in check by the king's negative which could always be interposed to prevent the adoption of an unwise or unnecessary statute. Again, the arbitrary exercise of the king's right of veto was itself restrained by the power which Parliament possessed of refusing a grant of supplies for the service of the Crown. The Crown in England has not vetoed a measure passed by the Legislature since the reign of Queen Anne, nor have the House of Commons withheld supplies from the Crown since the Revolution of 1688. Yet, in free America, both of the powers are exercised to-day, and the present Congress is hurling its anathemas against the President who, in his turn, replies by veto after veto (1879). Congress proclaims that it will withhold the supplies if the President vetos its measures. He does veto them, neverthe-

---

* Gilpin, 784, 787. Eliot, 151, 154.
† Gilpin, 783. Eliot, 151.
‡ "The dispensatory power claimed by the Stuarts would have been the full veto power." Lieber, Civil Liberty, 201.

less. Here is conflict, antagonism. Who is going to yield? One must do so, or anarchy will ensue. Although the ancient theory of the veto was abandoned in England, it has survived with us. It was specifically introduced into our law. All of the Presidents since Jackson have regularly exercised it. Since the foundation of the Government the veto power has been exercised by the Presidents of the United States about one hundred times. Washington returned two bills, one for the appointment of members of Congress, the other to reduce the army. Madison sent six veto messages to Congress. Monroe vetoed only one bill, Jackson twelve, Tyler nine, Polk three, Pierce nine, Buchanan four, Lincoln one, Johnson seventeen, Grant thirty-six, and Hayes about eight. The bills vetoed by Johnson were political. Nearly all those vetoed by Grant were for the relief of individuals. The Inflation Bill was the most important one. Hayes vetoed the Silver and Chinese bills. The others were the appropriation bills. There is no evidence that the American people desire to have the provisions of the law in relation to vetoes modified or amended. There was a time, however, as will be shown, when the question was earnestly discussed. It is one of the alarming signs of the times that there is not a greater agitation of this momentous issue. Congress (one branch of which is direct from the people) passes bills, which are merely propositions until the President assents to them; and if he refuse, it requires two-thirds of the members to override him. This one man is elevated above the will of the people. How is it possible to reconcile this extraordinary power with true representative government? Is this negative power a just part of the Executive? He should carry out the law, not impede it. To-day the Queen of England must sign her death-warrant if Parliament so direct, but the President of the United States vetoes any bill of which he may disapprove. On the 24th of January, 1842, Mr. Clay proposed certain amendments to the Constitution, to prevent the growth of this regal power, and in support of those propositions he said : "It (the veto) was known to all to have originated in the institution of the tribunitian power in ancient Rome; that it was seized upon and perverted to purposes of ambition, when the empire was established under Augustus, and that it had not been finally abolished until the reign of Constantine. There could be no doubt that it had been introduced from the practice under the empire into the monarchies of Europe, in most of which, in some form and under some modification or other, it was now to be found. But although it existed in the national codes, the power had not, in the case of Great Britain, been exercised for a century and a half past; and, if he was correctly informed on the subject, it had, in the French monarchy, never been exercised at all * * * * Every one must recollect how it (the agitation of this subject), had been turned against the unfortunate Louis XVI., who had been held up to the ridicule of the populace, under the title of "Monsieur Veto", as his wife, his queen, had been called "Madame Veto;" and although, after much difficulty, the power had finally found a place in the Constitution, not a solitary instance had occurred of its actual exercise. Under the colonial state of this country, the power was transplanted, from the experience which had been had of it in Europe, to the laws relating to the colonies, and that in a double form; for there was a veto of the colonial governor, and also a veto of the Crown, but what was thought of this power by the inhabitants of these States, when rising to assert their freedom, might be seen in the words of the instrument in which they asserted their independence. At the head of all the grievances stated in that paper, as reasons for our separation from Great Britain, was placed the exercise of this very power of the royal veto. Speaking of the king, the Declaration of Independence employed this language:—"He has refused his assent to laws the most wholesome and necessary for the public good. He has forbidden his governors to pass laws of immediate and pressing importance, unless suspended in their operations, till his assent should be obtained, and, when so suspended, he has utterly neglected to attend to them."

Mr. Clay said he "had taken the pains to look into the provisions of twenty-six State Constitutions, in relation to this matter of the veto, and the result was highly curious and interesting. The States were in this respect divided, as equally as their number would admit, into three distinct classes. Nine of them gave to the Executive the veto power, unless controlled by two-thirds of the Legislature. Eight other States conferred the veto but controlled it by a second vote of a majority, as was proposed in the amendment now under consideration, while the nine remaining States had not inserted the veto at all; and at the head of these stood one which had been called the Mother of States—Virginia." * * * *

At the period under consideration, the Senate consisted of fifty-two members; of that number a majority was twenty-seven; two-thirds amounted to thirty-six. Supposing a law to be passed by a bare majority (and in all great and contested questions, bills were wont to be passed by very small majorities) then there would be in its favor twenty-seven votes. The bill was submitted to the President, and returned by him with his veto. The force of the Presidential veto could not be overturned but by thirty-six votes. Here, then, the veto in the hands of the President was equal in its effect upon Legislation to nine Senatorial votes. Mr. Clay dismissed all considerations of influence derived from his office, "all the glitter and *éclat* of the President's high station, and all the persuasion directed to the interest of men by his vast patronage; all this he laid out of view, and looked merely at the numerical fact, that in the Senate the veto was equal to nine votes—and now in regard to the other branch," * * * * * "the Executive veto amounted in effect to forty representative votes."

The same process of reasoning applied to the present Congress would make the presidential veto equal to thirteen in the Senate and forty-nine in the House. Mr. Clay continued: "How did it happen that a man who, when in that character, and acting with his fellow Senators, had been considered upon a par with them, was no sooner transferred to the other end of the avenue than his will became equal to that of nine Senators and forty Representatives? How," he asked, "did this happen, and wherein was it just and right? Was it not sufficient that this man, after his political apotheosis, should enjoy all the glitter and distinction and glory attached to his office? Was it not enough that he wielded so vast and formidable an amount of patronage, and thereby exerted an influence so potent and so extensive? Must there be superadded to all a legislative force equal to nine Senators and forty members of the House of Representatives?" Mr. Clay said "he had hitherto viewed the veto power simply in its numerical weight, in the aggregate votes of the two Houses; but there was another and far more important point of view in which it ought to be considered. He contended, that practically and in effect, the veto, armed with such a qualification as now accompanied it in the Constitution, was neither more nor less than an absolute power. It was virtually an unqualified negative in the legislation of Congress. Not a solitary instance has yet occurred in which the veto, once exerted, had ever been overruled, nor was such a case likely to happen. In most questions where the veto could be exerted, there was always a considerable difference of opinion, both in the country and in Congress, as to the bill which had been passed. In such circumstances, when all the personal influence, the official patronage, and the reason which accompanied the veto, were added to the substantial weight of the veto itself, every man acquainted with human nature would be ready to admit, that if nothing could set it right but a vote of two-thirds in both houses, it might as well have been made absolute at once."

It may be urged here that during the administration of President Johnson, the bills were passed over his veto, but it must be remembered that the President's apostacy from his party was a most unprecedented occurrence. The effect of it was to leave the President standing with a small minority over which Congress frequently passed their bills. Mr. Clay's position seems to remain good otherwise. The silver bill vetoed by Grant was only passed in a modified form, and the bill in relation to the Chinese, which President Hayes vetoed, was not passed over his veto. To resume: Mr. Clay in his great speech continued:—" He now approached another view of it, to which he would ask the serious and undivided attention of the Senate. The veto power professed to act only while the legislature acted; then it was to terminate. Its effect was to consummate legislation. The officer of the Government, in whose hands the Constitution placed a power so formidable, was supposed in theory to remain profoundly silent as to the passage of great measures of public policy, until they were presented to him in a finished form for his approbation and sanction." This is the theory; but Mr. Clay contended that "really and in practice this veto power drew after it the power of initiating laws, and in its effect must ultimately amount to conferring on the Executive the entire legislative power of the Government. With the power to initiate, and the power to consummate legislation, to give vitality and vigor to every law, or to strike it dead at his pleasure, the President must ultimately become the ruler of the nation."

Mr. Clay then proceeded to draw attention to the fact, that a certain section in the bill to establish a bank of the United States was introduced as a measure of conciliation, in the hope it would secure the sanction of the President. Not a solitary man could have otherwise voted for that section. But the sacrifice was made in vain; the President vetoed the bill. Mr. Clay said: " Had not the feeling been we must take what the Executive offers, or get nothing? Yes, already the idea was becoming familiarized to the minds of freemen, to men of only the second generation after the days of the Revolution, of submitting to the dictation of the Executive, because without his assent they could do nothing. Mr. Clay warned the nation that if this veto power was not arrested, if it was not either abolished, or at least limited and circumscribed, in process of time, and that before another such period had elapsed as had 'intervened since the Revolution, the whole legislation of this country would come to be prepared at the White House, or in one or the other of the Executive apartments, and would come down to Congress in the shape of bills for them to register, and pass through the forms of legislation, just as had once been done in the ancient courts of France." Then to enable a nation of freemen to carry out their will, to set Congress free to speak that will, to redress the wrongs, and to supply the wants of those that sent them, Mr. Clay again declared "that the veto power must be modified and restrained. If not, the question that Congress would have to decide would be, not what is the proper remedy for the existing grievances of the country, not what will restore the national prospects; no, but what measures will be sanctioned by the chief magistrate." "The question was the old question, whether we should have in this country a power tyrannical, despotic, absolute, the exercise of which must, sooner or later, produce an absolute despotism or a free representative government, with powers clearly defined and carefully separated. That was the question to be decided." These words fell from the lips of one of the greatest statesmen this country ever produced. They were uttered nearly forty years ago in the most solemn and impressive manner. They were the embodiment of the experience of one who was almost continuously during a long life in the councils of the nation. Every sympathy of his heart was with the people. He was the great representative man of his day. He fairly won the name of "the great benefactor, the great commoner." No apology is necessary for quoting from the speeches of one so great, so good, so powerful. The words reproduced here are probably the best argument that can be made against the power which seems so inconsistent and conflicting with the principles of representative government. What American can read that speech without feeling indignant that the political sentiments formulated in the Declaration should have been so far departed from. This subject will be incidentally referred to at other points of this argument. It is thought, that when all the various acts of our Presidents have been contemplated, that no one will have the temerity to charge Mr. Clay with the ill-digested views of an alarmist. If he was not, then let us remedy this great wrong; sweep away this great error.*

At this present moment (March, 1879), there is occurring one of the greatest struggles which has ever taken place between the Executive and the Congress. Both branches of Congress are Democratic for the first time since 1860. The President is Republican. The Democrats have tacked on to the appropriation bills for the army, the executive and judicial departments, a repeal of the supervisory election law, and the law authorizing the use of the army in the preservation of the peace at the polls. The first of these laws is intended to give us honest elections in the large cities of the North, and the second to protect the recently enfranchised citizen in the exercise of his elective rights. This is an attempt, on the part of the Democrats, to compel the President to submit to their dictation. Still, they are working within their constitutional rights, and that fact must not be lost sight of.

* "At the head of the duties which remain for the Whigs to perform towards their country, stands conspicuously and prominently above all others— First, a reduction of the Executive power by a further limitation of the veto, so as to secure obedience to the public will as shall be impressed by the immediate representatives of the people and the states, with no other control than that which is indispensable to avert hasty or unconstitutional legislation."—[Address to the People, Niles' Reg., LXI., 35, 36.]

In 1855, the anti-Nebraska men, afterwards called "Republicans," in passing the Army Appropriation bill in the House attached a proviso forbidding the President to use the army to enforce the acts of the pro-slavery Kansas Legislature. In the aristocratic Senate—with the co-operation of a Democratic President—this act was denounced as revolutionary. The Slave South, with its sparsely inhabited states, had a tremendous power in the Senate. President Pierce was pliant to the wishes of the Democratic party. The Republicans, as they were then called, maintained the right of the House (without the co-operation of the Senate) to guard the purse and to impose any conditions whatsoever. Mr. Fessenden made use of these memorable words:—"Does he not know well, that in the English Parliament, from the earliest times, not only have appropriation and revenue bills gone together, but in cases without number, it has been the habit of that Parliament to check the power of the Crown, by imposing conditions to their appropriation of money? Does he not know that the only mode in which our ancestors of Massachusetts checked the powers of their royal governors was by granting money only on conditions? The power of supply and the power of annexing conditions to supply, have always gone together in parliamentary history; and their joint exercise has never been denounced as a case of revolution, or calling for revolution, or tending to produce revolution, in any shape or form whatever. It is a power essential to the preservation of our liberties." Mr. Seward, in his philosophical way, presented the argument on the same occasion as follows:—"Since the House of Representatives has power to pass such a bill distinctly, it has the power also to place an equivalent prohibition in any bill which it has constitutional power to pass. And so it has a constitutional right to place the prohibition in an annual Army Appropriation bill. It is a right one if necessary to effect the object desired, and if that object is one that is in itself just and eminently important to the peace and happiness of the country, or to the security of the liberties of the people. The House of Representatives, moreover, is entitled to judge and determine for itself whether the proceeding is thus necessary, or whether the object of it is thus important." Ben Wade thus expressed his thoughts: —"I say the House of Representatives have done right. Here we are told it is revolutionary, and therefore we must not breathe the breath of life into their action, but must permit it to go back to the House with an appeal to the House to recede. Sir, I do not know but what you may succeed under the idea that this is revolution; but, so help me God, I hope the man who proposes to recede a hair's breadth from the action of the House, will never find his way back again. Has it come to this, that if the House of Representatives do not think proper to frame a bill for the support of the army of the country, appropriating twelve millions in a way to satisfy the majority of this body, revolution shall follow, and the responsibility be upon the House." To those who look below the surface, it will be seen that this was really a conflict between the Executive and the people. The House is the only body which represents the masses; the Senate being a body not based upon equal representation. The Senate is not more Republican in its structure than the House of Lords in England. But this incident in our history marks not only the commencement of the great struggle between slave and free labor, but furnishes another illustration of the encroachments of the Executive; for the question was whether the President should be allowed to use the army in destroying the liberties of the people. Pierce had no sympathy with true government or liberty. If he had had a little more vim and courage, he would have made a first-class tyrant, but as it is, history has little to say of him. Notwithstanding these arguments, made by the first men of the nation, who held that the House of Representatives alone has the constitutional power to place a prohibition in the annual Army Appropriation bill, still, there can be but little doubt that the President has the legal power in effect of completely frustrating the legislation now proposed by the interposition of his veto (1879).* As an abstract question, he should not have. But it has been urged with considerable force that, concretely regarded, the President should exercise the right of veto on this occasion, for the reason that the movement against him is not in the interest of fair elections, either in the North or in the South, and by the repeal of these laws the Democrats will be enabled, if need be, to manipulate the elections so as to secure the success of their candidate.

It is also claimed that the President has the undoubted right by law to exercise the prerogative, and if the interests of liberty and good government can be temporarily subserved, he should do it; that many acts of Lincoln and Grant were even unauthorized by law, still, as they were performed in the cause of freedom, that it would be pushing an argument to the verge of absurdity to assert that they were wrong.

Admit that all the unequal and revolutionary conditions exist, as they were claimed to exist, should President Hayes exercise the extraordinary power conferred upon him? Would it not be establishing one more bad precedent, which the next President may appeal to in the furtherance of slavery and tyranny? Is it not better that he should forego the application of what he deems his constitutional right, even in this emergency, than to give to the enemies of Republican government a single argument, why the monarchical powers of our Executive should be continued in our fundamental law.

The reasoning from the general principle that he is necessary as a check upon Congress, is but the argument of force against force, revolution against revolution. With a true system of representation there never could be any tyranny. Congress must then express the will, the mind, and the con-

---

* We let the language stand as it was written at the time.

science of the people. The congress'onal form of government is the proper one.

Even in our transitional state, the office of President should be abolished, and with it all the survivals of kingship.

During the debate referred to, Mr. Hurd of Ohio said :— "It is revolution against every theory of the Constitution, * * * * * * for a member of this House, be he an intimate friend of the President or not, (referring to Mr. Garfield) to threaten the House with a veto from the President, if you dare do right. I do not believe that the majority of this House will be intimidated from its duty by a threat of the President, much less the threat of a President whose title to office is so doubtful, and whose tenure of office is yet so uncertain."

Mr. Blackburn of Kentucky said :—"Nobody has been surprised at the speech of the gentleman from New Jersey (Mr. Robeson). The performance would not have been complete, would not have been fairly sounded out, unless some member of the Privy Council of that imperialistic dynasty under whose administration the very vicious practice had grown up, which it was sought to reveal, had testified on the floor in its behalf. And now, by what sort of authority has the gentleman from Ohio come to threaten the House with a probable and possible action of the Executive? What provision of the Federal Constitution undertook to clothe anybody, either the President himself, or one of his Privy Council, even including his Premier, the Secretary of State, to sit as he has done on the floor of the House last Saturday, and by his presence and approval seem to intimidate, overawe and browbeat the American Congress? Who has commissioned the gentleman from Ohio to tell the House that it had better be careful, because the issue was made, and the President would not be coerced into a message of approval? Did the gentleman from Ohio, or any other gentleman, put such a low estimate on the self-respect, the integrity, the courage and the

manhood of the House, without regard to party, as to believe that such a threat, so flaunted, was to intimidate the law-making branch of the government, and shape its action on measures of legislation? If the gentleman from Ohio is to be excused (for certainly he cannot be justified) for parading before this House the *argumentum in terrorum* of a veto that is cut and dried to be put upon a bill which has not yet passed, and if he is to be pardoned for warning the House that the executive branch of the government will never yield its assent to this measure in its present form, I ask whether I am not warranted and justified in employing equal candor in assuring that gentleman and his associates that the dominant power in this Congress, the ruling element in this body, is also equally determined that until its just demands, sanctioned by all laws, human and divine, protected and hedged around by precedents without number, demanded by the people of this land without regard to section; clamored for, not by the South alone, but in Philadelphia as well as in New Orleans, in San Francisco and Boston, as well as in Charleston and Savannah, are complied with, this side of the Chamber, which has demonstrated its power, never means to yield, or surrender unless this Congress shall have died by virtue of its limitation." * * * "A principle cannot be compromised. It may be surrendered, but that can only be done by its advocates giving proof to the world that they are cravens and cowards, and lack the courage of their own convictions. We cannot yield, and we will not yield." * * *
"The issue is laid down. The gage of battle is delivered. Lift it when you please, and we are willing to appeal to that sovereign arbiter to which the gentleman from Ohio so handsomely alluded—the American people—to decide between us. We intend to deny to the President of this Republic the right to exercise such unconstitutional powers. We do not mean to pitch this contest on the grounds of objection to him who happens, if not by 'the grace of God,' by the 'run of luck'

to be administering that office. If from yonder canvas (pointing to a picture hanging to the east of the Speaker's chair), the first President of the Republic should step down to assume the powers which the grateful people of an infant Republic conferred upon him as their first chief magistrate— if he were here, fired by that patriotic ardor which moved him in the earlier and better days of this great government, to him we could never consent to yield unconstitutional powers, or to rest the liberties of the citizens in any man's discretion, nor would he receive it. It was not for the earlier, but for the later executives of this government to grasp and seek to retain such questionable prerogatives. You cannot have it. The issue is made. It is made on principle, not on policy, and it cannot be surrendered. Standing on such broad grounds, clothed in such a panoply, resting this case on the broadest principle of justice, we are content to appeal to the people of this land."

From the broad basis of representative government, the Democratic party is undoubtedly right in taking the stand that the Executive should not exercise his will against the legislative branch ; certainly not to threaten it, as it is charged. The philosophy of the present crisis seems to make it the interest of the Republican party to support the Executive, but let it be remembered that this is a dangerous position to assume, for the next President may be Democratic. If the Republican party is wedded to true progress and reform in government, then its every interest lies in establishing a representation based on population, and fair elections, and not in bolstering up the executive power of the nation. The Democratic party is reactionary and non-progressive, having for its chief object the strengthening of all the old theories of the Constitution, *e.g.*, State sovereignty and other heresies. Let the Republican party yield its present position and appeal to the people, and demonstrate to them that the present Democratic party has power inimical to the true interests of the country, acquired by the use of force and fraud in the South. Let the law be so amended that these great wrongs may be righted, and then the representative branch of the Government can no longer be controlled by the Bourbons who have seized upon it. Of course, every one should know how hollow is the position taken by the Democrats. They pretend that they do not want soldiery at the polls, when in point of fact they desire to rid themselves of those forces, merely to substitute the State militia, which will be employed in converting an election in the South into a farce. The following recital of what took place on one of the last days of this debate illustrates the insincerity of the Democrats:—

"The discussion was continued, and then Mr. New, of Indiana, moved that the sixth section of the Bill be amended by exempting sections 52–97 of the Revised Statutes from its operation. Immediately upon this motion being made, Mr. Baker, of Indiana, moved that to the proposed amendment be added his amendment, which provides that rifle clubs, and persons bearing arms, pistols, knives, bludgeons, and other weapons, be prohibited, under heavy penalties, from surrounding or being near any polling place during a Federal election." The Chairman, Mr. Springer, for the moment made no objection to this amendment. It was read by the Clerk, and Mr. Baker advocated it in a speech of much force. At this juncture, Mr. Sparks made the point of order that the amendment could not be considered together with that of Mr. New. Messrs. Conger and Baker were at once upon their feet, and very properly held that under the rules of the House this point of order came too late, the last amendment having been received by the Chair, read by the Clerk, and discussed on the floor. Still, Mr Springer seemed determined not to allow the amendments to be considered together, and Mr. Conger, with much indignation, which was certainly called for under the circumstances, was proceeding to discuss the merits of the case, when the Chair ordered him to take his seat. "No, I will not take my seat," cried brave Conger, quivering with suppressed passion. "Then I will send the Sergeant-at-Arms to compel you to sit down," shouted Mr. Springer. Great confusion followed, and from all sides there came loud cries of "Order!" "Order!" At last quiet was restored, and, amid defiant cries from the Democrats of "Appeal if you like, and we will vote you down," the Chairman, overriding every rule and precedent, decided that the amendment offered by Mr. Baker could not then be entertained. The Republicans were, of course, unable to help themselves, and the question recurred on the amendment of Mr. New.

It is quite apparent that if the Democrats had really desired to have the polling places in the South entirely free from bodies of armed men, they would have accepted the amendment of Mr. Baker. We have seen what they did do.

Another supreme absurdity indulged in by the Democrats was their attempt to draw an analogy between the laws of England, which provides that troops shall not be present at the polls, and the laws of the United States on the same subject. The reason why the reference was almost irrelevant to the issue here is, that a law in England prescribing that neither troops nor armed men shall be permitted within certain distances of the polling places on election days, would effectually and absolutely prevent such occurrence, while with us, with our State organizations, militia and other armed men might be in full force at the polls, and there would be no violation of any law of the United States. Here is the exact point. They wish to keep the United States forces away from the polls, in order to use to their heart's content the domestic militia and white league for the suppression of all opposition to Democratic rule.

Mr. Tucker, of Virginia, said that the President could not veto the Bill on account of the method of its passage. If he vetoes it at all, it must be on the merits of the Bill, and what were those merits? They take away from his Excellency the right to preside with his troops at the polls. Gentlemen said that there must be no coercion of the President. What right had the President to coerce Congress? It was coercion one way or the other. The President demanded unconditional supplies. Congress said, "We will give you no supplies except on conditions. We will give you the army, but you must keep that army from the polls." Would his friends from Ohio and Connecticut (Messrs. Garfield and Hawley), vote for the proposed repeal as a separate measure? Mr. Garfield — I would vote to repeal these clauses if brought up separately, but not to make them as you propose to make them. Mr. Tucker replied, "that his friend stood on the very narrow ground, that on the merits the law ought to be repealed, but that on account of the method of its passage the President ought to veto it. How could that be? What right had the President to say anything in regard to the method of its passage, if he had no objection on the score of its merits? The matters with which it was proposed to interfere were matters under the peculiar guardianship of the House of Representatives. The President represented the Electoral College. He represented the principle of the patronage of the Government. The Senate represented the States, but the House represented and was intimately connected with the people. That body now proposed to say that it would place the army in the hands of the President on condition that it should never be used at the polls. Would the President withhold his consent and say that unless Congress gave him the power to control elections he would let the Government die of starvation? Would he say, in the language of a highwayman, (if a President could use such language), 'Your money or your life?' The money I demand, or the life of the Government." Behold another illustration of the idea of executive influence upon legislation!

It would seem from this admission of Mr. Garfield that all he had been contending for was a matter of etiquette, a question of form, of regularity of procedure. The tacking on was a menace to the President. On the other hand, the Democrats claimed that they were not only acting within their constitutional powers in taking the step they did, but that they were right on the merits.

If the President really instructed his friends in Congress thus to disturb the whole country with this political debate, for the sole purpose of dictating the course of procedure to be taken in legislating on this subject, then it is one of the most glaring instances of presidential and unrepublican interference that has ever occurred. The meaning of it is this: The President does not object to the bill which you intend to pass, but he protests against your doing it in this way, and, if you do, he will veto the measure. This position savors of tyranny. But so long as we have a President, where is the remedy? In this contest between Congress and the President, the Democratic party has placed itself in a thoroughly inconsistent position, in as much as it championed the executive exercise of veto, during the administrations of Jackson, Pierce, and Buchanan. In its platform of 1856, it inserted a comprehensive statement of its position on this question. But it is not our purpose to criticize this party, only so far as it may throw light upon the general question of presidential power. The great matter for the consideration of the American people is whether it is right, first, to have a President who is not directly the representative of the people, but the creature of the Electoral College, which is chosen by the States; and, second, to give him, in any sense, a legislative power. Regarded as a constitutional question, he has that power, but as a question based on general principles of government by the people, he should not have it. Congress should have the sole law-making power. In legislation, the President should be a mere ministerial officer. If the signature of any executive officer be necessary it should be a mere formality, which he should have no right to withhold. The use of the veto by the President is a despotic encroachment on the powers of the Legislature. It is one of the great impending dangers to American liberty. The great consideration for the American people is, how long will a government stand, which is continually shaken to its very centre by violent and continued conflicts between its different branches, each charging upon the other revolutionary designs. Congress claimed the right to repeal certain laws, and the President replied that he forbore to enter again upon any general discussion of the "dangerous and unconstitutional principle" of the proposed laws. If we are to be guided by the lamp of experience, these antagonisms should be eliminated from the Constitution. History shows that they generally culminate in civil war.

CHAPTER IX.

IMPEACHMENT.

PRESIDENTS of the United States have committed acts prejudicial to the interests of the people, and subversive of the very principles of our Government. They have violated the provisions of the Constitution, neglected duties, and offended against the law. In some instances they have been guilty of high crimes and misdemeanors by acts committed, in others by acts omitted. While acting within the forms of law, they have abused discretionary powers. They have been charged by the first men in the nation with being usurpers and despots. The question naturally arises, whether there be not provisions for the trial of such offenders; whether they may not be instantly removed from office. If such provisions exist, are they efficient? The House of Representatives has the sole power of impeachment, that is, of bringing forward or proposing an impeachment, but the power to try all impeachments, after the arraignment by the House, is vested in the Senate. The Constitution provides: " The Senate shall have sole power to try all impeachments. When sitting for that purpose, they shall be on oath or affirmation. When the President of the United States is tried, the Chief Justice shall preside; and no person shall be convicted without the concurrence of two-thirds of the members present." * The trial of impeachment was given to the Senate, because in England it rested with the House of Lords, and, for the further reason, that the offences gen-

---

* Art. I., Sec. 3 Cons.

erally charged are not strictly legal or technical, but of a political nature of an extraordinary character, such as misdemeanors in office and violations of public trusts, which are difficult to define. In the House of Lords a mere majority suffices; in the Senate a two-thirds vote is required, and it must be borne in mind, too, that the Senate does not represent the people but the States. Since the adoption of the Constitution there have been five trials by impeachment: (1) That of Senator William Blount, in 1799, (2) Judge John Pickering, in 1803, (3) Judge Samuel Chase, in 1804, (4) Judge James L. Peck, in 1830, (5) President Andrew Johnson, in 1868. The country had been ruled by a Jackson, a Tyler, a Polk, but no impeachment was attempted. For some inexplicable reason, the people of the United States are averse to the exercise of this wise provision of the Constitution.; wise, particularly, in a Government which places its Executive in power for a fixed period. From the moment Andrew Johnson came to the Presidency, there was an open and violent conflict between him and Congress. Crimination and recrimination ensued. At the most critical period in our history, when the nation should have exercised all its wisdom in the settlement of the vexed questions of reconstruction, the time was mostly occupied in an abortive attempt to vindicate Republican Government and to enforce the plain provisions of the Constitution for the removal of a recreant or criminal Executive. In that great struggle the Executive proved the stronger. The world saw that we hesitated and then refused to punish the arbitrariness, usurpation, and crime of a President. So far as precedent goes, may not our future kings commit almost any act of unlawfulness or tyranny with impunity? May they not accompany those acts with taunts, menaces, and vulgarity?

The first eight articles in the impeachment set forth the acts of the President in the removal of Mr. Stanton and the appointment of Mr. Thomas, *ad interim*. There was a serious question whether the President did really violate the letter of the law. In answer to this position, it was urged that the misdemeanor lay in the intent and purpose; that the President could be guilty of an improper purpose although he acted under the color of law. The articles referred to charged that the President made these appointments and removals by intimidation and threats; that he conspired with Mr. Thomas to prevent the execution of the civil tenure act; that he conspired to seize the property of the War Department by force; and the 8th article charges the President with making the appointment for the purpose of getting control of the disbursement of moneys appropriated for the military service. The 9th article alleged that the President did declare to, and instruct General Emory that part of a law of the United States was unconstitutional. Article ten alleged that President Johnson, intending to bring the Congress of the United States into contempt made speeches, which were fully set forth, whereby he brought the office of President into ridicule and disgrace. To sustain these charges the shorthand notes of the reporters were put in evidence. They were complete and voluminous. To prove the revolutionary designs of Andrew Johnson, we shall quote a single passage only from one of his speeches. He said : " If you will take up the riot at New Orleans and trace it back to its source, or to its immediate cause, you will find out who was responsible for the blood that was shed there. * * * * I called upon your Congress that is trying to break up the Government. * * * But Congress, factious and domineering, had undertaken to poison the minds of the American people * * * * hence you will find that another rebellion was commenced having its origin in the radical Congress." The eleventh article alleged that President Johnson said, that the 39th Congress was not the Congress of the United States. Will not the reader of history pause in mute astonishment when he peruses the pages which record the impeachment trial of Andrew Johnson, and wonder why the Senate refused to find him guilty. The charges were proven. Does any one doubt that it was the intention of the President to undermine the affections of the people for the Government as represented in Congress, and to recognize his rebellious friends from the South, and their sympathizers at the North, as the Congress of the United States? Would he not have done this, although it caused civil war? Did he not intend to bring to naught the constitutional action of Congress? Did he not oppose the will of the loyal people of the United States?

One of the most remarkable features of the impeachment of Andrew Johnson was, that acts committed clearly in violation of the Constitution and subversive of good government, were not embodied in the articles. Did he not violate the law and usurp the powers of Congress in attempting to call the Confederate soldiers into the council of the nation before they had had an opportunity to wash their hands of the blood of Union men? Did he not issue proclamations in relation to civil affairs, basing his action upon his prerogative as commander-in-chief of the army and navy? In his answer to the tenth article, President Johnson avers: "That said article and specifications and allegations thereof, wholly and in every part thereof, question only the discretion and propriety of freedom of opinion, or freedom of speech as exercised by this respondent as a citizen of the United States, in his personal right and capacity, and without allegation or imputation against this respondent of the violation of any law of the United States, touching or relating to freedom of speech or its exercise by any citizen of the United States or otherwise." On the trial, it was claimed in support of this allegation that an act to be impeachable was necessarily an indictable act.* It must be some crime or misdemeanor against the letter of the law. The Constitution provides that the officer impeached

---

* "I put the case, suppose the President committed murder in the street. Impeach him? But you can only remove him from office on impeachment. Why, when he is no longer President, you can indict him. But, in the mean

can afterwards be tried for crime. The inference is plain, that the words "high crimes and misdemeanors" are not used in the Constitution in any technical sense.

Senator Bayard, on the Blount trial, said that "Impeachment is a proceeding purely of a political nature. It is not so much designed to punish the offender, as to secure the State. * * * It simply divests him of his political capacity." Neither the framers of our Constitution, nor writers on parliamentary and common law ever attempted to define an impeachable crime. It was held in England that an impeachment was no answer to an indictment. Impeachment has always been the mode of removing officers who imperil the public safety. The framers of our Constitution had in their minds the contemporaneous meaning of the words used by them in relation to trial by impeachment, and the authorities are numerous to the effect that : " When a Lord Chancellor has been thought to put the seal to an ignominious treaty ; a Lord Admiral to neglect his trust ; a Privy Counsellor to propound or support pernicious and dishonorable measures ;" he has committed an impeachable offence. Wooddesson, whose lectures were read at Oxford in 1777, declared that " Magistrates and officers * * * may abuse their delegated powers to the extensive detriment of the community, and at the same time in a manner not properly cognizable before the ordinary tribunal." He then goes on to say that the remedy was by impeachment. Madison said : " If the President got up a treaty by surprise, he would be impeached." Ingersoll said in the Blount trial, " The Duke of Suffolk was impeached for neglect of duty as an ambassador;

time, he runs away. But I will put another case. Suppose he continues his murders daily, and neither House is sitting to impeach him ? Oh ! the people would rise and restrain him. Very well, you would allow the mob to do what the loyal Justice must abstain from. . . . . General Schuyler joined us. 'What think you, General,' said I, by way of giving the matter a different turn; 'I am not a good civilian, but I think the President is a kind of sacred person.' . . . . Bravo! my *jure divino* man."—[Sketches of Debates in the First Senate of the United States, by Maclay, 152.

the Earl of Bristol that he gave counsel against a war with Spain, whose king had affronted the English nation; the Duke of Buckingham, that he, being admiral, neglected the safeguard of the sea; Michael de la Pole, that he, being chancellor, acted contrary to his duty; the Duke of Buckingham for having a plurality of office. * * * The Earl of Oxford for selling goods to his own use captured by him." Doctor Sacheverell was impeached for preaching an improper sermon. Although cases decided since the adoption of the American Constitution would throw no light upon the meaning of that instrument, still no decisions can be found where the ground of impeachment has been limited in England. Judge Story, in speaking of the Blount conviction, said that he was not found guilty of an indictable crime, that the offence " was not defined by any statute of the United States." William Lawrence, in his brief, stated that " the power of impeachment, so far as the President is concerned, was inserted in the Constitution to secure 'good behavior,' to punish 'misconduct,' to defend 'the community against the incapacity, negligence, or perfidy of the chief magistrate,' to punish 'abuse of power,' 'treachery,' 'corrupting his electors,' or, as Madison declared, 'for every act which might be called a misdemeanor.'" And Mr. Madison afterwards maintained that " the wanton removal of meritorious officers would subject him [the President] to impeachment and removal from his own high trust."

There is no need of consulting the authorities to prove how weak a defence President Johnson set up in answer to article ten. The President, not only subjected himself to the charge of making speeches filled with indecency, but replete with slander and treason. General Butler, speaking of that authority which has been vested in a single man under our Constitution, says, " Never again * * * can the people of this or any other country, by constitutional checks or guards, stay the usurpations of executive power."

The weakness and inefficiency of the provisions of the Constitution in relation to impeachment were thoroughly appreciated by many members of the Federal, as well as by the State Conventions. Judge Pendleton, in the South Carolina Convention, opposed the form of impeachment. Mr. Grafton, in the Virginia convention, said: "As this Government is organized, it would be dangerous to invest the President with such powers. How will you punish him if he abuse his power? Will you call him before the Senate? They are his counsellors and partners in crime!" Mr. James Monroe said, in the same convention, that he was opposed to the power of the President, and continued: "He is elected for four years, and not excluded from re-election. Suppose he violates the laws and the Constitution, or commits high crimes, by whom is he to be tried? By his own councils—by those who advise him to commit those violations and crimes? This subverts the principles of justice, as it excuses him from punishment. He commands the army of the United States till he is condemned." Mr. Martin, in his letter on the Federal Convention, says that there is little probability of the President ever being impeached; that under the laws it would be almost impossible to get the two-thirds vote. The Senate, he affirmed, is a Privy Council to the President; it is probable that many of its leading members may have advised or concurred in the very measures for which he may be impeached. The President can hold out one of the valuable offices to each Senator he wishes to influence. He can always secure the necessary one-third. How can a criminal be convicted who is constitutionally empowered to bribe his judges, at the head of whom is to preside the Chief Justice, who is appointed by the President himself? A strong President, with a vigorous will and a respectable following, never could be impeached. The slow, uncertain method of removing the Executive even failed against Andrew Johnson. During the storms of civil war, and of Presidential usurpation, it would be utterly worthless.

CHAPTER X.

THE CABINET.

The Cabinet has no separate entity or existence which the law recognizes. It is the mere creature of the President. Its members hold their positions subject to his will. They may express their views to him, but he is not in any manner controlled by them. They may urge, but the President acts. It matters little what the opinion or policy of a member of the Cabinet may be; it is the individual will of the President that rules.* It is the Executive who reaps the benefit of success; it is he who is responsible for failure. It is true that the practice of surrounding the President with a body called the Cabinet has grown up with the Presidency. It was natural and logical that this should be so; having established a king, we ought not to be surprised at his assumption of kingly prerogatives. To find authority for the establishment of the irresponsible advisers of the President, we shall be compelled to go to the monarchies of Europe before they became limited. The Constitution of the United States does not provide for any such officers. The departments themselves, over which these officers preside, are not provided for by the Constitution; they were created by Congress. They could be extended or abolished by the same power that called them into existence. The Department of State, originally known as the Department of Foreign Affairs, was created by

---

* "At present the Cabinet is selected by, and in substance retained during the will of the President. They are in a sense his clerks—not responsible to the people, but to him only. His policy is their policy, which the will of the people, however expressed, cannot change.—[The Third Term, by E. W. Stoughton, *North American Review*, March, 1880.

Act of Congress, July 27th, 1789. The War Department was created in August, and the Navy Department in April of the same year. Although the Post Office Department was organized in 1789, the Postmaster-General was only regarded as the head of a bureau until 1829, when President Jackson invited Mr. Barry to a seat in the Cabinet. Usage, since that time, has recognized the Postmaster-General as a Cabinet officer. With the history of our Presidents before us, it is strange that the chief of the Department of Agriculture has not been invited to swell the number of those erroneously termed the constitutional advisers of the President.

The Department of Justice was created in 1870. It had been called the Office of the Attorney-General. The Department of the Interior was created in 1849. Congress could merge these different departments or create new ones. How these Cabinet officers ever became the mere creatures of our President is one of the enigmas in the political history of the country. In seeking to find an origin, we can find only an analogy in the British Constitution, as it existed long before the American Revolution. Prior to 1688, the British Government was carried on "by virtue of Royal prerogative," that is to say, by the King in person, with the advice and assistance of Ministers appointed by himself, who were responsible to the Sovereign alone for the ordinary conduct of public affairs, while they were amenable to Parliament for any direct abuse of their functions. Under this system, Parliament had no voice in the selection of Ministers of the Crown, and whenever they entertained adverse opinions in regard to questions of administration, they had no means of making those opinions known, except by retrospective complaint and remonstrance. This system occasioned frequent conflicts which brought about civil war. In early times the great desideratum was how to preserve the balance of power between the different branches of the Government. Since that period the text writers, such as Blackstone, Paley, De

Lolme, all set forth the Constitution as we have just referred to it. The operation of the law of development has utterly destroyed their theory.

Mr. Rutledge, in the Federal convention, read a report of a committee of which he was a member, recommending, among other things, that "the President of the United States shall have a Privy Council, which shall consist of various persons (naming them), whose duty it shall be to advise him in matters respecting the execution of his office, which he shall think proper to lay before them, but their advice shall not conclude him, nor affect his responsibility for the measures he shall adopt." Mr. Madison moved that this committee be instructed to prepare a clause, or clauses, for establishing an Executive Council, or a Council of States, for the President of the United States, to consist of two members from the Eastern, two from the Middle, and two from the Southern States, with a rotation and duration of office as prescribed in the Senate. This was decided in the negative. That propositions for the establishment of a Privy Council to the President should have been made in the Federal convention by such prominent members of it, proves conclusively that the prevailing idea in that body, was that the Executive must be fashioned after that of Great Britain, and, strange as it may appear, after the model that had been virtually abandoned. This proposed Council could only examine such questions as the President might think proper to lay before it, and after its members had decided upon a certain course, that decision would not conclude the President. This proposition was in the very teeth of the law, as it actually existed in England at this time. How is this to be accounted for? Certainly not on the ground of ignorance of the law, or of the history of the Mother Country. The other proposition must, therefore, be true, namely, that it was the intention of the framers to establish a strong Government, with a vigorous Executive. The question for this generation to decide is, whether the framers acted logically, and whether they should not have formed a more national representative Government than they did. There is little evidence among us of a tendency to adopt the later and more liberal workings of the English Constitution. The ancient Privy Council belonged to the person of the monarch—the members of which were sworn to "advise the King to the best of their cunning and discretion." This Council has become obsolete in England only to be established here. For at least the last hundred years, there has been, in England, a decided inclination to abridge the powers of the Executive, in so far as they had been centred in the King; in our country the tendency has been in the opposite direction. In this respect, England has become more republican, we more monarchical. In our country the Cabinet has no actual power; in England it has been changed into the working Executive. The Queen is a figure-head, the President is a ruler. In England the Cabinet is the fourth power, as it were, standing outside of the Legislative, Executive, and Judicial branches of the Government. It is distinct and separate. Mr. Gladstone says: "The Cabinet is the threefold hinge that connects together for action the British Constitution, of King or Queen, Lords and Commons. Upon it is concentrated the whole strain of the Government, and it constitutes from day to day

* "Thus do the merits of the two systems—Committee Government and Government by a responsible Cabinet—hinge upon this matter of a full and free discussion of all subjects of legislation; upon the principle stated by Mr. Bagehot that free government is self government—a government of the people, by the people. It is, perhaps, safe to say that the Government which secures the most thorough discussions of public interests—whose administration most nearly conforms to the opinions of the governed—is the freest and the best. And certainly, when judged by this principle, Government by responsible Standing Committees can bear no comparison with Government by means of a responsible ministry, for, as we have seen—and as others besides Senator Hoar have shown—its essential feature is a vicious suppression of debate."—[Cabinet Government in the United States, by Thomas W. Wilson, *International Review*, August, 1879.

the true centre of gravity for the working system of the State, although the ultimate superiority of force resides in the Representative Chamber." Thus it appears that the British Cabinet has an entity and a power, while ours is the mere servant of the President.*

The American Cabinet is a secret and irresponsible conclave. It is a fit adjunct to the present form of the Presidency. Our Cabinet Secretary locks himself in his office. It is quite impossible to find out much about him. He may be learned or ignorant. His duty may be performed by himself or an employe. Whatever are his qualifications seems to be a matter that concerns only the President. The Secretaries are a species of staff officers of the President, and a personal staff at that.†

---

* Nothing, perhaps, can better explain the monarchical principle in the case of an American President, as contrasted with the formal acts alone permitted to the English King, than a reference to the respective attributes of the Cabinets of the two countries. The term Cabinet is in neither country known to the laws, though in both a word of universal use. Since the establishment of parliamentary government, the sole function of the King, which can have any political aspect, is the appointment of the ministers; but in this he acts a merely formal part. Public sentiment, through Parliament, indicates when a change in the ministry must take place, and points out the men to whom the administration of the government is to be confided, usually designating some one as the Premier. It is for the statesman, who may then be sent for by the King, to ascertain whether he can form such a Cabinet as will enable him to. control the action of Parliament. As the duties of the King cease when he has placed in the hands of the ministers the seals of their respective offices, and as it is an organic principle of the English Constitution that no act of the King is of any avail without being countersigned by a responsible minister, it may well be perceived that he can have no great motive for meddling with affairs of state, which he has no power of regulating. In England the officers of state administering the several departments, and who form the Cabinet, really constitute the Government, the head of which is the First Lord of the Treasury for the time being. In the United States, in no possible sense, are the different secretaries vested with any power whatever, except by the authority of the President, who is responsible for their acts, not they responsible for him.—[Wm. Beach Lawrence, *North American Review*, Nov., 1880.

† "But under the Congressional system the minister is necessarily a member of Congress, and as such he is exposed to the severest possible tests of his com-

Senator Beck recently offered a resolution, calling upon Secretary Sherman to come before the Senate, and furnish information under his control in relation to transactions in silver coin. What possible objection can there be to compelling the Secretaries to report in person before Congress? Are not the departments over which they preside the creation of Congress? Admirers of Presidential power would say, that to ask questions of a Secretary would be a violation of the Executive's prerogative. Should not the members of the Cabinet have seats in Congress, and should they not be compelled to report directly to Congress, or give verbal explanations and answers to questions proposed by Congress? Let us just enter upon a brief examination of the subject from the standpoint of the Constitution and the law. If we turn to the early pages of our history, we shall find that it was provided in the Act of 1789, organizing the Treasury Department, that the Secretary of the Treasury shall, from time to time, digest and prepare plans for the improvement and management of the revenue, and for the support of the public credit. * * * Shall make, report, and give information, to either branch of the Legislature, in person or in writing, as may be required, respecting all matters referred to him by the Senate or House of Representatives. This law is unchanged to-day, but has fallen into disuse. Hamilton made a report on the public credit, 1790, which he was required by Congress to reduce to writing. Mr. Clay showed, in the great debates on the subject of the removal of the deposits, that Congress had absolute control over the different departments and their officers. The present mode of communication between Congress and the Secretaries is unskilful, inexpedient, and unstates-

petence. As the head of a department of state, he has publicly to defend it against the attacks of hostile critics: he has publicly to answer detective questions in regard to it: he has openly to argue against sharp and clever opponents, and he has constantly to explain great affairs of state."—Reform in the Federal Executive, by George Mortimer Tibbets. 21.

manlike. The voluminous reports now made, need not be done away with, but they should be made perspicuous by verbal explanation. There are many Congressmen who would listen to oral elucidation, but never would fathom the muddy depths of obscurely written statements. The legislator naturally seeks the Secretary, and the Secretary the legislator. The one depends upon the other, and neither can act intelligently without association and instruction. As a matter of fact, they are in constant communication, but it is private. Why should it not be in the light of day? Why should legislation be influenced, as it now is, by the whispered tone of the lobbyist? Why should a Secretary glide into the halls of legislation, and with bated breath speak to his favorite member, and then hastily retreat before the opposition can propound an interrogatory? Why should a member be compelled to seek the Secretary in hidden places, to receive information which belongs to the nation? This irregular and illegitimate system is enveloped by suspicion —it is productive of corruption and of conflict.*

In April, 1879, Senator Pendleton introduced a bill, providing that the Secretaries shall be permitted to occupy seats on the floor of the Senate and House of Representatives,

---

* "The President cannot dissolve Congress, and he is in no way called on to resign his own office. Thus it is quite possible that the Executive and Legislative branches may be in a state of discord for years. On the other hand, a President of whom Congress thoroughly approves, may come to the end of his term of office when nothing calls for any change of men or of measures, and though he may be re-elected, yet his continuance in office is at least jeopardized, and the country is obliged to go through the excitement and turmoil of a Presidential election. * * * * In truth, the evil is one inherent in the form of Government; it may, by judicious provisions, be made less baneful, but it cannot be got rid of altogether. It is the weak point of Presidential Government,—a weak point to be fairly balanced against its strong points, and against the weak points of other systems. * * * If the President were elected by Congress, or by some body chosen by or out of Congress—if his ministers were allowed to be members of Congress, or to appear or speak in Congress, the evils of the system would be greatly diminished, while the essential principle of Presidential Government would remain untouched."—Freeman's Historical Essay on Presidential Government, page 391.

with the right to participate in debate on matters relating to their departments, and that the Secretaries shall attend the sessions of the Senate, at the opening of the sittings, on Tuesday and Friday of each week, to give information asked by resolution, or in reply to questions which may be propounded to them. This is one of the wisest propositions ever made in the history of our government. It attacks the almost unlimited power of the President. But, as in the case of most reforms which have been hitherto proposed, the Constitution of the United States is quoted against it. It provides that, " no person holding any office under the United States shall be a member of either House during his continuance in office." We do not believe that a fair construction of this section stands in the way of the proposition. How can it be claimed that a Secretary would become a member, if he merely reported to Congress orally, or was allowed to debate the affairs of his department? He would not be elected to either House. He would have no power to impeach, or even to vote. He would not have any privilege on account of the new duties. He would not be a member in any sense. Senator Morrill opposed this measure, and claimed that it was an attempt to "assimilate our Government to monarchies." If this be a reason why the bill should not become law, then, why not abolish the Presidency, for, in its entirety, it is a copy of monarchical prerogative? And further, it embodies and perpetuates the worst features of kingship, long since abandoned in England.*

The obligations resting upon members of the Cabinet in England, to debate and report, is the most important and salient part of the great reform made in parliamentary government. The substitution of the Cabinet for the King, is

* The worst disgrace that probably ever fell upon our Cabinet system was the endorsement which it received from Napoleon III., after the sanguinary *coup d'etat*. He demanded a Cabinet dependent upon the chief of State, and cited the powers vested in the President of the United States.

the great landmark in the causeway of free government. How could a United States Senator be so blind as not to see that, if the proposed law was assimilating our Government to a monarchy, that the monarchy to which we would be attempting to conform ourselves is in this respect a hundredfold more republican and representative than our system? Does not that kind of argument savor of demagogism? Was not the common law, which stands as the foundation-stone to our system of law (save in the case of one State), a heritage from the Mother Country? Did not the *habeas corpus*, the Petition of Rights, the Magna Charta, all of English origin, have a good effect upon this country? Is not the history of parliamentary government that of human progress and freedom? Mr. Pendleton said, in support of his bill, that "it is the way of the government of every civilized nation in the world which has a Legislature and Executive, except our own. * * * It is the reasonable, intelligent, progressive way—the way of improved legislation. No nation has ever abandoned it for the old way, more than the farmer has given up the mower and reaper for the scythe and sickle." With the absolute abolition of the Presidency, the present system of the Cabinet would necessarily fall. In the event, however, of the continuance of the Presidency, a system to which the American people seem to be so greatly attached, let the heads of the departments, at least, be placed under the direction and control of the law-making power. With the consummation of the plan of bringing the Secretaries face to face with Congress, and under its direct and absolute authority, we shall have made a great advance in the perfecting of free government in America.

CHAPTER XI.

EXECUTIVE POLICY.

The first act the President performs after inauguration, is to determine upon a line of action which has become known as the policy of the administration. This is thought to be his official duty. No such duty is conferred by the terms of the Constitution, and therefore its origin is vague and questionable. There is so much in the general powers of the executive which savors of the ruler, that the custom is regarded as both legitimate and lawful. Although it is true that the President is at the head of a separate, co-ordinate department of the government, which gives him extraordinary powers, still in many ways his individual will or purpose is somewhat circumscribed. The Constitution provides how he shall exercise that will or intelligence, and it would be fair to presume that all other methods were excluded. For example, it is provided that "he shall from time to time give to the Congress information of the State of the Union, and recommend to their consideration such measures as he shall judge necessary and expedient." There can be but one construction placed upon this clause. The President is to put in the form of a suggestion any measures he may deem expedient, and not to urge his opinion in any other way. It would seem to be intended that his will should be subordinate to the legislative branch. Further than this, that the mode suggested should be the only way of manifesting his individual thought. This course would in no way violate the spirit and genius of representative government. Personal pique, or passion, should spend its force in mere recommendation. If it took the form of legislation, then the President would execute. It is eminently proper that he should directly and specifically suggest to the representatives of the people that which he believes to be for the welfare of the nation. At any rate, it is now made his official duty thus to express himself. Few of our Presidents have been tardy in the creation of a policy. The process of crystalization of presidential thought and will has been rapid and effective. The nation soon feels the reins drawn over it as the new driver takes his seat. It realizes that it is being not only guided but directed. Does the road always lead to peace and prosperity? Has there not been a great deal of ignorant and reckless driving? Probably the most undignified and unrepublican manner for the President to manifest his individual purpose, is to go before the people with speeches and addresses. Every private citizen has the unqualified right thus to discuss the political issues of the day. The course of the President is laid down by the law. When he is chosen he should become the servant of the people. By delivering addresses he either refuses to exercise that submission which he should do as agent, or he presses his personal will with all that undue influence which his position as first public officer affords him. From both standpoints he is wrong. Does not the blush of shame come to the cheek of every American when he recalls the grotesque scenes which were enacted by President Johnson? Accompanied by the different members of his cabinet, by distinguished officers of the army and navy, the President arrived at one of the chief cities of this country. The civil authorities entertained him. A banquet was spread and partaken of. Meanwhile a promiscuous crowd of boys and men assembled under the windows of the apartments of the President, who, upon being informed of the fact, rushed to the balcony, and there delivered a ribald and scurrilous speech, hurling his anathemas against what he termed a radical Congress. In the place of recommending legislation to Congress, he stood up before the mob, with its jeers, taunts and abusive epithets, using the incendiary language of an agitator. His object was to reach the people through the press which he knew would report the harangue. He was struggling with Congress. He was hurling his individual will against representatives elected by the people. He threatened to displace all who opposed him. He coalesced with the enemies of the government. He encouraged treason. He brought loyalty into disrepute. There can be little doubt that the ever increasing hostility of the South to the North, which manifests itself so strongly in Southern society to day, had its inception in the policy of Andrew Johnson.

There was truth in the exclamation which came up from that mob addressed by him. "You are a traitor!" The President replied to the assertion in this manner; "Now, my countrymen, it is very easy to indulge in epithets ; it is very easy to call a man Judas, and cry out 'traitor,' but when he is called upon to give arguments and facts he is very often found wanting." He continued ; "Judas Iscariot, Judas ; There was a Judas once, one of the twelve apostles. Oh, yes, the twelve apostles had a Christ, (a voice ; "and a Moses, too," great laughter.) The twelve apostles had a Christ, and he never could have had a Judas, unless he had had the twelve apostles. If I have played the Judas, who has been my Christ that I have played the Judas with ? Was it Thad. Stevens ? Was it Wendell Phillips ? Was it Charles Sumner ?" Thus the disgraceful scene was continued. The crowd called upon the President in this way : " Mind your dignity, Andy ; don't get mad, Andy ; bully for you ! Andy." These are the words in which Andrew Johnson, then President, referred to the death of the martyred Lincoln. "There was, two years ago, a ticket before you for the Presidency. I was placed upon that ticket with a distinguished **citizen now no more,** (voices, it's a pity; too bad; unfortunate.') "Yes, I know **there are some** who say "unfortunate.' Yes, unfortunate for some that God rules on high and deals in Justice, (cheers). Yes, unfortunate. The ways of Providence are mysterious and incomprehensible, controlling all who exclaim 'unfortunate.'"

It is a sad commentary on our institutions that such a man **could** ever have been the President of this republic. He "swung **around** the circle" and, in blasphemous words, cast **his** will against the people who had elected him to office. He claimed that Providence had stricken down the person who was really elected for the purpose of making this ignorant bigot, not the Chief Magistrate of the nation, but its tyrant; that the Infinite made use of the assassin's bullet to place an uncouth politician at the head of the nation, in order that he might enact the *rôle* of ruler. Those monarchs who rule by divine right (as they claim) have at least the quality of being gentlemen, which Andrew Johnson had not. Never before **in** the history of nations, were the characteristics of tyranny and vulgarity so completely blended and combined as they **were** in the administrations of President Johnson.

Monarchical will and Presidential policy are synonymous. The first act of President Hayes was regal. **By** the action of his own will he promulgated the doctrine of the discontinuance of the use of the army in upholding Government in the States of Louisiana **and** South Carolina. The Constitution of the United States is plain on the point of national aid to legally constituted and *de facto* States, **but the** President, before any action of Congress could intervene, established it as a policy, **not** to do what was specifically set forth as his duty. The policy was put against the law. Why was not the whole **subject** submitted to Congress? There never could be a more momentous issue than that which was forced upon the nation after the election of President Hayes. Armed revolutions existed in these States against the Governors. The courts had been overthrown. These State executives were actual prisoners. They called for assistance from the National Government. The Constitution said, "Send troops!" The President replied, "I have formed a policy. I shall not only send no soldiers, but I shall withdraw those that now protect you." The two Governments fell. The policy also embodied the abandonment, in a general way, of all national protection, and with its promulgation, the organization of the Republican party in the South, which gave the freedmen the means of exercising the suffrage, fell to pieces, and now exists, if at all, only in name. Is it possible that these acts of the President were constitutional? Is it true that the genius of our system admits of the Executive forming an opinion upon such vital issues, and then acting without the direction and authority of Congress? If Governors Chamberlain and Packard were entitled to be protected as the respective Executives of South Carolina and Louisiana, then they should have received their constitutional rights. In any event, no one man should have the power to decide the question of withdrawal of the troops until legislative or judicial decision.

It should be the duty of an executive of a free Government, simply to execute the laws, not to make them by the enforcement of a policy. If the executive power were vested in a Council, then each member could advocate schemes of legislation in the legislative halls; certainly in the event of interpellation. The laws should not be even executed, as the President understands them, when there is any serious dispute as to their meaning or intent, for that might be but another form of exercising the regal potentiality. The President should have no will beyond that of Congress. Congress should be the director and guide. In that body should reside the will and conscience of the nation. The exercise of this power under the guise of a policy is essentially great, for the reason that it is undefined and uncertain. It is absolute monarchy. If the country be threatened by a conflagration, should not the people be warned by the ringing of an alarm bell? Let them awake to the impending danger of a one-man power, lest, sooner or later, the whole fabric of liberty be destroyed by the single will of some powerful and ambitious man

CHAPTER XII.

CAUCUS.

THE law as it was intended to operate was bad enough, for it placed the selection of the President in the hands of a body of men, who had no other duty to perform than to name him, and then retire from all responsibility. The evils of these provisions have already been described in a previous chapter. Abstractly, the law is weak and complicated; concretely, it is impracticable and unwieldly.* To make matters worse, and confusing, an irresponsible system of great potency has sprung up and attached itself like a fungus growth to the original plan. A few men in the township, representing nobody, except it be that mysterious body called the "machine" assembles, and appoints delegates to the County Convention. The State Convention sends delegates to the National caucus, called a Convention, and that body nominates the candidate for the Presidency. Be it remembered, that the delegates are not based entirely upon proportional representation, for the State representation, as in the Elec-

---

* "Though the office of President is elective, yet it is as completely beyond the reach of the great mass of the people as though it were hereditary. . . . Thus it appears that our right of suffrage in the election of our Chief Magistrate is an immensely complicated system of influence, interest, favor, confidence and proxy. A chain of influence composed of ten thousand links and divided into ten thousand branches descends with tortuous course to the great body of the people."—[Compend of History from the Earliest Times, comprehending a General View of the State of the World, with respect to Civilization, Religion and Government, by Samuel Whelpley (1806), cited by J. E. Chamberlin, in *International Review*, May and June, 1883].

toral Colleges, enters into the plan. Then the town sends delegates to the County, and the County to the State Convention, that nominates the presidential electors. The State election which follows determines which set of electors are chosen. At last, the counting of the votes of the Electoral Colleges takes place in the presence of Congress. The last process has become the most important of all. Here the various questions of regularity are finally determined. Thus the result of the lottery is accomplished by these numerous processes of the most intricate character. Indirectness, irresponsibility, and uncertainty are the characteristics of the whole procedure. The men who generally fill the position of delegates to the caucus and conventions are office-holders, or those who represent the office-holder. The political life of these men often depends upon the favor of public officers who hold places above them. This is what is known as the electoral college and caucus system. Its presence is an evidence of a decline in the methods of our statesmen and leaders. It crushes individual action. It lowers the standard of qualification. No man can serve his country and the caucus at the same time. Voting becomes a mere form in carrying out the will of the caucus.* Its insolence stifles discussion. The conscience of the sworn representatives is annulled. A new law-making power is created. The plan of the Constitution, as we have explained, is to elect the President by colleges composed of men who were independent of any dictation. The whole system has fallen into disuse, and now every elector is committed before his election, and the establishment of a grand caucus is the

---

* " Why is Polk, it was asked, placed over the heads of the most distinguished men of the nation ? The *Richmond Enquirer*, March, 1845, with a bitter sweet expression says, that ' the politicians had put their hands into the lottery box, when they could do nothing else, because of their want of Union, to draw out a prize, and the masses of the people had approved of Polk's name as willingly as they would that of any other with which they associated no definite idea.' " Von Holst, Vol. III, 20.

result.* Let us assume that some ambitious man, rich and powerful, and at the head of or controlling wealthy corporations, wishes to make himself President. He first proceeds to capture his own State. The majority of his party in his State are resident in one of its large cities. He is instrumental in having his friend elected mayor. The mayor has the appointment of the police department, which has special charge of the appointment of inspectors of elections. Thus, this would-be President has control of the political organization which directs the destinies of his party in the minutest detail. In this way he is able to say: "I own my city, which will determine the State, and the State having a large number of electors will control the national convention." With the aid of those who make politics a business and a trade, the primaries are held, delegates are elected, all of whom are pledged for the man who controls the large organizations. The State convention is held, and its delegates are in turn chosen and instructed to vote for some particular man. The national convention then meets. It is an all powerful, but irresponsible, body of men. It assumes powers which the people have not delegated. From the peculiar manner of the appointment of its members, the most intelligent and respectable portion of the community are excluded from its number. They are adepts in political chicanery. This is certainly a muddy source from which to expect the clear waters of representative government to flow. Do these men select the leader of their party? Do they agree upon the man of experience? Assuredly, No. Charles Sumner, in his great speech, of the 31st of May, 1872, in referring to the caucus in the country, claimed that it had succeeded in subjugating the Government. He continued: "The cau-

* "Seeing that the politicians had thus early learned the means of taking the choice of the President out of the hands of the non-official electors provided by the Constitution, the author had no doubt that the politician class would speedily consolidate its power, and lay the lasting foundations of a Republican aristocracy."—[J. E. Chamberlin, in *International Review*, May and June, 1883].

cus is at last understood as a political engine, moved by wirepullers, and it becomes more insupportable in proportion as it is directed to personal ends; nor is its character changed when called a convention. There, too, are wirepullers, and when the great office-holder and the great office-seeker are one and the same, it is easy to see how naturally the engine responds to the central touch." It is self evident that the actual workings of our governmental system practically subordinates the welfare of the people to the sinister interests of the mere politician. The caucus is a poison which is rapidly destroying the national life.*

In a parliamentary form of government, the really representative part of its system selects the foremost man of the nation; but the caucus in this country, of all political parties, nominates in most cases the obscure politician. Mr. Tilden, the nominee of the democratic party, 1876, had never been a representative in Congress, nor had held any position in the gift of the government. He had only been once in the legislature of his own state; and it is charged that he did not then personally attend to his duties. But he had been a state manipulator of organizations and caucuses. The voice, which had never been heard in the council halls of the nation, might now be directing our destinies only as a president may. To-day, surrounded and enveloped by charges of having attempted the purchase of electoral colleges and of state courts, of unsuccessful bribery, by means of cipher despatches, the black cloud of fraud and force overshadowing all, he, the creature of the caucus, stands up before the American people with an unequalled effrontery and claims to have been elected their President. He becomes a great claimant to a throne. Will he ever be crowned?

---

* "The caucus system—in short, a government within the government, at the worst account, the ship of State steered by the chief intriguers of the nation rather than by its intelligent leaders."—[J. E. Chamberlin, in *International Review*, May and June, 1883.]

The first thing which the national caucus asks is, "who is the available man?" The question alone, with few exceptions, strikes off the list the best men of the nation. Some one is nominated who has never had any experience in the science of government.* This mode of selecting the President has multiplied the bad features of our system. It appears that the President, whom we claim has many monarchical and unrepublican powers, is selected by the irresponsible caucus. The presidential office becomes the aim of the ambitious politician. The election is converted into a race for booty. Bargains commence before the nomination and increase with the progress of the contest. Office is promised, not to those who would serve the country, but to those who would best advance the interests of the candidate. Patronage bribery develops into a subtle science. New sources of corruption and intrigue spring up with every new administration. The bad effect upon public morals is incalculable. The incumbent dare not speak his own opinion, or do his honest duty. If he

---

* In one of the numerous letters of condolence sent to Clay, the conviction is expressed, "that a man of really towering ability would never again fill the presidential chair,"—[Von Holst, Vol. II., p. 695]. "The result of this election has satisfied me that no such man as Henry Clay can ever be president of the United States. The party leaders, the men who make presidents, will never consent to elevate one greatly their superior; they suffer too much in the contrast; their aspirations are checked; their powers circumscribed; the "clay" can not be moulded into an idol suited to their worship. Moreover, a statesman, prominent as you have been for so long a time, must have been identified with all the leading measures affecting the interests of the people, and their interests are frequently different in the several parts of our widelyextended country; what is meat in one section is poison in another. Give me, therefore, a candidate of an inferior grade, one whose talents, patriotism, and public services, have never been so conspicious as to force him into the first rank. He will get all the votes which the best and wisest man could secure, and some which, for the reasons I have stated, he could not."—[Priv. Corresp. of H. Clay,p., 508]. "Mediocrity has almost become a monopoly, without which one was not entitled to the highest office of the nation,"—[Von Holst, Vol., II. p. 697]. "And between them (Clay and Webster) stood the fortunate possessor * * * feeling that he was indebted for his triumph over the ' two giants' to his harmless mediocrity." Von Holst, Vol., II. 410.

express himself, it must be in the accents of the slave. It does not require a philosopher to point out the lesson to be learned from this condition of affairs. Behold the forerunners of despotism! Behold the demoralizing influences of the presidential election! If we continue the office of president, we must, at least, abolish the mode of his election, or we shall fall below the contempt of mankind. The effect is demoralizing upon the country. If the first republic of the age is to have a one-man executive of great power at its head, he should be a statesman who has taken an active part in public affairs—not an unknown man. Under the decrees of the caucus no man of transcendent qualities can be elected. Especially in a republican form of government should there be a continuous course for the statesman and patriot. The man of ability and brains should not be circumscribed by any branch of the government. He should be free to aspire to the highest office in the gift of the people. If he becomes the leader in the legislature, that fact should demand for him a position in the executive branch. Paradoxical as it may appear, pre-eminence in the legislative branch of government practically disqualifies for the executive. Hence, the tendency is not to get the strongest in intellect and ability, but the weakest, at the head of the government.

CHAPTER XIII.

REMARKS UPON THE CONSTITUTION OF THE "CONFEDERATE" STATES.

Our general allegation is that, in the inception of our Government many ancient and effete theories were embodied in the fundamental law, and that, since the formation of the Constitution, we have grown more monarchical and England has grown more Republican. Does the history of this Republic bear out that theory, for theory it must remain if not supported by facts?*

*We have already appealed to many political events in this country to sustain this position, and it is now our intention to refer to the course taken by about eight millions of our people in attempting to break away from the Union, and to establish a government of their own. This inquiry is pertinent to our argument for the reason that these people have resumed their allegiance to the government, and are now part and parcel of the body politic. They constitute a respectable portion of the masses who must in the future create by their thought, action, and history, whatever we shall be. Nothing, therefore, could be more interesting than to inquire (so far as the limits of the discussion will permit) what the Southerners' theories are in respect to Government. Their ancestors had

---

* "It (the Presidential election of 1876) will, for sad reasons, be fresh enough in recollection for some time to come, to afford the only compensation for its disgracefulness, by exhibiting the true physiognomy of the one-man power, as transmitted from its crumbling throne in Europe to sit upon the healthy heart of America."—["Republican Superstitions," M. D. Conway, 113].

fought for the right to form the Government of the United States. They and their children had lived under that Constitution for over eighty years prior to the rebellion. Let us inquire what interpretation the Southern people placed upon the United States Constitution, and what effect their living under this instrument had wrought upon their conceptions of government and liberty. In March, 1861, the Southern States that had seceded ordained a Constitution of their own. Our Constitution had been theirs; in race and tradition we had been one people; yet what did they do? It is a remarkable fact that the founders of the Confederate States of America adopted, in nearly all its parts, the language, articles, and order of arrangement of the Constitution of the United States. Of the Constitution of the Confederate States, Alexander H. Stephens says: "This work of the Montgomery Convention, with that of the Constitution for a Provisional Government, will ever remain, not only as a monument of the union, forecast, and statesmanship of the men who constituted it, but an everlasting refutation of the charges which have been brought against them. These words together show clearly that their only leading object was to sustain, uphold, perpetuate, the fundamental principles of the Constitution of the United States * * * * * * The Constitution of the United States was the model followed throughout, with only such changes as experience suggested for better practical working or for greater perspicuity." * Mr. Davis's book, from which we have just quoted, is, in our opinion, a labored argument to prove that the United States Government was, before 1861, a confederacy of independent States, having the right of secession. In addition to this, Mr. Davis claims the recognition and perpetuation of slavery, and upon the apex of the structure he places a "monocrat."

The Southern people proceeded to form their government.

---

* Rise and Fall of the Confederate Government, by Jefferson Davis, Vol. 1., p. 259.

Let us examine it more in detail. In the preamble of the Constitution of the Confederate States, its framers destroyed the possibility of their becoming a nation by providing that " each state, acting in its sovereign and independent character," formed the government. This was a mere compact between independent powers, which could be dissolved at the pleasure of any one of the contracting parties. They invoked " the favor and guidance of Almighty God " in the affairs of their aristocratic federative monarchy, thus seeking to impose upon the Infinite the task of framing a very bad system of laws. Slavery, feeling its wrong and weakness, has always sought the assistance of the supernatural. Priestcraft, pliant to its wishes, stood by with the theological blessing. Everything was done to blight the growth of the national idea ; and its Congress was forbidden to " appropriate money for any internal improvement intended to facilitate commerce, except for lights, buoys, and removing obstructions to rivers ; " in which cases such duties shall be laid on the navigation facilitated thereby."

The Government which these boasted students and lovers of Constitutional liberty formed, was a slaveocracy. Their Congress had no power to pass any law " denying or impairing the right of property in negro slaves," and all citizens of any state had the right of transit and sojourn in any other state with their slaves and property. It was also provided that in all new territory, the institution of negro slavery, as it then existed in the Confederate States, should be recognized and protected by Congress, and by the territorial government ; and the inhabitants of the several Confederate States and Territories should have the right to take to such territories, any slaves lawfully held by them in any of the states or territories of the Confederate States. The people who would form such a Constitution in the latter part of the nineteenth century could not be expected to have very republican ideas upon the subject of executive power. A fit capstone to such a structure would be a king. In the face of the history of Europe, the revolution against absolute monarchy in England, the French Revolutions, our own Revolution, and our experiences under the Constitution of the United States, they placed at the head of their government an elective king. The Constitution of the Confederate States provided that the executive power shall be vested in a President elected for the term of six years, but he shall be ineligible for re-election, and it re-enacted the system of our electoral college. Then, to the second section of Article II of the Constitution of the United States, defining the powers of the President, they added the following words: "The principal officer in each of the executive departments, and all persons connected with the diplomatic service, may be removed from office at the pleasure of the President," and all other civil officers of the executive department may also be removed at the discretion of the President. At the time this Confederate Constitution was framed, it was claimed by its friends to be the proper and legal interpretation of the Constitution of the United States. The pregnant lesson can be learned from the action of the Southern people, that, at least, they,—numbering some eight millions,—were not tired of the extraordinary powers conferred on the President of the United States, for the reason that they re-enacted those provisions and added others of a similar nature. The fact cannot be denied that the American people, as a whole, are wedded to the theory that a nation should have a strong and powerful executive. The result of conferring so much power upon Jefferson Davis was that he entered into a violent quarrel with the State of South Carolina. The Southern people saw that they had not only established a slaveocracy, but a monarchy. Next, the Confederate Congress had a vigorous discussion with Davis over the finances. The Southerners found that they had conferred too much power upon their executive. When a presidential form of government is regarded as too personal for a slaveocracy, it is time that nations calling themselves republics should abandon that system.*

* It may be noted that the Southerners, after the rebellion, did not seem over anxious to adopt the theories which had been placed upon, and embodied in, the law by the Northerners. The Southern press, which is one of the indications or evidences of prevailing opinion, continually asserted that it preferred a monarchy to our present government. We also desire to state, so far as our observation has gone, that in almost every instance it was thought that the monarchy should be in the nature of an absolute one.

CHAPTER XIV.

THE ADMINISTRATION OF ANDREW JACKSON.

Assumptions of power, and violations of the Constitution, have been charged against most of our later Presidents. Some of these various acts will be referred to, in order to show the actual working of the present American system; for the existence of arbitrary and despotic action, although unauthorized by law, yet having the sanction of the color of law, argues strongly against the general structure which protects and fosters them. Nor is it conclusive reasoning to claim that if the acts in question be proven unconstitutional, that there may not be sound argument against the Constitution itself. The fact is, monarchical power is exercised, and that, too, in the name of law. Vexed and complex questions of interpretation arise—arguments on the rostrum, and in the Courts, ensue.

There is considerable force in the statement that the President is vested by the Constitution with extraordinary power. He is the depositary of executive authority. He has conferred on him most of the monarchical prerogatives. If the commission of tyrannous acts be authorized by the Constitution, then that fact is good evidence against the instrument; if unauthorized, then, it is submitted, that a governmental system which makes such a condition of affairs possible, should be immediately reformed. No one who studies the character of Andrew Jackson will be surprised at the acts he committed while President. He was a duellist. He was fond of horse-racing and cards. He was a soldier; he had the instincts of one. His chronic condition was a thirsting for strife. He had defied Courts. He had imprisoned a judge.* Mr. Clay said of him, " War and strife, endless war and strife, personal or national, foreign or domestic, were the aliment of the President's existence. War against the bank, war against France, and strife and contention with a countless number of individuals. His wars with Black Hawk and the Seminoles were scarcely a luncheon for his voracious appetite." † President Jefferson had been guilty of making removals from office for political reasons, but the advent of Andrew Jackson to the Presidency marked a new era in the history of the country. It was the turning point of our national greatness as a Republican Government. His friends claimed that he had been unjustly deprived of his rights in 1825, just as the friends of Mr. Tilden now claim that he was defrauded of his office (as they phrase it). Is there no power to avert the reenactment of the scenes witnessed in Jackson's time ? The measures taken when Jackson was declared President were all characterized by violence, venom, and hate. " Our enemies must be punished ; our friends must be rewarded," was the cry raised. The office of President was treated as if it was a captured fortress. All found connected with it were

---

*Gallatin recalled him as "a tall, lank, uncouth-looking personage, with long locks of hair hanging over his face, and a cue down his back, tied in an eel skin, his dress singular, his manners and deportment that of a rough backwoodsman." [4 Hildreth, 692.] "Cold, dashing, fearless, and mad upon his enemies." [Putnam, 318.] "Turned loose in the regions of Florida, checked only by an uncertain and disputed boundary line running through half-explored forests, confronted by a hated foe, whose strength he could well afford to despise, General Jackson, in a war properly urged only against Indians, ran a wild and lawless, but very vigorous and effective career in Spanish possessions. He hung a couple of British subjects, with as scant a trial and meagre shrift as if he had been a mediæval free lance. * * * He flung the Spanish Commissioners into jail. He treated instructions, laws, and established usages, as teasing cobwebs, which any spirited public servant was in duty bound to break." [Adams, by Morse, 160.]

†All quotations made in this book from the speeches of Henry Clay, are taken from His Life and Times by Colton.

made prisoners. Those who formed the attacking party were comrades in battle. The will of the leader became law. All existing theories were subordinate to that will. He compelled his party to abandon the policy of protection. He then made a triumphal march upon the Capitol. He forced laws upon Congress; he took the public purse from their custody; he vetoed their bills.* The laws of Congress provided how the moneys of the United States should be kept and disbursed. The President tells his Cabinet that the matter of the removal of the deposits was his own measure, and that he assumed all the responsibility.†

Mr. Duane was dismissed from the Secretaryship of the Treasury because he **refused** to comply with the Executive order, and Mr. Taney was appointed in his place. On a report made by this substitute Secretary, Mr. Clay offered in the Senate the following resolution :—" *Resolved,*—That by dismissing the late Secretary of the Treasury, because he would not, contrary to his sense of his own duty, remove the money of the United States, in deposit with the Bank of the United States and its branches, in conformity with the President's opinion, and by appointing his successor to effect such removal, which has been done, the President has assumed the exercise of a power over the Treasury of the United States not granted to him by the Constitution and laws, and dangerous to the liberties of the people." The control of the National Treasury has always been regarded as the greatest guarantee for liberty in republican government; but, notwithstanding this fact, and the resolutions of the House of Representatives, that the deposits were safe, they were removed by Mr. Taney,

---

* " He held more power than any other American had ever possessed."
 * * * " He had had his desire upon all his enemies." [Sumner's Jackson, 386.

† " Our Presidents, indeed, have done that for which many citizens believed they had no warrant in law; for instance, when General Jackson removed the public deposits from the Bank of the United States."—[Lieber, Civil Government, 161.]

the Acting-Secretary, under the direction of the President. The greatest enigma is that the representative branch did not assert its powers and its rights. The reason why the President was not impeached was that he was stronger than the Congress. It was a question of force, and the predominance remained with the one-man power.*

Mr. Clay discussed the question of personal government in the following words:—" We are in the midst of a revolution, hitherto bloodless, but rapidly tending toward a total change of the pure Republican character of the Government, and to the concentration of all power in the hands of one man. The powers of Congress are paralyzed, except when exerted in conformity with his will, by frequent, and an extraordinary, exercise of the Executive veto, not anticipated by the founders of our Constitution, and not practised by any of the predecessors of the present Chief Magistrate. And, to cramp them still more, a new expedient is springing into use of withholding altogether bills which have received the sanction of both Houses of Congress, thereby cutting off all

* "These last lines give the key to the right understanding of the political bearing of the bank controversy, which was mainly the occasion of so rude a development of personal rule that we may very properly speak of the reign of Andrew Jackson."—[Von Holst, Political Hist. vii., p. 31.] " When a law has come into existence in a constitutional manner, the Constitution knows of only one authority, the judicial, which may declare it unconstitutional. But Jackson —as President—whose highest duty the Constitution makes it to 'take care that the laws be faithfully executed'—not only claimed the right to deny the constitutionality and force of a law, in the absence of such a decision by a Federal Court, and to make this, his conviction, the motive of official action; but he did so in the face of an express decision of the Supreme Court. He, indeed, would not allow that the decision in the case of McCulloch vs. State of Maryland, covered the whole question, because the Court had declared only that the establishment of a bank was constitutional, but not that all the provisions of the charter of that bank were constitutional." * * * * * * *
But Jackson went a step further. He denied entirely the competency of the Court to give a binding interpretation of the Constitution on such questions. In the veto message he says; " Each public officer who takes an oath to support the Constitution, swears that he will support it as he understands it, and not as it is understood by others."—[Von Holst, Political Hist., vol. ii., 48 and 49.]

opportunity of passing them, even if, after their return, the members should be unanimous in their favor.

The constitutional participation of the Senate in the appointing power is virtually abolished by the constant use of the power of removal from office, without any known cause, and by the appointment of the same individual to the same office after his rejection by the Senate. How often have we Senators felt that the check of the Senate, instead of being, as the Constitution intended, a salutary control, was an idle ceremony? * * * * * * The office cannot remain vacant without prejudice to the public interest, and if we reject the proposed substitute, we cannot restore the displaced, and, perhaps, some more unworthy man may be nominated." The executive assumptions were ramifying in all directions, and it was found necessary, in the argument of the question of the removal of the deposits, to mention many subjects. They were regal acts. To put it in the mildest form, they were unbecoming a representative executive. He disregarded the decisions of the Courts and the provisions of treaties. " The power of internal improvement lay crushed beneath the veto." * Mr. Clay proclaimed that "in a

---

* The power of the veto is exercised, not as an extraordinary, but an ordinary power; as a common mode of defeating acts of Congress not acceptable to the Executive. We hear one day that the President needs the advice of no Cabinet; that a few secretaries, or clerks, are enough for him. The next, we are informed that the Supreme Court is but an obstacle to the popular will, and the whole judicial department but an encumbrance to Government, and while on one side the judicial power is thus derided and denounced, on the other arises the cry "Cut down the Senate," and over the whole, and at the same time, prevails the loud avowal, shouted with all the lungs of conscious party strength and party triumph, that the spoils of the enemy belong to the victors. This condition of things, sir, this general and obvious aspect of affairs, is the result of three years administration, such as the country has experienced. * *
But, sir, in my opinion, a yet greater danger threatens the Constitution and the Government, and that is from the attempt to extend the power of the Executive at the expense of all the other branches of the Government and of the people themselves. Whatever accustomed power is denied to the Constitution, whatever accustomed power is denied to Congress, or to the Judiciary, none is denied

term of eight years, a little more than equal to that which was required to establish our liberties, the Government will have been transformed into an elective monarchy—the worst of all forms of Government." He contemplated the condition of public affairs with " feelings of deep humiliation and profound mortification." He said : " Thank God, we are yet free, and, if we put on the chains which are forging for us, it will be because we deserve to wear them." * * * * *
The two most important powers of Civil Government are the sword and the purse. The former, with some restrictions, is confided by the Constitution to the Executive, and the latter to the legislative department. If they are separate, and exercised by different responsible departments, civil liberty is safe; but if they are united in the hands of the same individual, it is gone. That clear-sighted and sagacious revolutionary orator and patriot, Patrick Henry, justly said, in the Virginia Convention, in reply to one of his opponents: " Let him candidly tell where and when did freedom exist when the sword and purse were given up from the people? Unless a miracle in human affairs interposed, no nation ever retained its liberty after the loss of the sword and the purse. * * * If you give them up you are gone."

President Jackson did not seem to be actuated by any principle, or process of reasoning. Passion and pique were the forces which controlled him. The Secretary of the Treasury, by the Act of 1789, was constituted the Agent of Congress. He was to report the fiscal condition of the country to Congress, not to the President. The President was restricted by the charter of the bank to the appointment of directors, and to the issuing of a *scire facias*. The Constitution required that no money should be drawn from the Treasury

to the Executive. Here there is no retrenchment; here no apprehension is felt for the liberties of the people; here it is not thought necessary to erect barriers against corruption."—[Speech of Webster in National Convention, Worcester, Mass., Oct. 12, 1832. Webster's Speeches, vol. 2, 125-128-142.]

except by an appropriation by Congress. President Jackson seemed to think that the will of the people, and the will of the President, were one and the same thing. Mr. Clay said that "The will of the President will be the whole of it. There will be but one bed, and that will be the bed of Procrustes; but one will, the will of the President. All the departments, and all subordinate functionaries of government, great and small, must submit to that will."

One of the most singular phases of the great contest over the deposits was a paper in which the President claimed that "Its responsibility (the measure of removal) has been assumed after the most mature deliberation and reflection, as necessary to preserve the morals of the people, the freedom of the press, and the purity of the elective franchise." All the absolute monarchs of the world have claimed to be not only the source of all civil, but of all religious authority. What a travesty on republican government, that its Executive should give as an excuse for an illegal act, that he wished to preserve the morals of the people! He was not the first man to commit political crime in the name of religion, but, it is to be hoped, that he will be the last of our Presidents who will attempt such an outrage on reason and decency.

In reading the speeches of the great minds of this nation against autocracy, one is struck with the force of their rhetoric, and the strength of their arguments. The leaders who spoke against the iron rule of Jackson stood nearer the founders of the Republic than we, and ought to have had a more perspicuous view than we of the purpose, object and destiny of this Government.

The President claimed that he had a right to execute the laws as he understood them, and as it pleased him.* The

---

* "In that important document, sir, upon which it seems to be his fate to stand, or to fall, before the American people, the veto message, he holds the following language: 'Each public officer, who takes an oath to support the Constitution, swears that he will support it as he understands it, and not as it is

Senate passed condemnatory resolutions, and the President protested. He wished the protest placed on the records of the Senate. This was carrying out his "armed interpretation" of the law in the most arbitrary manner. It was a sort of veto against one of the branches of Government, for the veto power may be only legally exercised against the action of both Houses. It was an unconstitutional act. John C. Calhoun, in a speech delivered May 5th, 1834, on a motion for the disposal of the President's protest, said: "But the part of this paper (the protest) which is most characteristic—that which lets us into the real nature and character of this movement—is the source from which the President derives the right to interfere with our proceedings. He does not even pretend to derive it from any power vested in him by the Constitution, expressed or implied. * * * To convert such duties into powers would, if admitted, render him as absolute as the autocrat of all the Russias. * * * He makes his interference a matter of obligation—of solemn obligation—imperious necessity—the tyrant's plea. * * * He claims to be, not only the representative, but the immediate representative, of the American people! What effrontery! What boldness of assertion! The immediate representative? Why, he never received a vote from the American people. He was elected by electors—the colleges. * * * If we consult what is due to the wisdom and dignity of the Senate, there is but one mode—meet it at the threshold.

understood by others.' Mr. President, the general adoption of the sentiments expressed in this sentence would dissolve our Government. It would raise every man's private opinion into a standard for his own conduct; and there certainly is, there can be, no government, where every man is to judge for himself of his own rights and his own obligations. Where every one is his own arbiter, force and not law is the governing power. He who may judge for himself, and decide for himself, must execute his own decisions; and this is the law of force. I confess, sir, it strikes me with astonishment, that so wild, so disorganizing, a sentiment should be uttered by a President of the United States."—*Speech of Webster, National Convention, in Worcester, Mass., October 12, 1832.* Webster's Speeches, 125.

Encroachments are most easily resisted at the commencement. It is at the extreme point—on the frontier—that, in a contest of this description, the assailant is the weakest, and the assailed the strongest. Permit the frontier of our rights to be passed, and let the question be not resistance to usurpation, but at what point we shall resist, and the conquest (over us) will be more than half achieved. * * * * I am mortified that in this country, boasting of its Anglo-Saxon descent, that any one of reputable standing—much less the President of the United States—should be found entertaining principles leading to such monstrous results; and, I can scarcely believe myself to be breathing the air of our country, and to be within the walls of the Senate Chamber, when I hear such doctrines vindicated. It is proof of the wonderful degeneracy of the times—of the total loss of the true conception of constitutional liberty."

But the imperious will of Andrew Jackson was not yet satisfied. The Senate had passed the complaining resolutions. This fact irritated the man who mistook the Government for a despotism. He demanded that the action be reversed, and issued his edict to the Senate.* A majority of its members were craven enough to submit. Mr. Clay made one

---

* "Has any English sovereign since Cromwell's time dared to send such a message to Parliament? Sir, if he (President Jackson) can tell us that some of us disobey our constituents, he can tell us that all do so; and if we consent to receive this language from him, there is but one remaining step, and that is, that since we disobey the will of our constituents, he should disperse us and send us home. . . . . Mr. President, the contest, for ages, has been to rescue Liberty from the grasp of the Executive power. . . . . Through all this history of the contest for liberty, Executive power has been regarded as a lion which must be caged. . . . . The President carries on the Government; all the rest are but sub-contractors. Sir, whatever *name* we give him, we have but ONE EXECUTIVE OFFICER. A Briareus sits in the centre of our system, and with his hundred hands touches everything, moves everything, controls everything. I ask, sir, is this republicanism? Is this a government of laws? Is this legal responsibility?"—[The Great Speeches and Orations of Daniel Webster, by Edwin P. Whipple, 381, 385 and 387.]

of the greatest efforts of his life to avert this supreme disgrace, and finding it impossible to do so, left the Senate while the vote which expunged the resolutions was being taken. During the debate, he said, "The Senate has no army, no navy, no patronage, no lucrative offices, nor glittering honors to bestow. Around us there is no swarm of greedy expectants rendering us homage, anticipating our wishes, and ready to execute our commands. How is it with the President? Is he powerless? He is felt from one extremity to the other of this Republic. By means of principles which he has introduced, and innovations which he has made in our institutions, alas! but too much countenanced by Congress and a confiding people, he exercises uncontrolled the power of the State. In one hand he holds the purse, and in the other brandishes the sword of the country! Myriads of dependents and partisans scattered over the land are ever ready to sing hosannahs to him, and to laud to the skies whatever he does. He has swept over the Government during the last eight years like a tropical tornado. * * * *
Sir, I hope the Secretary of the Senate will preserve the pen with which he may inscribe them (the black lines which were to be drawn through the words of the resolution) and present it to that Senator of the majority, whom he may select, as a proud trophy to be transmitted to his descendants. Then, hereafter, when we shall lose the forms of our free institutions, all that now remains to us, some future American monarch, in gratitude to those by whose means he has been enabled, upon the ruins of civil liberty, to erect a throne, and to commemorate especially this expunging resolution, may institute a new order of knighthood, and confer on it the appropriate name of the 'Knight of the Black Lines.'" In Mr Clay's Hanover County speech, delivered in 1840 he said :—
"In my deliberate opinion, the present distressed and distracted state of the country may be traced to the single cause of the action, the encroachments and usurpations, of the execu-

tive branch of the Government. * * * * That the Federal Executive had an awful squinting towards monarchy. * * * * Let us pause and contemplate the stupendous structure of Executive machinery and despotism which has been reared in our Republic. * * * * * The President had nothing to do but to say to his Secretary: 'Issue your warrant for such a sum of money, and direct the registrar and comptroller to sign it, and if they should talk about a regard for their oaths, and boggle at obeying, tell them to do what I command them, and if not, I will find men who will.' * * There was a third instance of this encroachment. * * * The Executive branch of the Government was eternally in action; it was ever awake; it never slept; its action was continuous and increasing, like the tides of some mighty river which continued flowing and flowing on, swelling, deepening, and widening in its onward progress, till it swept away every impediment and broke down and removed every frail obstacle which might be set up to impede its course."

The object of quoting thus fully from the speeches of Henry Clay, is to show what, in his day, was the thought of a large portion of the people of this nation on the subject of Executive power. He stood foremost in the councils of the country. He was at once its greatest orator and statesman. The last twelve years of his life were spent in denouncing the regal encroachments of Presidents Jackson and Tyler. About the close of his public career, he offered in the Senate three resolutions for the abridgment of these powers, by way of amendment to the Constitution. The first related to the veto; the second, that no member of Congress should be appointed to office; the third, to deprive the President of all control over the public purse.

The chief characteristic of Jackson's administration was that of personal government. He established himself as a ruler. He was, in his own opinion, a tribune of the people, and had care of their rights. The people were his people.

He published his desires and policy in a newspaper conducted by an intimate personal frend. In this way he pushed on, in his aggressive manner, leaving in his track pernicious and malignant results, which to-day seriously and injuriously affect this country.

No European Court of the seventeenth century was the scene of more flattery, espionage and servility. But the etiquette of the Court was wanting. A streak of brutality ran all through society at Washington. "The Nimrod wild-fires from the backwoods of Tennessee, the bear-hunters from the valley of the Big Muddy, and the *alumni* of Tammany Hall were always welcome guests."* Public officers, like other men, must be judged by their associations. Andrew Jackson was at the head of the great American Republic, and even if there were extraordinary power conferred upon him by law, in the event of any controversy in relation to the same he should have leaned toward the more representative part of the Government. Instead of this, he stretched his power to the very utmost. He went blindly on until he approached the verge of absolutism. And he did all this while he was the Executive of the Government of the United States. His stubborn and perverse nature was the cause of the pronounced and rapid development of all the defects of the Presidential system. An usurper, he claimed that he was acting within constitutional limitations; a creature of the colleges, he asserted that he was the true representative of the people.

* *Atlantic Monthly*, June, 1880.

CHAPTER XV.

ADMINISTRATIONS OF VAN BUREN, TYLER, AND POLK.

MR. VAN BUREN's administration, which followed General Jackson's, was not characterized by any marked event, except that he perfected the system of removals, to which we have already referred. He lacked Jackson's attribute of an iron will. His rule was an ebb-tide in the conflict between the Executive and Congress, that was soon again to be at its flood. A storm of commercial disaster swept across the country. Many financial schemes were proposed for relief, but most of them failed. The most prominent measure, which assumed the solemnity of law, was the Independent Treasury Bill. "The administration of Van Buren," it has been said, "was like a parenthesis— it may be read in a low tone of voice, or altogether omitted, without injuring the sense." In the election of 1840, which followed, the Whigs succeeded in placing General Harrison in the Presidential chair, which he occupied for about one month*. Immediately after his death, on the 6th of April, 1841, Mr. Tyler took the oath of office, and became the first Vice-President elevated to the chair of the President. He had been nominated on the ground of expediency. He had not been in accord with the party, which placed him second on its ticket. Although a Whig, he held a position inimical to his own party, on

---

* "Harrison was taken from his county clerkship in Ohio to be a candidate for the Presidency—not taken, indeed, by the people, but by a mere compromise of the politicians."—[J. E. Chamberlin, in *International Review*, May and June, 1883.]

the subject of the United States Bank. A hostility between Mr. Tyler and Congress soon developed itself, almost equal to that which existed in Jackson's administration. The Independent Treasury Bill was repealed. A general bankruptcy law was passed. The Whigs then demanded that the United States Bank be re-chartered. The bill was passed; the President vetoed it. It was again passed; again vetoed—upon which all of his Cabinet resigned.* It is not our intention to enter into the long conflicts which ensued between the Executive and Congress. Still, it will be pertinent to show that the great commoner, Mr. Clay, and other leading men of the time, thought that the President had assumed powers that should not be executed by the Chief Magistrate of a Republican Government. Mr. Clay affirmed that, "President Tyler has promulgated an address in the nature of a coronation oath, which the chief of the State in other countries, and under other forms, takes upon ascending the throne. * * * That the President claimed that a high trust had devolved upon him by the joint acts of the people and Providence." On another occasion, he said, "There is as complete and perfect a re-union of the purse and sword, in the hands of the Executive, as there ever was under General Jackson or Mr. Van Buren." Mr. Fillmore said: "The President had now told them in substance, that he had taken the power into his own hands,

---

* "Tyler is a political sectarian, of the slave-driving Virginian Jeffersonian school, principled against all improvement, with all the interests, and passions, and vices of slavery rooted in his moral and political constitution, with talents not above mediocrity, and a spirit incapable of expansion to the dimensions of the station upon which he has been cast by the hand of Providence, unseen through the apparent agency of chance." [Mem. of J. Q. Adams, April 4, 1841, IX, 457.] On the 6th day of April, he adds, "Slavery, temperance, land jobbing, bankruptcy, and sundry controversies with Great Britain, constitute the material for the history of John Tyler's administration. But the improvement of the condition of man will form no part of his policy, and the improvement of his country will be an object of his most inveterate and inflexible opposition." [Ibid., p. 459.]

and although the highest financial officer of the Government declared it as his opinion, that it was doubtful whether the duties could be collected which Congress has provided by law, the President told the House that any further law was unnecessary; that he had power enough in his own hands, and he should use it; that he had authorized the revenue officers to do all that was necessary. Thus, there would be, in fact, the question before the country, whether Congress should legislate for the people of the country, or the Executive." Mr. Thompson remarked, "that the President controlled the votes of nearly three millions of freemen by means of the veto power, and the power of appointment and removal.

In 1844, Mr. Tyler found himself without a party—the party which elected him repudiated him; the Democratic party refused to receive him. He had to form a party of his own. A game of shuttlecock was played with nominations and rejections. At last, the President, who had spent his time in trying to force Congress to adopt his projects of fiscal institutes, fiscal corporations, fiscal agents or fiscal exchequers, went out of power by the termination of the fixed period of his office.* In 1844, the great question before the country was the annexation of Texas. The Whigs opposed it, believing that the Democrats wished thereby to extend the slave-power. Political excitement was at fever heat. In that contest the Democrats elected their leader, James K. Polk, and Henry Clay's hope for the Presidency was forever lost. On the 4th of July, 1845, the Texan Legislature ratified the act of annexation, which had been passed at the close of

---

* Kent, in a letter of May 21, 1844, to H. L. Raymond, wrote to this effect:—" You will perceive that the impeachment power over 'high crimes and misdemeanors' is very broad, as defined and practised under the sanction of the common law, by which it is to be construed and governed. I think there can be no doubt that the enormous abuses and stretch of power by President Tyler afford ample materials for the exercise of the power of impeachment, and an imperative duty in the House of Representatives to put it in practice."—[Niles, Reg., **LXVI.**, p. 226.]

Tyler's administration, and the Lone Star took its place in the Union constellation. In 1836, the Texans had gained their independence from Mexico, and they claimed that it carried the Province of Coahuila, making the Rio Grande the separating line and not the Nueces. The Mexican Government would not accede to the position taken by Texas, which had now become a part of the United States. The President asserted that the boundary line was the Rio Grande, and took arbitrary measures to possess that disputed territory.* "Polk is just as responsible as Tyler for the choice of a method of annexation which, according to the opinion of the first jurists in the country, of a large minority of the House of Representatives, and of the majority of the people and the Senate, was unconstitutional." † Congress had passed a resolution, to the effect that it consented that the territory properly included within, and rightfully belonging to, the Republic of Texas, might be created into a new State, subject to the adjustment by the Government of all questions of boundary that might arise with other Governments. The President took no notice of this law, providing for an adjustment of the boundary with Mexico, but proceeded to decide the question himself, and to make use of the army and navy, as he had already done, to carry out his personal will. He marched his troops into the territory of Coahuila, and found the enemy naturally ready to defend their soil. Then, because the Mexicans were there found upon their own territory, the President declared that that condition of things constituted war. He took all these steps before Congress had a chance to express itself at all. The Constitution says, that Congress alone shall have the power to declare war. President Polk thought differently. After the war was once declared, the people were called upon to carry it on, wherever the troops of

---

* The instructions of the President were to advance and place the forces west of the Nueces.—[Exec. Doc., 30th Congress, 1st Sess., No. 60, 82, 83.]

† Von Holst, vol. iii.; 62.

the United States were ordered by the President. The
resolution provided that the Government of the United
States should adjust the question of boundary, and President
Polk claimed by some process best known to himself, that he
had become the Government. Louis XIV. thought the
same thing. The President went on in his course, and instructed Commodore Connor, commanding the Gulf squadron,
that, in the event of Mexico declaring war, to take possession
of Tampico, while Commodore Sloat, who commanded the
Pacific fleet, was to take San Francisco and other ports. Of
course, the rest was easy. The troops were then ordered to
march into the territory of Mexico; they met with resistance,
and the President formally declared that war existed between
the two countries. It has been said of Polk, that he played
a double game against England and Mexico; against England the strong, a warlike policy, with sword in the scabbard;
against weak Mexico, a peace policy with a drawn sword.
That is, the President blustered towards England when he
meant peace, and talked peace to Mexico when he meant war.
He said that he would not declare war against Mexico unless
she first made war, but he nevertheless sought a conflict and declared war himself.* Mr. Garrett Davis addressed the House
on the subject of the Mexican war on the 14th of May, 1846,
as follows:—" But I do not intend that this consideration, or
any other, shall divert me from full and free inquiry how, and
by what authority, this war was begun. And if I establish, as
I have no doubt I will, that it was undertaken and commenced
by the President during the present session of Congress, in
disregard, and by the usurpation, of the sole and exclusive authority of Congress to make war, I will speak my censure of
such bold abuse of power in the strongest terms that I can
command. In taking this course, I will manifest anything

* The House of Representatives passed a resolution accusing Polk of having begun the Mexican war needlessly and unconstitutionally.—[Von Holst,
vol. iii., 337.]

else than unfriendliness to my own country, or sympathy for her enemies. James K. Polk is not the gallant army, which he has precipitated into needless carnage and peril. He is not the Government, which is the Constitution executed rightfully, administered in all its powers by the appropriate departments and officers. He is not the country, but President as he is, only a small part, an atom of it. Clothed with a little brief and fugitive authority, he has used that with the purposes of an usurper, in sport of the lives of his countrymen, and in the destruction of the peace of nations; his condemnation becomes the highest of all duties, and the member of Congress who "cries aloud and spares not" is much to be preferred to him who, from blind zeal of a partisan, or the venality of a tool of power, shouts "Cæsar can do no wrong," or to him who from any motive whatever can stifle the indignant reprobation with which every freeman's soul must heave upon such an occasion. * * * * I charge and arraign James K. Polk with having, as President of the United States, during the present session, usurped the power of Congress by making war upon Mexico, a nation with whom the United States were at peace. * * * * We were at peace with Mexico, and yet it was into this portion of her territory that Mr. Polk, by his own mere will, ordered an American army to march, forcibly to subvert the jurisdiction of Mexico, and to erect upon its overthrow that of the United States.

"Such invasion, in either state of the case, is not defence, but aggressive war; and this power the Constitution in no case whatever vests in the President, but solely and exclusively in the representatives of the States, and of the people in Congress assembled. When our territory is actually invaded, I have conceded what all men know, that the Constitution and the laws authorize him, and make it his duty to repel it with the military and naval forces of the country. His power stops there, and he can undertake no offensive operations whatever without the authority of Congress. This limitation upon the President is one of the Constitutional bulwarks of popular liberty; when it is overthrown, the fall of the citadel is inevitable, and despotism rises upon its ruins."

Thus the evidence is cumulated that an American President, who was endowed with extraordinary power as the Commander-in-Chief of the army and navy, was not content, but proceeded to declare war, and to direct the invasion of a neighboring nation. The war was continued, and the sympathies of the nation went out to the gallant army which had invaded Mexico, that thickly inhabited country, abounding in natural fortresses. The glory of Buena Vista, Palo Alto, and Chapultepec, shed its lustre around the administration of Polk. The territory of the United States was greatly enlarged. Gold was discovered in California. The people soon forgot the despotic acts of the President, and he, unjust as it may seem to us to-day, reaped the benefit of his own unconstitutional course. The people looked to the central head, and ascribed to him all the credit and the glory of successful war. If that war ever was necessary, it might have been carried to the same successful termination without the instrumentality of personal Government. Any belief in contravention of this last assertion is but one of the political superstitions of the past, which the people of a representative Government should have long ago outgrown.

CHAPTER XVI.

ADMINISTRATIONS OF TAYLOR, FILLMORE, AND BUCHANAN.

The Taylor-Fillmore administration, which followed Polk's, is made conspicuous in American history by the great slavery agitation. Those intellectual giants, Webster and Calhoun, met and debated the question, whether the Union constitutes us a nation. The South wished to carry their slaves into Texas and the new territories, and manifestoes of dissolution, were formulated and signed. The South opposed the admission of California as a free State. Clay, the author of the Missouri Compromise, proposed a grand consolidation of all compromises, in the form of the Omnibus Bill of 1850. The Bill was lost.

President Pierce, who followed in 1853, though not famous for his strength of character, yet managed to a considerable extent to stem the rising tide of liberty. He exercised the veto power nine times.

In January, 1854, Stephen H. Douglas introduced a bill into Congress, which precipitated the impending crisis between the systems of slavery and liberty. The proposition, which in the following May became law, permitted the inhabitants of the then Territories of Kansas and Nebraska, to decide for themselves whether the new States should be free or slave. As these territories lay north of thirty-six degrees and thirty minutes, the law was a virtual repeal of the Missouri Compromise. Pro-slavery outlaws rushed into Kansas, and formed the Lecompton Constitution, authorizing slavery.

The aggressive spirit of the South alarmed the North. Nathaniel P. Banks was elected Speaker of the House; Henry Wilson succeeded Edward Everett in the Senate; and Anson Burlingame followed William Appleton in the House. Charles Sumner was assaulted by a Southerner, in the Capitol, for words spoken in debate.

In 1856, James Buchanan, who had been President Polk's Secretary of State, was elected President of the United States. If President Buchanan had declared, as Chief Justice Taney actually did, that negroes, whether free or slave, were not citizens of the United States, and that they could not become so by any process known to the Constitution; that they could neither sue, or be sued; that a slave was a personal chattel; that he could be removed through any State or territory; and that, therefore, the Compromise measures were unconstitutional and void, such declaration would have been a fitting prelude to his administration, which was uninterruptedly conducted in the interest of the South. He used his immense powers to assist the slaveholder in making war upon the Government.

If there were no incident in the history of the country which proves the absolute necessity of a provision for the removal of the President without unnecessary loss of time, save the one furnished by the administration of James Buchanan, then the event, which is said on good authority to have taken place at that time, establishes the necessity of this most needed provision of law. Buchanan scattered our navy to the winds; he sent arms and ammunition into the sections threatened by insurrection; he ordered small bodies of troops where they could easily be overpowered; and, above all, he did not raise his hand to protect his Government from impending overthrow. But he did more. On the authority of the Hon. Thomas L. Clingman, the President sent one of his own "Privy Council" to North Carolina, to bring about the secession of that State. The following is his speech, cited in Mr. Stickney's work, already quoted: "About the middle of December (1860), I had occasion to see the Secretary of the Interior on some official business. On my entering the room, Mr. Thompson said to me, 'Clingman, I am glad you have called, for I intended presently to go up to the Senate to see you. I have been appointed Commissioner, by the State of Mississippi, to go down to North Carolina to get your State to secede, and I wished to talk with you about your Legislature, before I start down in the morning to Raleigh, and to learn what you think of my chances of success.' I said to him, 'I did not know that you had resigned.' He answered, 'Oh no; I have not resigned.' Then, I replied, 'I suppose you resign in the morning.' 'No,' he answered, 'I do not intend to resign, for Mr. Buchanan wished us all to hold on, and go out with him on the 4th of March.' 'But,' said I, 'does Mr. Buchanan know for what purpose you are going to North Carolina?' 'Certainly, he knows my object.' Being surprised by this statement, I told Mr. Thompson that Mr. Buchanan was probably so much perplexed by his situation that he had not fully considered the matter, and that, as he was already involved in difficulty, we ought not to add to his burdens, and then suggested to Mr. Thompson that he had better see Mr. Buchanan again, and, by way of inducing him to think the matter over, mention what I had been saying to him. Mr. Thompson said, 'Well, I can do so, but I think he fully understands it.'

"In the evening I met Mr. Thompson at a small social party, and as soon as I approached him, he said, 'I knew I could not be mistaken. I told Mr. Buchanan all you said, and he told me he wished me to go, and hoped I might succeed.' I could not help exclaiming, 'Was there ever before any potentate who sent out his own Cabinet ministers to incite an insurrection against his Government?' The fact that Mr. Thompson did go on the errand, and had a public reception before the Legislature, and returned to his position in the Cabinet, is known; but this incident serves to recall it."

Search through the pages of history, and it will be impossible to find a case where even an absolute monarch plotted for the destruction of his own government. If we had a government at that time, then Buchanan was a traitor, and should immediately have been punished. Mr. Stickney thinks that he acted from party motives—that this was the cause. No. The cause lies further back, in the very inception of our Government. Buchanan was at the head of a government, of very limited powers for holding itself together, as he thought. His theory seemed to have been, that a monarchical President was not restricted in any action he should decide upon. He had a number of persons about him who owed their political existence to him—they were his private advisers. One of this conclave, being a citizen of one State, went as a Commissioner to another, to induce that State to make war upon the Central Government, which he was then pretending to serve.*

The fact is, that this confusion of morals, results from a confusion of laws. How can a government be at the same time representative and confederative—republican and monarchical?

The conflict between slavery and freedom had long been carried on. On the one hand, it was asserted that slavery was a "divinely-appointed institution;" on the other, that it was a violation of the laws of God and man. Personal liberty bills were passed to counteract the Fugitive Slave law. John

---

* "Presidential intrigues cost us the war with Mexico, the repeal of the Missouri Compromise, the Kansas-Nebraska Act, and the civil war in Kansas. Presidential intrigues wrought up the sectional misunderstanding until ' Yankees and Southerners' formed legendary and fabulous notions of each other. It was on account of the importance of the Southern vote to all presidential aspirants that the Southern 'arrogance' and the Northern 'truckling' were developed."
—[Prof. William G. Sumner, in *Princeton Review*, Jan., 1881.]

Brown, driven to desperation by witnessing the massacre of entire Northern families, invaded Virginia, accompanied by twenty associates, and seized the United States arsenal at Harper's Ferry, with the intent of getting arms to liberate the slaves. Those who were not killed at the onset, were tried, convicted, and hanged. Although this movement was legally considered a mere insurrection, still, regarded in a more philosophical light, it was the advance skirmish of the great rebellion that was so soon to follow. In 1860, Abraham Lincoln was nominated for the Presidency, and it was soon apparent that the South fully appreciated that its revolutionary efforts to force slavery upon the free territories was thoroughly understood at the North, and that, beyond all peradventure, its candidate would be defeated. The South commenced to organize war.* It is popularly believed that slavery was the sole cause of the war of the rebellion. It may have been one of the prominent elements of discord, but the overshadowing and controlling cause was the presidential system. A matter of difference arose between two sections of the country upon the subject of slavery, which was thought to create an irrepressible conflict. No issue should be undeterminable in a true republic. There exists in this view of our law, its great danger and evil. The South saw that a Republican President was certain to be elected in 1860 by a minority of the people. It was familiar with the political opinions of Mr. Lincoln, and believed that his action as President would be unfavorable to its interests. If the people of the United States had been living under a representative government, with an executive whose purpose,

---

* " As to the Elective Presidency, it is the curse and bane of the country: more than once it has brought on convulsions serious enough to paralyze commerce and fill the community with alarm; once it has brought on civil war. Unarmed civil war is, in fact, a fair description of the state in which it now keeps the nation two years at least out of every four."—[Prof. Goldwin Smith, in *The Bystander*, Jan., 1883.]

design and wish were to carry into effect the will of the masses, the South would probably have remained loyal and submitted the issue to the decision of the ballot. In that event the result would have been peacefully and quietly accepted. But we all know that the President is elected by colleges and not by the people; the Senate represents the confederated States and not the masses. The South saw no way, save by revolution, to perpetuate its favorite institution, and at the same time resist the action of a personal government. In the autumn of 1860, South Carolina, Mississippi, Florida, Alabama, Georgia, Louisiana, and Texas, passed secession ordinances, and Virginia, Arkansas, Tennessee, and North Carolina, soon followed. The first six formed a Confederacy at Montgomery, Alabama, on the 8th of February, 1861, called the Confederate States of America. Buchanan, of course, remained President of the United States until March, 1861, and during all of this time he was silent, while the revolutionary government seized treasury funds, custom houses, ships, and forts, which were within its assumed jurisdiction. Congress was loyal, the President disloyal, to the Government. Not making any particular point as to the four vetoes which President Buchanan, interposed, he uniformly used his high office for the benefit of the revolutionary element in the country, and against liberty, order, and law. In the exercise of his kingly powers the President ordered troops into positions where they could easily be overpowered; he abandoned fortified places, in order that they might be expeditiously captured; he sent arms and ammunition into the South, that they might be forthwith seized; and he ordered ships to foreign seas, that they might not be employed in re-asserting the supremacy of law.

In January, the steamship "Star of the West," unarmed, on her way to provision Fort Sumter, in South Carolina, was fired upon by the Southerners, and forced to return to New

York. In fine, it does not require a very elaborate analysis of the administration of James Buchanan, to prove that he exercised the powers of an elective monarch, and monarch-like, almost without exception, on the side of slavery, and against liberty.

We have had no intention of making a full examination of the various acts of the administration of President Buchanan, further than to show what steps led to the greatest event of American history.*

* " The 'Life of Buchanan,' by Mr. Curtis, is a very big work about a very small man. Buchanan was a typical politician, and the natural offspring of caucuses and Presidential campaigns. . . . . Dante has a place for him among those who are hateful alike to God and to the enemies of God. His biographer evidently deems him a legal Abdiel of the Constitution, but then Mr. Curtis is himself too great a constitutional legist to see any difference between the moribund slavery, with which terms were made in the compact of 1788, and the aggressive Slave Power of 1861."—[Prof. Goldwin Smith, in *The Bystander*, October, 1883.]

CHAPTER XVII.

ADMINISTRATION OF ABRAHAM LINCOLN.

IF any one should attempt the criticism that there is an effort made in these pages to condone or palliate the acts of President Lincoln, notwithstanding their tyrannical and unconstitutional character, if that could be so proven, then he assists the purpose and object of this essay by showing the salient imperfection of a system which makes the commission of such acts possible. It is undoubtedly true that grave constitutional questions were raised in relation to many acts of President Lincoln. But is there any doubt that he conscientiously exercised his presidential power in the interest of liberty and human rights? In reflecting upon the power exercised by President Lincoln, it would seem that he had been guided by the motives, and influenced by the principle, enunciated by Cicero to Brutus, while the issue was pending between the second triumvirate and the party of Brutus and Cassius: "By what right, by what law, shall Cassius go to Syria (as pro-consul)? By that law which Jupiter sanctioned when he ordained that all things good for the republic should be just and legal."* Congress did not authorize every act done by the President. The latter exercised what were then known as war powers. The fact that he was found on the side of liberty and good government was an accident pertaining to the man; that he had extraordinary and monarchical power was a matter of crystalized, settled and

---

* Trollope's "Life of Cicero," II., 218; cited by Hurd, "Theory of Our National Existence," 515.

fundamental law. President Lincoln, as a man, might waver or err; the law was fixed and determined. *A priori*, he was as liable to have been allied with wrong as with right, slavery as with freedom, treason as with loyalty. That this great and good friend of human rights died in the service of liberty, while the words of his assassin, "*sic semper tyrannis,*" were still ringing in the air, is most true. That the man who stood foremost as the great emancipator was stricken down in the name of liberty, is the most startling and inexplicable event in the history of the world. Slavery struck the blow at liberty. The pistol-shot was but an incident of a brutal, degrading system which traded in the flesh and blood of man.

It is only necessary to read the President's first inaugural address to prove that neither emancipation nor war measures were at first intended. He undoubtedly desired only to enforce the Constitution as he found it. The course of events changed all this. He said, on March 4th, 1861, "I have no purpose, directly or indirectly, to interfere with the institution of slavery in the States where it exists. I believe I have no lawful right to do so, and I have no inclination to do so." He quoted the platform upon which he had been elected, denouncing the lawless invasion of any State or territory as the gravest crime; adding, that he would enforce the reclaiming of fugitive slaves. In answer to a committee appointed by a convention in Virginia, the President, on the 13th of April, 1861, said :—"The power confided to me will be used to hold, occupy and possess the property and places belonging to the Government, and to collect the duties and imposts; but, beyond what may be necessary for these objects, there will be no invasion, no using of force, against or among the people anywhere. * * * While the strict legal right may exist in the Government to enforce the exercise of these (Federal) offices, the attempt to do so would be so irritating and so impracticable withal, that I deem it better to forego, for the time, the use of such offices."

Major Anderson surrendered on the 14th of April, and on the 15th the President, by proclamation, called for seventy-five thousand men. In the same proclamation the Senators and Representatives are summoned to assemble on the 4th day of July. Thus it appears that from the 15th day of April to the 4th day of July all measures for the suppression of the greatest rebellion of modern days were under the complete control of a single man. Governor Ellis, of North Carolina, in reply to the proclamation, said, that he regarded "the levy of troops made by the Administration, for the purpose of subjugating the States of the South, as a violation of the Constitution and a usurpation of power." Governor Jackson, of Missouri, replied, "Your requisition is illegal, unconstitutional, revolutionary, inhuman, diabolical, and cannot be complied with."

On May 3d, 1861, the President called for thirty-nine volunteer regiments of infantry and one regiment of cavalry, and the enlistment of eighteen thousand seamen. The President also ordered an increase of the regular army to the extent of eight regiments of infantry, one of cavalry, and one of artillery.

All of these acts were done two months before Congress came together. No king could have done more. Although there is no doubt that the loyal people were in perfect accord with the President in this great emergency, still is it not right that we should pause and ask ourselves whether these are not alarming and dangerous precedents? May not this same power some day be used against the true interests of the Government and people? On the 6th day of August, Congress nevertheless legalized the increase of the regular army, as well as the acts, orders and proclamations of the President respecting the army and navy. In his first message, President Lincoln said of these acts, that "these measures, whether strictly legal or not, were ventured upon under what appeared to be a popular demand and a public necessity, trusting, then as now, that Congress would readily ratify them. It is believed that nothing has been done beyond the constitutional competency of Congress." It was not pretended that the acts referred to were within the constitutional powers of the Executive, nor need we draw attention to the fact that the power to declare war rests wholly with Congress. In the same message the President says, that after the first call for militia it was also considered a duty to authorize the Commanding-General, in his discretion, to suspend the writ of *habeas corpus*. The Opposition claimed that he whose duty it was under the Constitution to execute the laws should not himself violate them. It was insisted upon that Congress, not the Executive, was vested with this power. The President claimed that he exercised the right to save the Government itself; that " it was with the deepest regret that the Executive found the duty of employing the war power in defence of the Government forced upon him." Is not a representative government defective under which such acts could be explained as a conscientious exercise of what is indefinitely termed the "war power?" May not some future President do these same acts in the interest of anarchy, revolution, and slavery? Presidents have done so before. The ordinary means of administering justice had in many places failed. There were no courts in the territory repossessed. The President continued: "Under these circumstances, I have been urgently solicited to establish, by military power, courts to administer summary justice in such cases." He said he had no doubt that the end was just and right in itself, but he had " been unwilling to go beyond the pressure of necessity in the unusual exercise of power." He then referred the whole matter to Congress.

In England, arrests were only made by the authority of Parliament. It is fair to infer that the ministers did not make arrests, for the reason that the elementary writers do not even mention the subject. "If an English sovereign were now to immure a subject in defiance of the writ of

166   THE ABOLITION OF THE PRESIDENCY.

habeas corpus, the whole nation would be instantly electrified by the news."* Those who contend that our ancestors intended to confer upon the President the right of the suspension of the writ of *habeas corpus*, claim, in effect, "that the prerogatives wrested from the Plantagenets, Tudors and Stuarts, were renewed by the framers of our Constitution." President Jefferson, on being informed of the arrest of Aaron Burr, on the charge of conspiracy and treason against the United States, asked Congress to suspend the writ. In this respect President Jefferson followed English precedents. Judge Marshall afterwards held that it was the Legislature that had the power to suspend the writ.

Notwithstanding the English and American precedents, on the 27th of June, 1861, General N. P. Banks arrested the Chief and members of the Board of Police of Baltimore as conspirators against, and as hostile to, the authority of the Government of the United States. Prominent men in all parts of the country were daily arrested. All of these arrests were made by direction of the President through the War Department.

In May, 1861, John Merryman, of Baltimore, Md., was arrested, charged with holding a commission as lieutenant in a company in armed hostility against the Government; with being in communication with rebels, and other acts of treason. He was sent to Fort McHenry. He at once forwarded a petition to Chief Justice Taney, reciting his arrest and praying for a writ of *habeas corpus*. The writ was issued. General Cadwallader, who was in command, refused to respond, alleging that he was authorized by the President to suspend the writ. The Chief Justice issued an attachment directing the United States Marshal to produce the body of General Cadwallader, to answer for his contempt. The Marshal replied that he was not permitted to enter the fort, and that he was informed there was no answer to the writ. The

* Macaulay's England, II, 30.

Chief Justice stated that he ordered the attachment because, on the face of the return, the detention of the prisoner was unlawful on two grounds; 1st, that the President, under the Constitution and laws of the United States, cannot suspend the privilege of the writ of *habeas corpus*, nor authorize any military officer to do so; 2d, that a military officer has no right to arrest and detain a person not subject to the rules and articles of war. The Chief Justice afterwards said that the Marshal had legally the power to summon out the *posse commitatus*, but it was evident that he would be resisted. The Chief Justice remarked that he would report the proceedings to the President, and call upon him to perform his Constitutional duty to enforce the laws, in other words the process of the Court.

Our Government, it is claimed, consists of three co-ordinate branches, each having its particular sphere; each having power to enforce its own mandates. In contemplating the actual workings of the system, what do we witness? The suspension of *habeas corpus* rests with Congress, yet it is exercised by the President. The Supreme Court decides the writ unlawful; it is unable to enforce its decree, and calls for assistance upon the President, who refuses. This looks as if one, at least, of the co-ordinate branches on that occasion had disappeared from active participation in the affairs of Government.

The learned justice indulged in a very exhaustive argument. He said:—"As the case comes before me, I understand that the President not only claims the right to suspend the writ of *habeas corpus* himself, at his discretion, but to delegate that discretionary power to a military officer, and to leave it to him to determine whether he will or will not obey judicial process that may be served upon him. No official notice has been given to the courts of justice, or to the people, by proclamation or otherwise, that the President claimed this power, and had exercised it in the manner stated in the return." He continued: "That when the conspiracy of

Aaron Burr became so formidable as to justify (in the opinion of Mr. Jefferson) the suspension of the writ, he referred the whole matter to Congress. No one suggested that Mr. Jefferson might exercise the power himself. The clause authorizing the suspension is devoted to the Legislative Department, and has not the slightest reference to the Executive. In the second article of the Constitution, which organizes the Executive Department, there is not a word that can furnish any grounds to justify the exercise of this power." The opinion continues: "I can see no ground whatever for supposing that the President in any emergency, or in any state of things, can authorize the suspension of the writ of Habeas Corpus, or arrest a citizen, except in aid of the judicial power. He certainly does not faithfully execute the laws if he takes upon himself legislative power of suspending the writ, and the judicial power, also, by arresting and imprisoning a person without due process of law." * * *
"The Government of the United States is one of delegated and limited powers—neither of its branches can exercise any of the powers of Government beyond those specified and granted."

From the earliest history of the Common Law, if a person was imprisoned, no matter by what authority, he had a right to the writ to bring his case before the King's Bench. The learned justice quotes the following from Blackstone's Commentaries on the Laws of England:—"But the glory of the English law consists in clearly defining the times, the causes and the extent, when, wherefore, and to what degree, the imprisonment of the subject may be lawful. This it is which induces the absolute necessity of expressing upon every commitment the reason for which it is made, that a Court upon a *habeas corpus* may examine into its validity, and according to the circumstances of the case, may discharge, admit to bail, or remand the prisoner. * * * * But the happiness of our Constitution is, that it is not left to the Executive power to determine when the danger of the State is so great as to render the measure expedient. It is the Parliament only, or the legislative power, that, whenever it sees proper, can authorize the Crown, by suspending the *habeas corpus* for a short and limited time, to imprison suspected persons without giving any reason for so doing." Chief Justice Taney then continues: "And if the President of the United States may suspend the writ, then the Constitution of the United States has conferred upon him more regal and absolute power over the liberty of the citizen than the people of England have thought it safe to entrust to the Crown; a power which the Queen of England cannot exercise at this day, and which could not have been lawfully exercised by the Sovereign even in the reign of Charles the First."* The Chief Justice concludes as follows:—" Such is the case now before me; and I can only say, that if the authority which the Constitution has confided to the Judiciary Department and judicial officers may thus, upon any pretext or under any circumstances, be usurped by the military power at its discretion, the people of the United States are no longer living under a Government of laws, but every citizen holds life, liberty and property at the will and pleasure of the army officer in whose military district he may happen to be found." †

Attorney-General Bates, in an elaborate opinion, dated July 5th, 1861, took an opposite view of the power of the President to arrest suspected persons, and suspend the writ of *habeas corpus*. After stating that the President is the active officer; that he must take the initiative; that he must begin operations; he continues as follows: "The duties of the office comprehend all the executive power of the nation, which is expressly vested in the President by the Constitu-

---

* But the opinion is not confined to drawing analogies between the English Government and our own. C. J. Taney quotes Story, " Commentaries on the Constitution," vol. 3, section 1, 336; also, Chief Justice Marshall, in the case of *ex parte* Bollman and Swartwout, reported in the 4th of Cranch, 95.

† McPherson's " Hist. of the Rebellion," 155-158.

tion, and, also, all the powers specially delegated to the President, and yet are not in their nature executive powers; for example, the veto power, the treaty-making power, the appointing power, the pardoning power. These belong to that class which, in England, are called prerogative powers, inherent in the Crown. And yet, the framers of our Constitution thought proper to preserve them, and to vest them in the President, as necessary to the good government of the country. * * * All the other officers of Government are required to swear only to support this Constitution, while the President must swear to preserve, protect, and defend it, which implies the power to perform what he is required in so solemn a manner to undertake. And then follows the broad and compendious injunction to take care that the laws be faithfully executed. And this injunction, embracing as it does all the laws, Constitution, treaties, statutes, is addressed to the President alone, and not to any other department or officer of the Government. And this constitutes him in a peculiar manner, and above all other officers, the guardian of the Constitution—its preserver, protector, and defender. * * * The manner in which he shall perform that duty is not prescribed by any law, but the means of performing it are given in the plain language of the statutes, and they are all means of force—the militia, the army, and the navy. The end, the suppression of the insurrection, is required of him; the means and instruments to suppress it are lawfully in his hands; but the manner in which he shall use them is not prescribed, and could not be prescribed without a foreknowledge of all the future changes and contingencies of the insurrection. He is, therefore, necessarily thrown upon his discretion as to the manner in which he will use his means to meet the varying exigencies as they arise. If the insurgents assail the nation with an army, he may find it best to meet them with an army, and suppress the insurrection on the field of battle. If they seek to prolong the rebellion, and gather strength by intercourse with foreign nations, he may choose to guard the coast and close the ports with a navy, as one of the most efficient means to suppress the insurrection. And if they employ spies and emissaries to gather information, to forward secret supplies, and to excite new insurrections in aid of the original rebellion, he may find it both prudent and humane to arrest and imprison them. And this may be done, either for the purpose of bringing them to trial and condign punishment for their crimes, or they may be held in custody for the milder end of rendering them powerless for mischief until the exigency is past. In such a state of things, the President must, of necessity, be the sole judge, both of the exigency which requires him to act, and of the manner in which it is most prudent for him to employ the powers entrusted to him, to enable him to discharge his Constitutional and legal duty; that is, to suppress the insurrection and execute the laws. And this discretionary power of the President is fully admitted by the Supreme Court.* This is a great power in the hands of the Chief Magistrate; and because it is great, and is capable of being perverted to evil ends, its existence has been doubted or denied. It is said to be dangerous in the hands of an ambitious and wicked President, because he may use it for the purposes of oppression and tyranny. Yes, certainly it is dangerous; all power is dangerous, and for the all-pervading reason, that all power is liable to abuse; all the recipients of human power are men, not absolutely virtuous and wise. Still, it is a power necessary to the peace and safety of the country, and undeniably belongs to the Government, and, therefore, must be exercised by some department or officer thereof. * * * As to the second question, having assumed, in answering the first question, that the President has the legal discretionary power to arrest and imprison persons who are guilty of holding criminal intercourse with men engaged in a great and

---

* Martin *vs.* Mott, 12 Wheaton's Reports, 19; 7 Curtis, 10.

dangerous insurrection, or persons suspected, with 'probable cause,' of such criminal complicity, it might seem unnecessary to go into any prolonged argument, to prove that, in such a case, the President is fully justified in refusing to obey a writ of *habeas corpus*, issued by a court or judge, commanding him to produce the body of his prisoner, and state when he took him, and by what authority, and for what cause he detains him in custody, and then yield himself to judgment 'to do, submit to, and receive, whatsoever the judge or court, awarding the writ, shall consider in that behalf.' * * * If, by the phrase, the suspension of the privilege of the writ of *habeas corpus*, we must understand a repeal of all power to issue the writ, then, I freely admit, that none but Congress can do it. But if we are at liberty to understand the phrase to mean, that in case of a great and dangerous rebellion, like the present, the public safety requires the arrest and confinement of persons implicated in that rebellion, I as freely declare the opinion, that the President has lawful power to suspend the privilege of persons arrested, under such circumstances; for he is especially charged by the Constitution with the 'public safety,' and he is the sole judge of the emergency which requires his prompt action. This power in the President is no part of his ordinary duty in time of peace; it is temporary and exceptional, and was intended only to meet a pressing emergency, when the judiciary is found to be too weak to insure the public safety—when (in the language of the Act of Congress), there are 'combinations too powerful to be suppressed by the ordinary course of judicial proceedings, or by the powers vested in the marshals.' Then, and not till then, has he the lawful authority to call to his aid the military power of the nation, and with that power perform his great legal and Constitutional duty, to suppress the insurrection. And, shall it be said, that when he has fought and captured the insurgent army, and has seized their secret spies and emissaries, he is bound to bring their bodies before any judge who may send him a writ of *habeas corpus*, 'to do, submit to, and receive, whatsoever the said judge shall consider in that behalf?' * * * The power to do these things is in the hands of the President, placed there by the Constitution and the Statute law, as a sacred trust, to be used by him in his best discretion, in the performance of his great first duty—to preserve, protect, and defend the Constitution."*

Sufficient has been quoted, to show that the Attorney-General was of the opinion that the President had the power which the Supreme Court denied him. While the discussion continued, the President acted. Arrests were made; the writ was not obeyed.

Horace Binney, in his work on "The Privilege of the Writ of *Habeas Corpus* under the Constitution," says : "In this matter of suspension of the privilege of the writ of *habeas corpus*, the Constitution of the United States stands in the place of the English Act of Parliament. It ordains the suspension in the conditioned cases—by the act of the competent department—as Parliament does from time to time. Neither is mandatory in suspending, but only authoritative. Each leaves discretion to the Executive power. The difference is that Parliament limits a time, and provides for the effect by technical terms. The Constitution connects the suspension with the time of rebellion, and provides for the effect, as it did for the privilege, by words that comprehend the right, and deny for a season the enjoyment of it." †

The comparison which Mr. Binney attempts seems defective, for the cases are hardly analogous. In the one case, a single man arbitrarily exercises a certain power; in the other,

---

* The following are the cases cited by the Attorney-General:—The Rhode Island Case, 7 Howard, page 1 ; Fleming vs. Page, 9 Howard, page 615 ; Cross vs. Harrison, 16 Howard, page 189 ; The Santissima Trinidad, 7 Wheaton, page 305; Martin vs. Mott, 12 Wheaton, page 29. McPherson's "History of the Rebellion," 158-161.

† "McPherson's "Hist. of the Rebellion," 161.

a Parliament by a vote specifically, and for a definite time, decrees the suspension, the details of which are actually carried out by the Cabinet. The Crown has no power at all. The suspension does not depend upon the exercise of any one will.

Professor Theophilus Parsons, in a lecture on the Executive branch of the Government, on the 5th of June, 1861, remarks: "The question is, has the President this power? The Constitution does not expressly give this power to any department of Government, nor does it expressly reserve it to Congress, although, in the same article, it does make this express reservation as to some of the provisions contained in the article, This may be a mere accidental omission, but it seems to be more reasonable, and more consonant with the principles of legal interpretation, to infer from it an absence of intention to confine it to Congress. * * * * My conclusion is, therefore, that in case of invasion from abroad, or rebellion at home, the President may declare, or exercise, or authorize, martial law at his discretion."

It is the loosest kind of reasoning to hold that such stupendous power should rest upon an inference, an implication; and we have herein an illustration of the unsettled, unfinished, and indeterminate condition of our fundamental law. Would it be necessary in England to request the opinion of a professor or barrister, in order to determine which branch of the Government had the right to suspend this writ?

On the 4th of May, 1863, Clement L. Vallandigham was arrested on account of acts committed for the benefit of the enemies of the country, and for publicly expressing sympathy with those in arms against the Government of the United States. The specification sets forth passages from a speech delivered about May 1st, 1863. On the 5th of May, Mr. Vallandigham applied to Judge Leavitt, of the United States Circuit Court, for a writ of *habeas corpus.* Upon its return he refused to discharge the prisoner, holding, in substance, that the legality of the arrest is determined by the extent of the necessity of making it, and that necessity by the will of the military officer. On the 16th of May, he was found guilty by a military commission, and sentenced to be placed in close confinement in Fort Warren, Boston Harbor, during the continuance of the war. On the 19th of May, 1863, the President sent a cipher despatch to General Burnside, directing that Mr. Vallandigham be sent to the headquarters of General Rosecrans, to be put by him beyond the military lines, and in case of his return to be kept in close custody for the term specified in his sentence. On the 16th day of May, there was a meeting of Democrats held at Albany, N.Y., at which meeting a series of resolutions were passed. They denounced the arrest and the course of the administration as a fatal blow at the supremacy of the law, and called upon the President to reverse the action of the military tribunal. On the 12th of June President Lincoln replied, in a letter, in which, among other things, he said: "Under cover of 'liberty of speech,' 'liberty of the press,' and '*habeas corpus*,' they (the insurgents) hoped to keep on foot amongst us a most efficient corps of spies, informers, suppliers, and aiders and abettors of their cause in a thousand ways. They knew that in times such as they were inaugurating, by the Constitution itself, the '*habeas corpus*' might be suspended; but they also knew they had friends who would make a question as to who was to suspend it; meanwhile, their spies and others might remain at large to help on their cause. Or if, as has happened, the Executive should suspend the writ, without ruinous waste of time, instances of arresting innocent persons might occur, as are always likely to occur in such cases; and then a clamor could be raised in regard to this, which might be, at least, of some service to the insurgent cause. It needed no very keen perception to discover this part of the enemy's programme, as soon as, by open hostilities, their machinery was properly put in motion. Yet, thoroughly imbued with a reverence for the guaranteed rights of individuals, I was slow to adopt the strong measures which by degrees I have been forced to regard as being within the exceptions of the Constitution, and as indispensable to the public safety. Nothing is better known to history than that courts of justice are utterly incompetent in such cases. * * * *. The Constitution itself makes the distinction; and I can no more be persuaded that the Government can constitutionally take no strong measures in time of rebellion, because it can be shown that the same could not be lawfully taken in time of peace, than I can be persuaded that a particular drug is not a good medicine for a sick man because it can be shown to not be good food for a well one."

The President, after indulging in this rather peculiar style of constitutional argument, draws attention to the incident in American history where President Jackson arrested both the lawyer who had procured a writ for the release of an editor, and the judge who had granted it. There is no dearth of headstrong and even tyrannical acts in the life of Andrew Jackson.

The Democrats of Ohio addressed a communication to the President on the same subject, to which Mr. Lincoln replied, and to such reply the Committee rejoined. The argument in the rejoinder is very extensive and exhaustive. The following are some of the conclusions of the Committee: "Your assumption of the right to suspend all the Constitutional guarantees of personal liberty, and even of the freedom of speech and of the press, because the summary remedy of *habeas corpus* may be suspended, is at once startling and alarming to all persons desirous of preserving free government in this country. In derogation of the constitutional provisions making the President strictly an executive officer, and vesting all the delegated legislative powers in Congress, your position, as we understand it, would make your will the rule of action, and your declaration of the requirements of the public safety the law of the land. Our inquiry was not, therefore, ' simply a question, who shall decide, or the affirmation that nobody shall decide, what the public safety requires.' Our Government is a Government of law, and it is the law-making power which ascertains what the public safety requires, and prescribes the rule of action; and the duty of the President is simply to execute the laws thus enacted, and not to make or annul laws. If any exigency shall arise, the President has the power to convene Congress at any time to provide for it; so that the plea of necessity furnishes no reasonable pretext for any assumption of legislative power."

What the powers of the various officers are must be arrived at by examination and discussion of these subjects. At the present time, there is a great diversity of opinion concerning the extent and limit of the different departments. The peace of the country demands that all these questions be settled, so far as law or decision may ever settle anything. Was it not questions spawned by conflicting constructions of our boasted fundamental law that arrayed one half of the country against the other half, in one of the bloodiest wars in the annals of history? If the right of secession was the logical and Constitutional view of the law, then the North was wrong, and the United States Government to-day holds the Southern States to the compact of the Union by no stronger bond than the mere force of arms. But, the question fraught with the greatest danger is: What are the powers of the President? Should he be elective? What shall be the mode of election? Shall we have a President at all? Should not the source of all power be the legislative, and should not its committee execute its decrees?

In February, 1864, Mr. Vallandigham's case came before the Supreme Court, on a petition that a *certiorari* be directed to the Judge Advocate-General for a revision of the proceedings of the Military Commission. It was denied. Judge

Advocate Holt wrote an opinion in which he claimed that the Court could with equal propriety be asked to issue an injunction against Congress to reverse these proceedings. A short time afterwards, Mr. Vallandigham returned to this country. The President, being personally advised of the circumstance, simply said that the fact of his return had not been officially brought to his notice, but should Mr. V. make his presence known by objectionable acts, the Executive stood ready to execute its order. The whole discussion in relation to the department of the Government which should suspend the writ of *habeas corpus*, was brought to an end by Congress authorizing the President to act in his discretion; and on the 11th day of September, 1863, there was a general suspension of the writ by the President.

It remained for President Lincoln to assume the greatest power in order to accomplish the greatest good. The Constitution indirectly recognized the institution of slavery. The Southerners believed that slavery would be destroyed if President Lincoln was elected. They rebelled against the Government. They made human bondage the corner-stone of their new political structure. They attempted to establish a slaveocracy on firm foundations. They appealed to the arbitrament of arms. In the North, slavery came to be regarded as the cause of the irrepressible conflict between the two sections. The philosophy of events called for the abolition of slavery. Congress would not take the step. It was at last urged that the war itself, as prosecuted by the Government, was for the freedom of the slaves. It was believed that a national necessity was at hand, and that a blow at slavery would bring the war to an end. President Lincoln no longer hesitated. Did the Constitution authorize him to act? No! Was he empowered to act by Congress? No! Nevertheless, on the 22d of September, 1862, he issued his proclamation declaring his intention, and on the 1st day of January, 1863, he enrolled himself in the world's history as the great emancipator. That proclamation, among other things, provided:—" Now, therefore, I, Abraham Lincoln, President of the United States, by virtue of the power in me vested as Commander-in-Chief of the army and navy of the United States, in time of actual armed rebellion against the authority and Government of the United States, and as a fit and necessary war measure for suppressing said rebellion. * * * * And by virtue of the power and for the purpose aforesaid, I do order and declare that all persons held as slaves within said designated States, and parts of States, are, and henceforward shall be, free; and that the Executive Government of the United States, including the military and naval authorities thereof, will recognize and maintain the freedom of said persons. * * And upon this act, sincerely believed to be an act of justice, warranted by the Constitution upon military necessity, I invoke the considerate judgment of mankind, and the gracious favor of Almighty God."

President Lincoln had issued a proclamation on April 19th, 1861, declaring the acts of pretended privateers, under the authority of certain States, punishable as piracy; * he had declared war, raised troops, increased the regular army, instituted blockade, ordered arrests of citizens, and suspended the *habeas corpus*, before he issued the Proclamation of Emancipation. These acts he called acts of necessity. If they were acts of necessity, they were not acts of law. "A necessity for violating the Constitution in order to maintain the Constitution is contradiction, and the argument is not bettered in the least by calling it the necessity for preserving 'the integrity of the Union,' or 'the life of the nation,' or 'the national existence.' If the limitations imposed upon a Government holding delegated powers are inconsistent with attaining these great objects, they are not the objects for which such Government was instituted, and the necessity cannot be supposed." †

* McPherson's " Pol. Hist. of the Rebellion," 149.
† Hurd's " Theory of Our National Existence," 201.

It is quite evident that President Lincoln regarded his oath to support the Constitution as one of allegiance to some Sovereign power, independent of the Constitution itself. The law seems to have acted upon his mind as an evidence, like any other evidence, which might lead him to a correct comprehension of the wish, desire or will of the people. But he did more. He failed to take instruction and direction from the masses, either through legislation or other organized effort, in order to learn their will, and established and promulgated his own standard of right and wrong.

It certainly is an anomaly to witness a President of a Republic exercising such powers, affecting such immense interests, not by virtue of the law, but by operation of his own will. It was held by many that the Proclamation of Emancipation was not warranted by the Constitution, and that it was "an assumption of power dangerous to the rights of citizens, and to the perpetuity of a free people." One of the grotesque features of that political controversy was this, that in the name of liberty the acts of the President were denounced. But the great friend of the people had determined that our country should no longer be a hunting ground for human game. President Lincoln immortalized himself by striking off the chains of four millions of slaves. But the consideration which forces itself upon us is whether he did not exercise a kingly prerogative in doing so. We assert that he did. While he performed this laudable act, in the interest of human rights, he at the same time struck a blow at Representative Government.

CHAPTER XVIII.

ADMINISTRATION OF ANDREW JOHNSON.

At the outbreak of the rebellion, President Lincoln increased the regular army, and virtually conducted war; but, at the same time, he called an extra session of Congress to consider, not only the general direction of the war, but the constitutionality of the acts he had already performed. It required an egotist like Andrew Johnson to claim that he had full power to reconstruct the nation, and, at the same time, to lecture the people upon the beauties of the Constitution, as he understood them. The old slaveholders were terror-stricken when they heard that Johnson had become President. "Why," said they, "he comes from the lowest white people of the South. He naturally hates us; he will hang us all." Every one knows that he became their best friend. The war had ended. There was no civil government in the South. Those States were not represented in Congress. The Military Commissions were the only Courts. The great problem was how to bring back into the Union those communities which had been making war against the Government. The President had power to convene Congress. Can the imagination conceive of a more extraordinary occasion for the exercise of this power? Why did he not submit those momentous questions to the people through Congress? But, no; this little Cæsar attempted to execute the stupendous task himself. What were the rights of the loyal men of the South? What was to be done with the States lately in rebellion? What should be the terms of readjustment?

All these vexed questions this single man endeavored definitely to settle for the American people. He did not consult them. In no part of the civilized world would the Sovereign have failed to call the representative branch of the government together, in order to pass upon matters of such importance to the public weal.* He commenced by orders and proclamations. On the 29th of April, 1865, he endeavored to restore commercial intercourse with the people of the South, and under the same date to proclaim amnesty and pardon to nearly all who had fought to destroy the Government. On the 9th of May, he published another order, "To establish the authority of the United States, and to execute the laws within the geographical limits known as the State of Virginia." This document contained many high-sounding terms, many cautions and directions. It was, however, an outrage upon the principles of representative government. It recognized Francis H. Pierpont, who had been chosen by a small body of men, assembled at Alexandria, in April, 1864, as the Governor of that State. This recognition was a fraud perpetrated in the name of law. But the most characteristic procedure of Andrew Johnson was, while openly and flagrantly violating the law of the land, to claim that he was acting in pursuance of the Constitution. In most of the rebellious States there was no person who assumed to be entitled to the governorship; so, it was necessary to make appointments. This difficulty was surmounted by proclamations, appointing

---

* "But, for reasons which I abstain from any attempt to unfold, he saw fit, like a daring mariner, sailing forth, without chart or compass, upon an unknown sea, to assume the high and perilous responsibility of dealing with it (reconstruction) alone. * * Animated by the prevailing desire for reconstruction; favored by the long recess of Congress; coveting, perhaps, the glory of the achievement, and possibly not insensible to the allurements of a less elevated ambition, he resolved, like Alexander, to cut the Gordian knot, and overlooking, or disregarding, the lurking dangers of the enterprise, to advance at once, by the shortest and easiest road, to its accomplishment.'—[" The Powers of the Executive Department of the Government of the United States," by Alfred Conkling, 8, 9, 12].

provisional governors charged with various duties. The first one related to North Carolina. Its preamble sets forth that, "Whereas the President of the United States is, by the Constitution, made Commander-in-chief of the army and navy, as well as chief civil executive officer of the United States, and is bound by solemn oath faithfully to execute the office of President of the United States, and to take care that the laws be faithfully executed; * * * and whereas the rebellion has deprived the people of the State of North Carolina of all civil government; now, therefore, in obedience to the high and solemn duties imposed upon me by the Constitution of the United States, * * * I, Andrew Johnson, President of the United States, and Commander-in-chief of the army and navy of the United States, do hereby appoint William W. Holden Provisional Governor of the State of North Carolina." Then follows the imposition of certain duties upon his newly-created officer, and a direction to the military commander of the department, and all officers and persons in the military and naval service, to aid and assist the said Governor in carrying into effect the proclamation of the President.

Reconstruction was a matter of civil government. It belonged to the law-making power. If ever there was a subject for legislation, this was. There were no laws on the question to execute, so it follows that there was no legitimate province for the Executive. He should not have done the first act. What did he do? From what source did he derive his power? First, he says, by virtue of his office as Commander-in-chief of the army and navy. Certainly, neither the army nor the navy had anything to do in bringing about reconstruction, except so far as they might be called upon to assist the proper officer in the execution of the law. This habitual pretence of Johnson's, in always having some claim of authority for his acts, made him a dangerous man. There can be no better way of showing the absurdity of this assumption, than by stating it. Reduced to an absolute statement, it meant that as Commander-in-chief he had power to legislate for the nation. That is all. And this took place in free America.

The President assumes the absurd position that he has the right, first, to make the laws, and then to execute them. This has always been called tyranny. Is there anything in the organization of a Republic which requires us to put a different construction upon such an assumption of power?

Then, the President speaks of the solemn duty imposed upon him by the Constitution to do these things. He fails, of course, to specify the clause. This would have been impossible. He afterwards capped the climax by directing the army and navy to aid the satraps whom he had appointed by military order.

It so happened that Tennessee, Arkansas, and Louisiana already had political organizations which made it even unnecessary for the President to issue his proclamations in these States, according to his own theory.

The provisional governors thus appointed proceeded to frame constitutions for these respective States, none of which were submitted to the people. Most of the gentlemen who were elected to fill the offices had not time to doff their Confederate uniforms. That is, they were traitors. The President was equal to the occasion. He sent a telegram asking for their names, that he might extend executive clemency in the shape of a pardon. All these various acts were done with precipitancy, brusqueness and haste. In other parts of the world, where kingship obtains, its most tyrannous exercise of power is tempered by culture, refinement and learning; its mandates are promulgated with pomp and circumstance; its will is couched in dignified and courteous language.

But Congress assembled. The Representatives of the people, who had been successful in striking down the hydra of rebellion, met. They set to work to consider the problem of constructing out of the broken fragments of a great government, one embodying, in some crystallized form, these "burning questions." The "man at the other end of the avenue" rebelled against the action of Congress.* They, on their part, were not inclined to endorse the extraordinary measures taken by this accidental President. He wanted to become a great Napoleon, but he could not even rise to the dignity of *Le Petit.* He had the intention, the desire, but he lacked the nerve, the courage, the ability. The civilized world was looking towards us to see what a people great enough to crush a gigantic civil war would now do. The usurper at last yielded to the impulses of rage and passion, and indulged in a series of exciting harangues.† He addressed mobs in Washington. He threatened to recognize a few of his followers in Congress, together with certain Confederate officers elected under his provisional governments as the Congress of the United States. He denounced the loyal members in Congress as usurpers and enemies. It should also be borne in mind, that the members who were in large majority in Congress were elected by the same section of the communities that elected Johnson to the Vice-Presidency. He was not satisfied with his unseemly and grotesque buffoonry in the capital, so he "swung around the circle" of

* "Under the administration of the late President Johnson, the virtual immunity of the Executive was completely proved. Johnson simply snapped his fingers in the face of Congress, as its laws fell one after another at his feet—dead letters. The power which looked upon him with loathing represented far more than two-thirds of the American people; and, with all his resource of bribery, he could not prevent each of his vetoes from being set aside by the requisite constitutional majority of two-thirds of both Houses of Congress. But the laws fell dead all the same.—["Republican Superstitions," by M. D. Conway, 108.]

† "As the President, to the amazement of the whole civilized world, yielding himself up to the dominion of passion, has seen fit, in a long series of violent and most unseemly public harangues, commencing with that addressed to a mob assembled in front of the Presidential mansion on the birthday of Washington, to denounce this Congress as usurpers and public enemies, to deny their authority, and encourage disobedience to their enactments, it may not be amiss to pause here a moment, for the purpose of exhibiting this unprecedented conduct of the Chief Magistrate of the Nation in its true light."—["The Powers of the Executive Department of the Government of the United States," by Alfred Conkling, 24.]

the country, making maudlin speeches. The issue he forced was between autocracy and representative government. Congress instituted an inquiry into the condition of the late Confederate States, as to whether they should be represented in either branch of Congress. Bills were passed by Congress and vetoed by the President. They were passed over the vetoes. A Bill protecting all persons in their civil rights was also passed over the veto. Andrew Johnson was a traitor to the people who had elected him to the position which made it possible for him to become President. He opposed their will, their measures; he was compelled to associate with their enemies; he became an apostate to the principles of the loyal people of the country; he used the great powers of his office to defeat the results of the war, which had cost the nation so many lives and so much treasure; he encouraged disloyalty. In a general way, he did what the rebel army would have done if it had remained in existence. He acted as a self-willed tyrant. He did everything he could to enforce his own wishes against those of the people. He endeavored to do what was clearly within the province of Congress. He refused to convene Congress. He appointed officers unknown to the Constitution or the law. The Constitution provides that "The United States shall guarantee to every State a republican form of government." He proclaimed himself the Government within the meaning of the clause. He placed his own interpretation upon this section. His most ardent friends can hardly insist that he acted in good faith when he asserted that he was the United States Government; and that Congress should not interfere with his wild and revolutionary schemes.* In addition to these usurpations, this

---

* "The Executive," wrote Roger Sherman, from the Convention of which he was a member, to the elder Adams, "is not to execute its own will, but the will of the Legislature, declared by the laws."—[Pitkin's Hist., vol. 2., p. 289.]

"He (President Johnson) is not to take it upon himself to supersede the law, or to supply its deficiencies by devices of his own invention, even for the

elective king gave his personal order that property of an immense amount should be turned over to the States lately in rebellion, and to citizens who had scarcely disbanded their rebellious forces. Whence did he derive this authority—as the depositary of executive power, or as Commander-in-chief? It will remain always a mystery how the Executive of a representative government could even have attempted to exercise such extraordinary power. Any system, whatever its form or name, under which such outrages against popular rights and good government could take place, must be, in some essential, radically wrong. Will the American people take warning, or will they perish in the general destruction, which must sooner or later overtake them, if these great defects are not remedied? The exercise of regal prerogative by our Presidents has done more to impair our idea of nationality than anything else. If this condition of things continue, we shall lose our characteristic of American citizens and become mere subjects. No nation can be truly free that allows its destinies to be directed by the will of one man.

accomplishment of legitimate objects, of a nature requiring the agency of the Executive; and still more censurable would it be for him to enter upon the pursuit of objects not committed to his charge by the Constitution or the laws. If, in his opinion, existing laws require amendment, or new laws are needed, he is bound to invoke the interposition of the Legislature, instead of usurping its powers. If an intelligent subject of a despotic government had come among us immediately after his (Johnson's) accession to the Presidency, ignorant of the organic structure of our political institutions, would he have been likely, during the recess of Congress, to discover, from passing events, that our government was less despotic than his own? And if he had remained here long enough to read the message of the President at the opening of the next session of Congress, would he not have sought in it in vain for the recognition of any right in Congress to exercise an effective control over his will in prosecuting his scheme of construction?"—["The Powers of the Executive Department of the Government of the United States," by Alfred Conkling, 63, 138, 139.]

CHAPTER XIX.

ADMINISTRATION OF ULYSSES S. GRANT.

If it were thought that our position would be strengthened by an arraignment of the Presidents, for acts alleged to be arbitrary and unlawful, then a long list of indictments could be quoted against General Grant, for he, like Lincoln, exercised powers in relation to which grave constitutional questions have arisen. It was thought he was a Cæsar, who, having once come into power, would never peacefully surrender it. It was charged that he had used the army to interfere with the organization of a State Legislature, and to force returning boards to declare his political friends elected. Grant did not hesitate to concentrate the army at Washington, in order to inaugurate a President "who had been rejected by the people."* "Under color of his office alone, without any treaty, or act of Congress, or any judicial process, he seized and delivered up to Spain a Spanish subject, who had sought shelter on our shores; and under color of protecting a State against domestic violence, he turned out one legislature, and put in another, in three of the States.†" These are grave accusations, and, if they are true, Grant should have been hurled from power. In addition to criticisms that came from the people

---

* Judge Black, in *North American Review*, May, 1880.
† D. D. Field, in *North American Review*, May, 1881. Mr. Field might have added, that on another occasion, he sent a United States war vessel to Spain, to capture a fugitive from justice, fleeing from prison, where he had been incarcerated for violation of a State Statute, and in a case where there was no extradition treaty to authorize the act.

at large, there was a criticism that took its rise in the brain of one of America's brightest and noblest men. Mr. Sumner spoke for a minority of the great Republican party, which believed that Grant had infused too many attributes of personal government into his administration. There can be no question that Charles Sumner spoke honestly and bravely. He may have been deceived into giving high color to the picture he drew; still, unquestionably, the American people can gaze upon it with profit. In the great speech which Mr. Sumner made in the United States Senate, on the 31st of May, 1872, he arraigned President Grant upon many different charges. He said: "The President, without warning, precipitated upon the country an ill-considered scheme for the annexation of a portion of the island of San Domingo, in pursuance of a treaty negotiated by an aide-de-camp. Reluctant Senators were subdued to its support, while treading under foot the Constitution in one of its most destinctive republican principles. The President seized the war-power of the nation, instituted foreign intervention, and capped the climax of usurpation, by menace of violence to the Black Republic of Hayti. * * * Too plainly it was becoming the instrument of one man and his personal will, no matter how he set at defiance the Constitution and international law. * * * A President must turn into a king before it can be said of him that he can do no wrong. * * * Not only are Constitution and law disregarded, but the Presidential office itself is treated as little more than a plaything and a perquisite— when not the former, then the latter. Here the details are ample, showing how, from the beginning, this exalted trust has dropped to be a personal indulgence, where palace cars, fast horses, and seaside loiterings, figure more than duties; how personal aims and objects have been more prominent than the public interests; how the Presidential office has been used to advance his own family on a scale of nepotism, dwarfing everything of the kind in our history, and hardly equalled in the corrupt governments where the abuse has most prevailed; how, in the same spirit, office has been conferred upon those from whom he had received gifts and benefits, thus making the country repay his personal obligations; how personal devotion to himself, rather than public or party service, has been made the standard of favor; how the vast appointing power, conferred by the Constitution for the general welfare, has been employed at his will to promote his schemes to reward his friends, to punish his opponents, and to advance his election to a second term; how all these assumptions have matured in a personal government, semi-military in character, and breathing the military spirit, being a species of Cæsarism, or personalism, abhorrent to republican institutions, when subservience to the President, is the supreme law; how, in maintaining the subserviency, he has operated by a system of combination, military, political, and even senatorial. * * * It is easy to see that Cæsarism, even in Europe, is set at a discount; that 'personal government' has been beaten on that ancient field, and that 'Cæsar, with a Senate at his heels,' is not the model for our republic. King George III. of England, so peculiar for narrowness and obstinacy, had retainers in Parliament, who went under the name of 'the King's Friends.' Nothing can be allowed here to justify the inquiry, have we a King George among us? or that other question, have we a party in the Senate of the 'King's Friends?' * * * Government of laws, and not of men, is the object of republican government—nay, more, it is the distinctive essence, without which it becomes a tyranny." Mr. Sumner then charges President Grant with an unrepublican subordination of the war department to the general in chief. "From the Executive Mansion, pass now to the war department, and there we witness the same Presidential pretensions, by which law, usage, and correct principles, are lost in the will of one man. * * * It was said of Gustavus Adolphus, that he drilled his Diet to vote at the word of command. Such, at the outset, seemed to be the Presidential policy with regard to Congress. We were to vote as he desired."

Next follows the charge of interference in local politics. Mr. Sumner continued: "Why the grand inquest of the nation, which brought Andrew Johnson to the bar of the Senate, should have slept on this conglomerate misdemeanor, every part of which was offensive beyond any technical offense charged against his predecessor, while it had a background of nepotism, gift-taking officially compensated, and various Presidential pretensions beyond all precedents. All this will be one of the riddles of American history, to be explained only by the extent to which the War Power had succeeded in subjugating the Government. * * * Higher than party, are country, and the duty to save it from Cæsar." *

These are the words of one of America's greatest sons warning the people of this country against the ambitious tendencies of a most powerful citizen. Mr. Sumner reflected the opinions of all the opposition, and of many of the party that had elected Grant to the high office of President.

Although a mere private citizen, he seems to have been regarded abroad, wherever he went, as in some way representing this Government, and we, the people, ascribed to him as much importance as if he were still our chief Executive. At all public entertainments he was assigned the position which would have been accorded to some ruler or emperor. Whether it was right for General Grant to accede to European interpretations and assignments of rank, was a matter for him to decide, as he was at that time his own master, and had no longer any official relation with the Government. The tendency of all people is to elevate a single person to the

---

* In the quaint style of Hobbes, it is written: " Whoever beareth *the person of the people* beareth also his own NATURAL PERSON. And though he be careful in his politic person to procure the common interest; yet he is more, or no less, careful to procure the private good of himself, his family, kindred and friends;

position of ruler. The idea is simple. It appeals to all orders of intellects. It can be understood by all. Around this centre all nationality and patriotism are grouped. A nation comes to know the characteristics and nature of an individual. It learns to believe in the man. Certain contingencies are likely to take place. It does not require a great amount of political knowledge to form an opinion as to the course of their favorite statesman, whose character they have studied. Under these circumstances, let a person be chosen to an office, with power conferred upon it equal to that of the Presidency of the United States, and it will make but little difference whether the law actually gives him the right to act in a particular direction or not. He determines a policy. He acts. No argument that the law has been violated will avail. He is the chief officer of the nation. He stands alone. He is a separate power in himself. The lines with which we attempt to mark the limits of his power are shadowy and ill-defined. A party, real or imaginary, stands back of him demanding action. In either event, the President acts. The sentiment of hero worship, which to a great extent prevails among the American people, will endorse him. Under our form of government, we do not think so much of what Congress may do. A great multitude declared: "Give us President Grant! We know him. He is strong! He will rule!"

Unquestionably, there appeared to be a great demand for a vigorous government in 1879, in relation to the South. The argument was, that force should be used against force; even revolution against revolution. This principle is essentially wrong. Better councils, however, prevailed, and the passing panic, or spasm of enthusiasm, did not induce this people to trust General Grant with power that might have enabled him to destroy our liberties.

and, for the most part, if the public interest chance to cross the private, *he prefers the private.*"—Cited in "The People and Politics, by G. W. Hosmer, M. D., 300.

Mr. Black, in the *North American Review*,* claims that Washington saw plainly the great defects in our Constitution, which permitted successive elections, and that so great was this consideration, to his mind, that he sought retirement after his second term, in order to establish a shield in the way of precedent against this danger inherent in the law."† Is it not startling to contemplate, if this view be correct, that Washington, who was a member of the convention which framed the Constitution, should have discovered such a grave error in it, so soon after its adoption; not a mere incongruity or inconsistency, but a defect which threatened the overthrow of the entire fabric. Is it not remarkable that the American of to-day shows such an apathy to the warnings of history; such a reluctance to discuss and to remedy these faults, which affect the very national existence? The subject seems to be fraught with such weighty considerations, that the public mind hesitates to contemplate them, and seems rather inclined to drift on with the hope that all will be well.‡ If the people of this country believe that Grant is a bad, ambitious, and withal incompetent man, then, certainly, that is the end of all question of again conferring upon him Presidential honors. But, on the other hand, if the people believe that he is a good, safe, and capable man, is there any other consideration which should militate against his re-election? Let us suppose that the people believe him to be the saviour of our country; that their hearts are full of gratitude to him for his many services —still, are there not potent arguments against the third term, which exist entirely distinct from General Grant, or from anything that may concern him. While it may be claimed that

* May, 1880.
† "How can there be a doubt that, superadded to these personal considerations, was the thought that his example might serve as a restraint in case of the appearance of a popular leader, who should seek to subvert the Government through successive elections." Quoted by Black, in *North American Review*, May, 1880.
‡ This was written in 1879, upon the subject of a Third Term.

there can be no good or sufficient reason ascribed for not continuing to avail ourselves of the services of an efficient officer, still we are forced to contemplate how far this generality is modified when considered in connection with the Presidency. The American people have never hesitated to confer a second term. In the case of the re-election of Lincoln, it seemed absolutely necessary that we should not change "our commander-in-chief" while a battle was in progress. But the sentiment against third terms is deep and widespread; and the custom of a hundred years seems to have crystalized into an unwritten law as binding as the specific provisions of the Constitution. Then our Executive is entrenched in a citadel, which cannot be successfully carried within the period of four years. The philosophy of our position would undoubtedly lead us to the conclusion that a third term would be a step toward office for life, if not to hereditary rank itself. *

It would seem that the English people were recently about to request Gladstone to form a Cabinet, and yet we hear of no outcry against his acting a second time. The reason is, that the system of the English Government is such that in case of this distinguished statesman being once more called to act as Premier, and then failing to retain the confidence of the Commons, he would be again compelled to retire. This action would be immediate and direct. But in the event of General Grant's being re-elected, the constitutional term of his office would be four years. There would be no practical way of removing him, and with the immense power conferred on him, he could defy the people. The principal peril lies in

---

* Gunning Bedford, of Delaware, argued for triennial elections of the Executive, with an ineligibility after three successive elections. The Convention voted, by at least seven States against Connecticut, that the Executive should not be twice eligible. [Gilpin, 779; Elliot, 149.] Gouverneur Morris had loudly put forward his wish to make of the Senate a thoroughly aristocratic body, and of the President a tenant for life. . . . It agreed with this view, to repose the eventual election of the President in the Senate. . . . "He was aware

the definite, unyielding and fixed period of the office of President, and the dangerous character of his prerogatives. If it were not for these facts, we would hear no more of imperalism in this country over the mere proposition to re-elect Grant, or any one else, than we heard of Cæsarism in England in the discussion of the advisability of calling Gladstone to the head of the Cabinet. We may believe Grant to be pure and good ; still, as the presidency is now constituted, would it not be establishing a dangerous precedent to place him at the head of the nation for a Third Term ?

One of the most convincing evidences of the innate weakness of our form of Government is the fact that the people of this country are compelled, apparently, to turn to any one particular man in an emergency, for assistance and support. Woe to that country whose destinies are involved in the fortunes of any one man, however great and pure he may be ! *

The true, logical, and efficient way to destroy imperialism in this country, is to abolish the system which makes it possible. With the destruction of presidential and the establishment of representative congressional government, we could, with impunity, place any man at the head of the executive branch, were he never so bad, ambitious, and inefficient, for it would then be known that at any moment he could be relieved from the cares of State.

---

that the outgoing President would be apt to be a candidate for re-election ; and desired nothing better than such a juncture between the President and Senate as would secure a re-election during life." [Bancroft's " History of the Formation of the Constitution of the United States," 176, 177.]

* John Randolph, writing of Jefferson, in 1780, said :—" And if the head of that very great, and truly good man can be turned by adulatory nonsense, they will endeavor to persuade him that our salvation depends on an individual. This is the essence of monarchy, and with this doctrine I have been, am, and ever will be at issue." " John Randolph," by Adams 49, 50. A prominent Southerner said recently, that if " Grant wants to be Emperor of this country, or even to head a constitutional monarchy, he would find plenty of Southern backing."

CHAPTER XX.

ADMINISTRATION OF RUTHERFORD B. HAYES.

RUTHERFORD B. HAYES was President of the United States in law and in fact. Numbers of people throughout the country, however, have denied this statement. Members of both branches of Congress declared from their seats that he was counted in by fraud ; that the Electoral Commissions' decision was wrong. If anyone were desirous of massing evidence tending to prove that presidential contests are insensate struggles for extraordinary power, he would need only to turn to the pages of history which describe the events preceding the inauguration of President Hayes. Long before the electoral colleges met, it was known that there would be two sets of returns from a number of States. Vermont, Oregon, Florida, South Carolina, and Louisiana, each forwarded two returns. If all of these questions were decided in favor of President Hayes, he would be elected by one vote. The country was on the verge of civil war. The Electoral Commission was created. Its early decisions indicated that the rulings would be in favor of President Hayes. The House became a scene of disorder. Filibustering was rampant. The democrats attempted to prevent the declaration of the election of a President until after the fourth day of March. Dilatory motions were made. Mr. Lane of Oregon, moved for a recess. Mr. Hale made a point of order that it was a dilatory motion. The Speaker said he was unable to classify it in any other way, and ruled that when a law directs anything to be done by either House, it is not in order, by any motion, to obstruct or impede the execution of that constitutional law. It was then resolved that the count of the electoral vote proceed in conformity with the decision of the Electoral Commission. Upon this resolution, forty nine democrats voted with the republicans—most of the democrats hailing from the South. What was the motive of these Southern democrats in voting to place a republican President in power? Was it the patriotic one of avoiding civil war? It was specifically and deliberately charged, that prominent members in the republican party, high in the confidence of President Hayes, had given solemn and earnest assurance that the white South should govern the South, on condition that no obstacle should be thrown in the way of the electoral count. The bargain was complete. The old story repeats itself, and a President agrees once more to use the monarchical powers of his office in the interest of those who voted against him. All citizens, of whatever color, creed, or condition, have by law the right of suffrage, and should be allowed to exercise it. The republican party was largely made up in the South of the newly enfranchised citizens, who had not the physical courage to stand up and enforce their rights against the white population. By a system of fraud, intimidation, and assassination, the political power of the blacks was actually destroyed. All white men who dared to organize them were ruthlessly driven out of the South. Northerners who had any political association with them were called "carpet-baggers;" Southerners, "scallawags." Social degradation and ostracism, and all punishments, even death itself, were inflicted, if necessary, to bring about complete submission to the dominant slave democracy—slave democracy, because they are still actuated and inspired by the injustice and tyranny incident to a condition of slavery.

The white South saw that by solidly carrying their States with their **increased representation,** resulting from the enfranchisement **of** the blacks, **together** with the co-operation of **a few Northern States, they** could place the candidate endorsed by them, in **the** Presidential chair. **They would** then control, **not only** their own States, but the **Government** itself. The great financial and economical affairs of the nation would then to a large extent be under **their direction.** As a matter of political honesty and sequence, **did the** President have any **duty to** perform ; **any** pledge to keep ? **It** cannot be denied that the whole **campaign was** made upon the Southern issue. All citizens **in the South were to be** protected. When the first **news of the election arrived,** the democratic candidate seemed chosen. **President Hayes,** believing himself defeated wrote under **date of the 8th of November** : " I do not care for myself, * * **but I do care for the poor** colored men of the South. * * **Northern men cannot live there, and** will leave. The Southern **people will practically treat the** constitutional amendments as nullified, and then **the** colored man's fate will **be worse than** when he was **in slavery.** That is the only **reason I regret the news as it is."** Now what did he do when **he came into office ?** Did he **make use** of his constitutional **power to protect life and political** rights in the South ? Did he ever apply **the law to Southern** States in the manner he did to Northern ones ? Did he execute the laws ? The Constitution provides that :—" The United States shall guarantee **to every State in** the Union a republican form of government, and shall protect each of them against invasion ; and, on application **of** the legislature, or of the executive (when the legislature cannot be convened) against **domestic violence."**

The President was authorized **by Act of Congress to call** forth the militia **of** any **State or** States to suppress insurrection, and to employ the naval forces for the same purpose. **Packard** was undoubtedly the Governor **of** Louisiana ;

Chamberlain of South Carolina. Hampton was marching armed men through the streets of Columbia, and Nichols had already seized the police force of New Orleans, and overthrown the judiciary of the State of Louisiana. Packard and Chamberlain were actually prisoners of a mob. Did not the President know that the withdrawal of the United States troops would put the two revolutionists, Hampton and Nichols, in power? The rightful Governors, not only protested against the withdrawal, but asked for assistance under the plain provisions of the Constitution which had been complied with. These two States were not only not protected against domestic violence, but the only protection they had was withdrawn.* The legal Governors of South Carolina and Louisiana were denied protection and compelled to flee. The two usurpers took their seats. "The unbefriended, uneducated, simple black people."† saw their government seized by a remorseless enemy, their political organizations broken up and destroyed, their white allies driven from their midst, their leaders, if need was, assassinated, and all their political rights trampled under the feet of a ruthless so-called democracy. The prophecy of the President, in relation to the poor colored people, came true. Did he raise his strong arm to avert the calamity? No, he did not, and to day 1877-8 thousands of this race are fleeing from their oppressors. It is one of the political enigmas yet unsolved, why it is that American Presidents, almost without exception, are loath to use the extraordinary power conferred upon them in the interest of liberty and representative government. Is it because the policy of kingly power demands that it shall be employed for the benefit of absolutism and slavery? President Hayes refused to support republican government

---

* Subsequent to these events, the President was not slow to send troops into Indiana and Western Virginia to suppress a labor demonstration.

† Words of William M. Evarts.

in these two States. Force was triumphant. The colored people looked for protection, to the government which had liberated them. True, social order now exists in the South, but is not humanity in prison? Quiet reigns among the blacks; but is it not the quiet of despair?

The President, by refusing assistance to the Republican governors, negatively exercised his great powers against human rights, as he affirmatively did, by sending into the State of Louisiana a committee which, in the name of the Executive, so far interfered with its internal affairs, that the Legislature was broken up, and an usurping one substituted. By what provision of law was this done? Was it not an assumption of power unprecedented even in the annals of American Presidents?

The question may be asked, is it consistent and logical to claim that President Hayes should have given Governors Packard and Chamberlain the assistance applied for by them, under the clear provisions of the Constitution? Undoubtedly, the States should be protected against domestic violence. The Constitution makes it the duty of the President to give this protection. As a matter of duty, he had no discretion. The provisions requiring the President to furnish troops is a duty imposed, not a mere power conferred. It amounts to this, that so long as the Presidential system exists, it should be administered, as far as possible, in the interest of freedom and representative government. The law should be radically changed—the elective kingship should be swept from the Statute Book; but until the American people can be persuaded to take that step—to make that great change—let our Presidents execute the law, leaning as much as possible to the side of representative government. A President should not refuse to execute the law. If he did, he would thereby make himself a violator of it. Because we believe that the power of removal should not be given to the President, that is no reason why we should object to his removing an incompetent officer. There is no other way of doing it. Because we are opposed to the President's being Commander-in-Chief, that is no reason why we should deny him the right to order troops to Washington to protect that city against a foreign foe. No other officer could do it. Because we believe that the powers conferred upon the President are kingly, that is no reason why all his acts are abstractly unjust or wrong. Acts done strictly within the limits of the Constitution may be subversive of all the inalienable rights of man, while those exercised without any authority of law, strike the fetters from the slave. What did President Hayes do? He had an opportunity, under the Constitution, of protecting two States against domestic violence. He not only did not protect them, but he withdrew the only protection they had. By what authority did he do this? Is it replied, as Commander-in-Chief of the army—a monarchical power given him by the Constitution, by the exercise of which he claimed a right to neglect a plain duty imposed upon him by the same instrument. He exercised this Constitutional right against liberty. The Constitution put it in his power to deprive two States of the protection of the American flag. The course taken in these instances by President Hayes, is once more the old story of the one-man power deciding important issues which should have been submitted to the whole people. Then again, has the President adhered to the rules in relation to the Civil Service, laid down in his inaugural address? Has he not rewarded his friends by appointment to office? Has there not been a suspicious circumstance in the frequent recurrence of appointees hailing from the State of Ohio? The fact is, that the President has suspended officers of well-known ability and honesty, and replaced them by scheming politicians. that his nominations have been confirmed by Democratic senators, does not prove much in favor of reform. Their shibboleth has always been, "to the victor belong the spoils." When a public officer succeeds in getting the approval of his enemies, it is time to inquire if he has not been untrue to his friends. Mr. Stickney, in his work already quoted, speaking of the administration of President Hayes, remarks : " Civil Service Reform meant only that public servants were to be appointed for nothing whatever but their fitness. A very large number of the men who had to do with carrying the election in certain doubtful States, in favor of the present President, have been appointed by that President to offices under the general government. Who is there that believes that these appointments have been made for the fitness of the men ? Most men believe that these appointments have been made because of some agreement or understanding that, if certain votes were counted in a certain way, the men who did the counting should be paid for it—with the people's offices. No one thinks the President made the bargain. He only took its fruits, and paid the price. And the main feature of the last Presidential election is this, that the unelected candidate is charged with having made an attempt, which failed, to buy electoral votes with his own money, and the elected President is believed to have paid for electoral votes with the people's offices. For a President of the United States to buy votes with his own money, is a thing bad enough ; for him to buy them with either promises or gifts of the people's offices is somewhat worse. His money is his own, to do with as he wills ; the offices are the people's, which he, their chief magistrate, is bound to bestow on the fittest men, and not to use in any way for his own profit ; and, both in law and in morals, it makes slight difference whether a President of the United States himself makes the bargain to buy votes, or simply carries out the bargain made by other men, and pays for the votes after they are cast in his own favor." The President must have seen that many of his acts were blows at the very people who had supported him. In any event, he made speeches endeavoring to explain the policy which he had adopted. He embarked upon a voyage of argument. He tried to baffle the storm of discontent which was gathering around him. In this respect, it may be said, he was successful, for his administration went on to a peaceful close. The people saw that they had no power to change the course of the administration, and they wisely submitted.

CHAPTER XXI.

ADMINISTRATIONS OF GARFIELD AND ARTHUR.

The election of James A. Garfield to the Presidency furnishes one of the few exceptions to the rule, that our system elevates men of mediocre ability, of requisite obscurity, or of military fame. Although a brilliant orator and a vigorous thinker, he, like so many of our Presidents, owed much to the fact that he had been a general in the volunteer army of the United States. The forces which carried him on in his public career were irresistible. He had not met with a single reverse. The moral powers were nationality and freedom ; the physical force was war. He sympathized with the great monopolies and corporations of this vast, growing commonwealth. He saw, what he called, the Government looming up before him in all its magnificent strength and power. That idea at times embodied the conception of the Constitution, then of the States in unison, then the people as a mass ; but underlying all was the subjective crystalization of his own will, and that will was a sovereignty of itself. Imperial drafts upon the lives and property of the people were of constant occurrence. He built up, in his own imagination, an empire without limitation in power, to be administered by those who were temporarily, but for fixed periods, the power-holders. In legislating, he claimed the right to stand upon a higher law, higher than the written law. For nearly twenty years he lived in an atmosphere of war and implied prerogatives, exercising, and helping others to exercise, extraordinary powers, which were far removed from the letter of the law. One revolution caused another revolution. It was force used against force, power against power. He did not stand alone, for the most honored names of the land are linked with his. The error, if error there be, lay in the dominant spirit of the times in which he lived. Brilliant oratory, expansive thought, tireless activity, and boundless ambition, marked the causeway over which he travelled. He went on like a conqueror, until a shaft from a clear sky struck him down, and the grave closed over all that remains of him, except the memory of his aspirations, his thoughts, and his deeds. For his abilities we have admiration; for his misfortunes, sympathy; for his public career, criticism. The fact that James A. Garfield was nominated and elected President of the United States, and exercised the duties of that office for nearly four months, give his statements and doctrines, made or expressed, prior or subsequent to his election, a great significance and importance. "In the course of debate on the confiscation legislation, arising at the first session of the Thirty-Eighth Congress, Mr. S. S. Cox, also a representative from Ohio, had asked him whether he (Mr. Garfield), would, to aggravate the punishment of the traitor, or to punish the innocent children of the rebels, break the Constitution?" Mr. Garfield replied, "I would not break the Constitution for any such purpose. * * * I would not break the Constitution at all, unless it should become necessary to overleap its barriers to save the Government and the Union." * In the course of a debate which arose a few months later * * *

---

* I felt that measures, otherwise unconstitutional, might become lawful by becoming indispensable to the preservation of the Constitution, through the preservation of the nation. Right or wrong, I assumed this ground, and now avow it. I could not feel that, to the best of my ability, I had even tried to preserve the Constitution, if, to save slavery, or any minor matter, I should permit the wreck of Government, Country, and Constitution altogether." . . . [Letter of Abraham Lincoln to Colonel Hodges, dated Washington, April 4th, 1864.]

these remarks were recalled to Mr. Garfield's notice, and on that **occasion he repeated the** statement of his position. On the same occasion, immediately after the remark already cited, **as** to a right **of** revolution, and his determined purpose **to resist it** by force, Mr. Garfield said: "What is the Constitution **that** these gentlemen are perpetually flinging in our faces whenever we desire to strike hard blows against the rebellion? It is the product **of** the American people; they made it—and the creator is mightier than the creature. The **power** which made the Constitution **can also** make other instruments to do its great work in the **day of** its dire necessity." The question being asked **by** another member, whether he **had not,** in the same remarks, alluded to his having taken **at** the Speaker's desk, together with the other representatives from **the** State of Ohio, the **oath to** support the Constitution, Mr. Garfield answered, "I did, and I am very happy the gentleman **has** reminded me of it at this time, and I remember, in the very preamble of that Constitution, it is declared to be ordained and established for the purpose of promoting the general welfare, and providing for the common defence; and on that **very** ground, based on **that** very statement of its declared object, I not only lifted up my hand to swear to support the Constitution before God, but it makes me now sorry there had not been a sword in it when I lifted it up, to **strike** down **any,** and all, who would oppose the use of all the means God has placed in our power **for** overthrowing the rebellion forever."

In reply to another question from **Mr. S. S. Cox,** Mr. **Garfield said,** during the same debate, "What I have uttered **is this: When** asked **if I would,** under any circumstances, **override the** Constitution, I said **this, and** this only,—premising, as I believed, that the Constitution was ample enough in itself to put down this rebellion, **that its** powers were most **capacious, and that there was no need to** override it; that if such a time ever should come that the powers of the Consti-

tution were not sufficient to sustain the Union, if that impossible supposition should ever prove true (laughter from the Democratic side of the House), then I would say, that we have a right to do our solemn duty, under God, to go beyond the Constitution, to save the authors of the Constitution."
"Some will say, probably, that such declarations show, at least, that there must be some very material limitation to that veneration for the Constitution, which outside observers have supposed to be so universal in our minds. More critically considered, however, such language may rather be taken as betraying one of those phases which all fetish worship exhibits. While all goes well with the devotee, he exalts his idol with song and sacrifice, and boasts its omnipotence as he invokes its terrors against rivals and enemies crouching about some other jungle shrine. But if fortune is adverse, and his lusts fail of gratification, the idolator begins sulking before the senseless block, refuses incense and homage, rails at its obstinacy, and, as things grow worse, strips it of its ornaments, and even gives Mumbo Jumbo a douse in the horsepond. The fetish, however, is none the worse for this usage. When the day of adversity is passed, the deity becomes respectable again to the enslaved imagination of the votary; and when he has seen his desire satisfied on his enemies, he brushes up his soiled faith, renews his broken vows, and sets his god up again, with fresh paint and brighter feathers—a somewhat changed, but no less powerful divinity, to answer the needs of the superstition that gave it being." * From these extracts of speeches and letters, it is quite evident that, at least, one school of politicians believes that the written Constitution of the United States is not always to be followed. The other class holds, that it is the duty of all in authority, first to determine what the meaning of that instrument is, and then blindly to adhere to it. It would seem that both

* Hurd's "Theory of Our National Existence," 517.

Lincoln and Garfield regarded their oaths as giving allegiance to some power standing outside of that instrument. In effect, that there was no Constitution to be faithful to, when the individual judgment was in antagonism to it. The intellect and the conscience were to decide each measure that came up for decision. Logically, President Garfield stood in the same position as the Secessionist. They both recognized the existence of the creators of the Constitution; they both claimed the privilege to decide for themselves and everybody else; they both placed their standard of right and wrong in the place of the supreme power. In this sense, at least, extremes seem to meet. It has always been claimed that the theory of Story, Webster, and Lieber, is that the person, or persons, known "for the time being as constituting a National Government," held the political power.

It is very true that there must be temporary power-holders in the legislative, judicial, and executive branches of the Government, but, what we cannot understand, is, that the power-holder should decide anything for himself; that is to say, when there is any doubt whatever in his mind as to a given question, why should he first act, and then "leap into the arms" of the people? why not first get the will of the people, from the people, and then act? In that event, there would be no leaping over the Constitution by the individual decision of the power-holder, but the whole matter would be decided by the masses themselves.

The occasions when the trustee of the masses should act immediately must be few and far between. All questions of importance could be easily submitted to the people. There is nearly always ample time, except, possibly, in rare instances of defence. Could not the people have voted upon the questions arising out of the Mexican War, the Oregon Boundary, the Louisiana Purchase, the Confiscation Acts, the Emancipation of Slaves? All of these questions were arbitrarily acted upon by the power-holders. They generally invoked the supernatural in the place of the people, who should be the grantors of all authority—the creators of all government. Why do we continually have this proposed exercise of a higher law, which means, after all, the personal will of him who uses it; and he who exercises it generally calls upon the supernatural, which has never manifested either approbation or dissent. It may be, that that is the reason why the Infinite is so often invoked to bolster up a wrong. This higher law, when it means individual judgment, is but another form of divine right.

In 1881, the National Republican Convention met at Chicago, composed, as it was, necessarily, of irresponsible men, holding no offices, and in no wise accountable to the people. According to the custom which had grown up, they were assembled to nominate a President. Of the forces that entered into that Convention we do not intend to speak. We desire simply to state, that neither of the two men who had been prominently before the people was nominated. One candidate was a leader in Congress, and seemed entitled to the position through long service; the other had been in the Executive chair for two prior terms, and had no other record as a civil officer, save the one gained in that capacity. General Garfield had not been prominently spoken of, and, in fact, he had been devoting his energies to place in nomination a third gentleman of distinguished service in the Government. The two opposing forces charged furiously against each other for several days, until, at last, a panic took place in the ranks of one of the contending parties, its adherents going over to the banner of Garfield, and in the general scrimmage that ensued he was crowned conqueror. We shall not stop to criticise this method. We shall content ourselves by referring the question to those who remember the course and action of that body, leaving them to decide whether there was anything in it that indicated reason, propriety, or statesmanship.

We would willingly draw the veil over the disgraceful scene which thereafter took place in the City of New York. But in truth and justice we cannot. It has been stated upon evidence, which seems to be incontrovertible, that a number of gentlemen, among whom was the Republican Presidential candidate, entered into a bargain, reduced to writing by the terms of which the future patronage of the Government was contingently pledged for the advance of large sums of money, to be used for campaign purposes. At the same time, a Wall Street financier, more familiar with " corners and futures " than diplomacy, was the chief actor in this drama. According to the contract, he was to make the advances immediately required to corrupt the people of a State, and afterwards to furnish funds necessary for the General Election. For these services he was to be appointed Secretary of Treasury, or Minister to one of the first nations of the world. The money was furnished, the preliminary battle won, and the campaign proved successful. President Garfield kept his part of the contract, and the banker was made Foreign Minister. The liberties of the people were thus bartered for gold. The cupidity of Shylock and the vulgarity of the pawnbroker, played an important part in the execution of this contract.* We shall not attempt in this essay, to repeat what seems to be based upon good authority, that Garfield was fully imbued with the idea, that

---

* This bargain and sale of an Office of the Government reminds us of the act of King John, who, in 1213, " conveyed England with all its appurtenances to Pope Innocent, who re-conveyed it to him in fee-farm, subject to a rent of 1000 marks , and that this conveyance and re-conveyance were considered strictly within right is evidenced by the fact that the rent was paid throughout the reigns of Henry III, Edward I, and Edward II, and part of that of Edward III, for nearly a century and a quarter. And among the numberless other evidences of the King's vested rights of private property in the kingdom of England, I shall only advance that as late as 1271, Edward I, while yet heir-apparent, devised the kingdom with all its appurtenances to his executors to administer the same for the benefit of his heirs."—[A Definition of Liberty, by Isaac L. Rice, *North American Review*, January, 1883.

it was necessary for him, having been elected President, to form an aggressive policy for the welfare of his own fellow-citizens, and the admiration of the world. His Secretary of State, whose plans the President was anxious to forward, was a pushing, aggressive, and brilliant politician. It was said, "Now we shall have activity in all commercial, industrial, and financial affairs at home, and the influence and prestige of the United States will be carried throughout North and South America, by placing our Government at the head of a combination of American Nationalities, having for its ultimate object the enforcement of an ultra view of the Monroe doctrine." We all remember how nearly this country was involved in war during the few months of the Garfield administration. What would have been the administration of General Garfield no one can now divine. But it may not be uninteresting to inquire into the peculiar views of the President, in addition to the examination already made. Prior to his election, he made use of the following words, in a serenade speech, delivered in the city of New York: "Just yonder, down by the Battery, more than a hundred years ago, a young student of Columbia College was arguing out the ideas of the American Revolution and the Union, against the treason and disloyalty of his college Presidents and Professors, and by and by going into the army of the States, with General Washington, and fighting the battles of the Republic; and then, on his drumhead, in camp, before he was 21 years old, writing a letter that contained in it every germ of the Constitution of the United States. That scholar, statesman, soldier, and great chieftain, Alexander Hamilton, of New York, made this Republic glorious by his thinking, and gave, in large part, New York's great contribution to the ideas that made the Union of our States." Hamilton, according to the thought of Garfield, was the bright particular star which illumined our political firmanent. But Hamilton was a monarchist of the Tudor sort. He believed that the people should be governed, not govern. His scheme of government was Empire. He divided the people into two classes, the rich and well-born, and the masses. He maintained that the people were turbulent and changing ; checks must be placed upon them. There must be two branches of the legislature ; the members of one must be appointed for life. There must be an Executive who dares execute regal powers, and should hold, as a hereditary prince, or as an elective one, for good behavior. He believed in ceremony, and prescribed a system of absurd formalities to govern the intercourse of the President with the people, and Washington, conforming to these rules, "went in a coach and six, attended by outriders in livery, and followed by members of the administration in a coach and four, with numerous and stately retinue, to open Congress, and then delivered his message like a king's speech. Congress having agreed upon an address in reply to the speech, attended the President in a body to present it. All forms of etiquette were arranged to the minutest particular, after the manner of European Courts."*

We think that a drum-head, in a military camp, was an appropriate place to outline such a Constitution. If we then recollect that General Garfield believed in the exercise of individual will, even if the exercise of it overleaped the Constitution itself, it would seem that he had within him the "potency and power" of a strong personal administration, which would range from the removal of a postmaster to the command of the army and navy.

A few days before the assassin fired the fatal shot, the President was at the White House, discussing with certain gentlemen the troubles and embarassments which had begun to hedge his administration. The factions, envies, and hatreds, of different communities, were referred to. He was called upon to exercise more than a kingly power in reward-

* Essay by **Chauncey F. Black.**

ing and revenging. He was also asked to act as a judge, in order to decide claims for office based upon conflicting statements. During this interview, one visitor assured him of his earnest sympathy, and said, "You are now, for the first time in your life, invested with the distribution of power and patronage, and you can now fully realize that the position of ambition does not bring unmixed pleasure." The President at this arose from his chair, and putting his hand on the shoulder of his friend, said, "Yes, I see plainly, that he who wears the crown, must bear the cross." It is also related by an intimate friend of the President, who accompanied him on a trip to Elberon, just before the shooting, that one bright, starlight evening, they were taking a stroll near the breakers, and in full view of the ocean, when the President turned suddenly to his companion, and said, "Now, is it not strange, and is it not a striking commentary on the protection and security afforded by free institutions, that a President of the United States can go about in this way, practically unattended, without a body guard, and without the paraphernalia that encompasses other rulers."* A few days later, with these words upon his lips, comparing himself to the rulers of other nations, and while exercising powers of removal and appointment of officers of the Government, in reward for services, if not in revenge for unfriendly acts, he met the fate of Cæsar, of Henry of Navarre, of William the Silent, and of Alexander of Russia. Should not all thoughtful men pause long enough to seek out, if possible, the cause of these direful effects? Looking at the violent deaths of potentates in other

---

* It should be stated in this connection, that Presidents Lincoln and Johnson had a special body-guard, consisting of two companies of infantry, stationed both at the White House, the winter, and the Soldiers' Home, the summer residence of the Executive. President Lincoln was always escorted by a company of cavalry in passing from the White House to the Soldiers' Home. To-day there are bills pending before Congress, making it a crime to compass the death of the President, or any one acting under his authority. In ancient England, it was a crime to imagine the death of, or to scandalize, the king.

countries, we are apt to exclaim, "How natural it is that their deaths should have been as they were." But may we not find the relation of cause to effect in the circumstances which surrounded the assassination of two of our Presidents? Strange as it may appear, if we include in this statement the Presidents of the South American Republics, whose Constitutions were fashioned after ours, there is, within a given time, a much larger proportion of Presidents who have suffered violent deaths from political causes, than kings reigning in monarchical countries. If we were to express our own opinion, in the determination of the cause of the assassination of Presidents Lincoln and Garfield, we should say, philosophically speaking, that it was the Presidential system. We believe that both Generals Hamilton and Garfield had wrong conceptions of the executive form of Government; that the advocacy of these false doctrines by the one, and the execution of them by the other, had a potent effect in producing the violent death of each. However that may be, on the 2nd day of July, 1881, James A. Garfield was stricken down by the act of a man afterwards judicially found to be sane.

The first great defect found to exist, at this time, in our Presidential system, was, that the Senate had adjourned without choosing a President *pro tem.*, and as there was no Congress in session, there was no Speaker of the House. So the life of President Arthur alone stood between us and anarchy. These facts created an impending crisis as to the succession of the Presidency. The Constitution confers most potent power upon the President, but fails to provide for a succession in the case of death, resignation, or disability. Where such unusual powers are delegated, it is first essential that it be known to whom they are given, in order to hold the person exercising them responsible for arbitrary or wrongful acts. President Garfield never performed, authorized, or approved, a single executive act after he was shot. Who did perform the necessary acts between that date and the time of his death? Certainly, not President Arthur. He forbore to act, with remarkable self-restraint. The Constitution provides, that when the President dies, resigns, is removed, or is not able to discharge the powers of his office, the same shall devolve on the Vice-President. It requires the Vice-President to assume and perform the duties whenever the President is unable to do so. It was claimed that a lot of irresponsible secretaries, or personal clerks of the President, should have decided when it was necessary for the Vice-President to act. This is simply absurd. The Vice-President clearly had the right to judge of the inability under which he should have become President of the United States. So far as President Arthur is concerned, he acted from a patriotic purpose in refraining from intruding himself into the office. President Garfield's clerks did everything they could to prevent President Arthur from assuming the duties of the office. A system of laws which makes such an interregnum possible is rickety and defective. This possibility of anarchy, through defect of the Constitution, and the laws establishing the existing system, is urged as one reason why the present executive form is wrong. What was our position before the world, from the 2d day of July to the 19th of September? Our Government was certainly without a responsible head. The events of that period, however, seems to have exploded the theory that there is any real necessity for having the executive powers of the Government centred in the will of any one man. The other fact proven is, that while the law centres the executive power in a single will, a number of officers, unknown to the Constitution, ran the Government. But the experience of those eventful days shows, that if the executive power is vested in a number of officers created by law, and responsible to the people for their acts, and have seats in Congress, that the most feasible and effective form of government has been discovered; and by adopting such a method we could abolish the Presidency in this country, which has always been an ever-disturbing element in the body politic. The course pursued by the American Cabinet during the disability of the President, was not so bad in itself, and if this act, in view of the law, had been Constitutional, it would have been commendable. The objection is to its assumption of power, after having lost its chief, and its irresponsibility under the law.

If we had been living under a representative Congressional form of government when President Garfield was shot, the legislature would simply have passed some act supplying the defect in the *personnel* of the Government. By the accident of environment there was no great struggle of war, or issue of peace existing while Garfield lay helpless and suffering, which required much decison, or exercise of power; but suppose there had been, would not the great aversion which the American people have to the Presidential office being interfered with, even by the Vice-President, have caused them to prefer that irresponsible men should carry on the affairs of state. It mattered little to them that such a course might involve the entire nation in confusion and conflict.

It may be said that the present working of the American plan, as to the Vice-Presidency, is bad. The Vice-Presidents are not selected with a view to their assuming the office of chief magistrate, although, strange as it may appear, four of them have already been called to exercise the office. We have certainly been very unfortunate in relation to three of them, and the fourth is still in office. While acting as Vice-President, it is true that he has little of importance to do, and except he be a personal and intimate friend of the President, he officially leads a lonely and perfunctory life. "The office of Vice-President, especially under the present system, would seem to be altogether objectionable. His duties, under ordinary circumstances, being of the most formal character, his selection is often made without regard to the possible succession. This office was unknown to any of the original proceedings before the Convention; and there would seem to have been no other motive in introducing it at the final adjustment, than that of having something to give to both of the two candidates voted for by each State in the electoral colleges, as hereinbefore indicated."*

In 1788, it was ascertained by the Commons that George III. was deranged. Pitt moved certain resolutions, the second of which was in the following words: "It is the opinion of this committee, that it is the right and duty of the Lords, spiritual and temporal, and Commons of Great Britain now assembled, and lawfully, fully and freely representing all the estates of the people of this realm, to provide the means of supplying the defect of the personal exercise of the royal authority, arising from His Majesty's said indisposition, in such manner as the exigency of the case may appear to require."† The king was virtually deposed, and the Prince of Wales made regent. ‡

* William Beach Lawrence, *North American Review*, Nov., 1880.
† Tomline, Mem. of Wm. Pitt, vol. ii., p. 407.
‡ "Questions which concern the very existence of the Government and the liberties of the people, were suggested by the prolonged illness of the late President, and his consequent incapacity to perform the functions of his office. It is provided by the Second Article of the Constitution, in the fifth clause of its first section, 'In case of the removal of the President from office, or of his death, resignation, or inability to discharge the powers and duties of said office, the same shall devolve on the Vice-President.' What is the intendment of the Constitution, in its specification of 'inability to discharge the powers and duties of said office,' as one of the contingencies which calls the Vice-President to the exercise of Presidential functions? Is the inability limited in its nature to long continued intellectual incapacity, or has it a broader import? What must be its extent and duration? How must its existence be established? Has the President, whose inability is the subject of inquiry, any voice in determining whether or not it exists, or is the decision of that momentous and delicate question confided to the Vice-President; or is it contemplated by the Constitution that Congress shall provide by law, precisely what should constitute inability, and how, and by what tribunal, or authority, it should be ascertained? If the inability proves to be temporary in its nature, and during its continuance the Vice-President lawfully exercises the functions of the Executive, by what tenure does he hold his office? Does he continue as President for the remainder of the four-

President Arthur, upon his accession to office, abandoned many of the positions occupied by his predecessor. He extricated the Government from its involved relations with Chili and Peru, and all the attendant evils. He abandoned the autocratic course laid out by Garfield, having for its object, extended appointments and removals ; and, if we are correctly informed, has made fewer than any prior President, in proportion to the officers now under his control. But he has been charged with the attempt to force one of his staff officers—the Secretary of the Treasury—upon the State of New York, as its Governor. If this charge be true, then he only attempted what the King of England did, when he sent his favorites to America to be governors of the colonies. The people rebuked the President for this act, apparently believing that he was guilty of it, and the President, on his part, seems to have profited by the experience, So far as our observation goes, at the present time (May, 1883), there is no Executive interference with the free exercise of the ballot by the people.

The President receives a large salary. It is ample for his support. He should be careful to carry his sense of personal dignity to the fullest extent, and should not make use of the public property in any way whatever. He should respect the letter and the spirit of the law. In taking this course he should not use the war-vessels of the Government as pleasure yachts. He should, if he so fancy, provide himself with one, in the same manner as any other gentleman. President Arthur has used the naval vessels for the purpose of recreation, and this course is not consistent with

years' term? or would the elected President, if his inability should cease in the interval, be empowered to resume his office? And if, having such lawful authority, he should exercise it, would the Vice-President be thereupon empowered to resume the powers and duties as such? I cannot doubt that these important questions will receive your early and thoughtful consideration." [Message of Chester A. Arthur, December 6, 1881.]

his honorable life. Then it must also be borne in mind that the salary of the President has been recently doubled, and further, that certain yearly appropriations, made ostensibly for furniture for the White House, have largely increased. In 1881 there was appropriated for furniture, repairs, and greenhouses, the sum of twenty-seven thousand dollars; in 1882 thirty-nine thousand dollars; in 1883 forty-eight thousand dollars. There is voted yearly, directly and indirectly, about one hundred thousand dollars for the benefit of the Executive Mansion. The affectation of court life which now exists at Washington seems to preclude the idea of an economical government.

The course of the present administration proves the correctness of our position, namely, that departmental officers may conduct the affairs of State without the presence of the Chief Magistrate. President Arthur was absent about the same time President Garfield was ill, and during that time the swamps of Florida, the canons of the Rocky Mountains, the geysers of the Yellowstone, the fisheries of the St. Lawrence, and many almost inaccessible places were visited. These pleasant journeyings establish the fact that the working of this Government need not depend upon the direction of one man.

President Arthur has created, or submitted to the creation, of the new-fangled device of a President's flag, to be hoisted to the top-mast whenever he passes on board a war vessel. The officer chargeable with instituting this imperial symbol should be immediately dismissed from the service. While a certain bombastic Vice-Admiral was basking in the sunlight of Grant's administration, and looking forward to the time when he would be admiral himself, he caused an ensign, which resembled the St. George's Cross, to be raised on the flagship of the brave Farragut. The strange and nondescript device caught the eye of the Admiral, who demanded, "What do you call that gridiron thing up there?" Some one told him that it was the new

Admiral's flag. "Who ordered it to be hoisted?" he asked. He was informed that the Vice-Admiral had. "Take that rag down at once," he thundered, "the Stars and Stripes are good enough for me." The gridiron came down with a run, and that was the last time it was ever unfurled. We commend this anecdote to the attention of the President.

The fact is, there is fast growing up in this country, under the teachings of certain politicians, a sentiment which will not be satisfied until we have, not a kingship as it exists in Europe to-day, but one with all the effete and decaying powers of absolutism. If the Presidency is to be continued, the man temporarily filling it who shall be guilty of high crimes and misdemeanors, must be deposed; and if he should be disabled from performing his duties, he must be pushed aside. The fact is, that the individual who fills the office for the time is deified; he becomes superhuman in the eyes of those who crave for patronage and power. His platitudes become household words. His children become objects of adoration, or are appointed to office beyond their fitness to fill it. His wife is a heroine; her dress and habits are copied throughout the land; words of reverence, love and affection, are bestowed on the man at "the other end of the avenue." To criticise him, is to be disloyal. All this nauseating and undemocratic subserviency is un-American and wrong. We can go on without the Presidency with all its tendencies to monarchy. The Executive Council would then be pliant to the will of the people, and at the same time strong in the execution of the law.

CHAPTER XXII.

THEORIES OF O'CONOR, LAWRENCE, SMITH, AND BARTLEY.

THE distinguished lawyer, Mr. Charles O'Conor, has deemed the following changes advisable in our political system. First.—The separate State Governments should be abolished. This seems now to be a Republican idea, but, certainly, no sound thinker among the leaders of that party will ever promote its adoption. The dissensions and civil war in which their party was born, nurtured, and matured, grew out of the State organizations; without them its bloody-shirt sectional cries must cease to animate, and their party perish. The benign tendency of the separate State systems to embroil the country in civil war was well explained in the Federalist, No. 28. Second.—The quadrennial Presidency should be abolished. An excutive chief might be selected by lot from the legislative corps for the ensuing month, on some late day in each month. Third.—The Senate should be abolished, and the Representatives chosen for a short term, substantially as at present. They should have no power to make any but general laws. By stringent regulations they should be prevented from assembling in Congress to enact laws, except on those rare occasions when a general existing law actually required amendment or a new general law was needed. Fourth.—The Congress should be rigidly confined to making laws which are absolutely necessary, leaving all transactions and business, as far as possible, in private hands, and to the action of private enterprise. Instead of becoming a banker, and issuing paper money, as the Greenbackers suggest, the power of Government over money should be confined to minting the citizens' metals, and compelling the security of proper circulation. The only standard of value, should be coined gold. There should be no protection to any trade or community in preference to others, nor any excises or duties on imports and exports. Government should not, as the Greenbackers advise, become a carrier of goods or passengers, an expressman, or a telegraph operator; but on the contrary, it should cease to be a letter carrier. The telegraph and express systems have rendered unnecessary our enormous post-office patronage. Borrowing money by the State, or any of its agencies, should be forbidden. No army or navy should exist, except *flagrante bello*. And indeed wars would rarely occur after the trade of politics was set aside. The militia could amply protect us from foreign invasion or domestic disorder. Through the merchant marine and other means, an adequate naval force could, on an emergency, be promptly improvised. The entire range of charity, including hospitals and schools, should be left, like divine worship, to the spontaneous impulse of individual volition. This arrangement would be fraught with vast benefits—alike to the rich, whose best feelings and benignant activities it would stimulate, and to the necessitous, whose wants it would tenderly relieve. Fifth.—Inferior local courts for the administration of justice should of course be instituted, and a Supreme Appellate Court, without original jurisdiction. Judges in the latter should be sufficiently numerous to form several separate chambers, with equal authority, and equal membership. The chambers, like the present jury-box, should be supplied by lot from the entire body at short intervals, so as to prevent packing. Sixth.—The repudiation of paternal government, or laws not general, should be extended to all subordinate administrations, thus avoiding boards and councils in local districts, as cities, towns, **villages**, etc. Seventh.—A **Chief** Executive, and **a** legislative authority **being** necessary, while **the** system should provide for them, it should contain **strict** guards against **the** evils **to** which they tend. **The** executive office, being **of** brief duration, should immedi**ately, or** directly, appoint to all offices except Representa**tives** in Congress. The term of office, in **all** cases, should **be during** good behavior, the power of removing all officers appointable by him, except Judges of the Supreme Court, being absolute in the Chief Executive. He should **not** be allowed, however, to make any removal, except on the day immediately preceding that of his **own** successor's election, unless the Supreme Court Chamber, sitting in the district of the officer removed, **or** all the chambers, should approve the removal as necessary to the public interest; nor should a vacancy produced by any such removal be filled by the officer making it, unless the latter act was sanctioned by a like approval from **the** necessity **of an appointment before** the ensuing month. The Chief Executive and the Supreme Court of Judges should **be** impeachable for malversation **in office.** They should be liable during, or within, a reasonable limited period after their **official** terms by **a** tribunal **of** say, fifty Representatives chosen by lot, whose power on conviction should be unlimited in other respects, and might extend to the punishment of death on a four-fifths vote. Eighth.—Suitable precautions might promote intelligence and purity in exercising the elective franchise, and prevent frauds upon it. **There should be** a fixed Registry law, and **no** person **should** be allowed to vote, except in the **district of** his permanent registered **residence, or otherwise** than *viva voce.* The voter should also be required to file a ballot, written and signed by himself, in the presence **of** the inspectors, which should **be** preserved **long** enough to afford certain proof of his act, in case of a contest. The franchise should be withheld from all persons in Government employ, and their subordinates in any public work or service. Ninth.—Taxation should be enforced with absolute equality upon all property not belonging to the Government, without exemption or distinction of any kind, thereby restraining the unworthy devices by which wealthy men, and the politicians, escape the duty of contributing to the public fisc. The needed taxes might soon become so slight as to be almost unfelt, as was the case before our civil war. Effectual provision should be made for the exclusive devotion of the public domain to public uses, or to the encouragement of actual settlers thereon. Tenth.—The existing public debt, of every description, including that created by States, and all other civil divisions, should be exempted from enforcement by ordinary private action, and should not be renewable. Measures should, nevertheless, be instituted to enforce its payment, both as to principal and interest, in gold coin. The interest should thus be paid punctually as it may fall due, and the principal as soon as reasonably practicable.

The abolition of the State governments, as recommended in the first section, is good, salutary, and necessary. It is true that their existence, throughout our history, has always been a fruitful source of civil war and dissension.

The President to be selected by lot for the period of one month (second section), is unscientific and absurd.

The third section recommends the abolition of the Senate; and if we are correct in our interpretation of the language, namely, that nothing is to be created in its place, then we are in accord with the suggestion.

The fourth section is, in the main, good, as describing what the scope of legislation should be. We think that while special and unnecessary legislation should be avoided, as far as possible, that the legislature should remain the temporary depositary of the supreme power, its members acting from instructions given to them in pursuance of a proper system of submission of all important issues to the people themselves.

The suggestions in relation to the elective franchise are good. The present system, existing in most of our States, and controlling the general machinery of the ballot, is based upon fraud and cowardice. A man who is afraid to vote openly is a poltroon, and should be disfranchised. The recommendations that follow are beyond the province of this essay to consider.

In a carefully prepared article, published in the *North American Review*, November, 1880, by Mr. William Beach Lawrence, the well known writer on Constitutional and International subjects, points out the monarchical principle in our Constitution. He not only illustrates that principle by many arguments against the assumption of power by our Presidents, but he shows that actual regal power was conferred by the law. He also claims that Congress has overleaped the constitutional barriers. We will admit that, in many instances, Acts of Congress, judged by the strict construction of the law, have been unconstitutional. It is here, however, where we diverge from the course taken by Mr. Lawrence, in our desire to suggest a plan of government for the future. He was a firm believer in the federative idea, based upon a written Constitution, that the General Government should be one of limited powers, and that the real sovereignty should rest in the States in Union. It was natural that he should recommend the Swiss Constitution, with its confederation of cantons and an aristocratic State Council. He admits that there are objections to an executive, consisting of a single person in confederative or composite States, that do not apply to an homogeneous country. Take the United States, for example, whose interests, North and South, during the whole period of slavery, were avowedly antagonistic. It cannot be doubted that a single executive, possessing the immense prerogatives enjoyed by the President of the United States, might influence legislation, as well as the administration of the Government, in favor of his section to the prejudice of the others. Some attempts were made, during the disputes with regard to the tariff and slavery, to devise a plan by which the rights of each section might be protected. Mr. Calhoun proposed a dual Executive, having a legislative and executive action, as one of the means of preserving the balance of power between the two sections. Mr. **Lawrence goes on** to say, that he knows of nothing more suitable **to our condition** than the present Constitution **of Switzerland.** This government is **a** league of semi-independent States. **It** vests the supreme legislative and executive authority **in a** parliament of two chambers, a State Council, and **a National Council.** In the first, **the** members are elected, **two from each canton, in the** second, by equal representation. The chief executive authority is deputed **to** a Federal Council, consisting of seven members, elected **for three** years by the Federal Assembly (which is composed **of** both chambers), and as such represents the Supreme Government of the Republic. The President and Vice-President of **the** Federal Council are **the** first magistrates of the Republic. Both are elected by the Federal Assembly for the **term of** one year, and are not eligible till after the expiration **of** another year. It will be perceived that our Senate system appears in the plan, that the members of the Council are elected for a period **of three** years, and its President for **one year.** Although there is a great improvement in their executive over ours, still it lacks the Cabinet feature **of** the British Constitution; the Executive is inflexible, and the basis of the whole **structure is** not representative in the truest sense. It is a Confederation. **For** these reasons, **we** cannot approve of **that form** of government.

Mr. Goldwin **Smith has** written much upon the subject of this essay, chiefly in magazines. We have not **been able to** procure **a full** copy of his writings, but we have **before us an** extract from **an article** entitled, "The Ninety Years' **Agony** in France," which was published a few years **ago in** the *Contemporary Review*.* Mr. Smith

---

* Republished in the *Radical Review*, May 12, 1883.

says, "A single head of the State is a fancied necessity." "Your President is evidently the British king reproduced in an elective form." "The Swiss Constitution, which, instead of single man, has a Council with a President, whose function is only to preside, presents great advantages in this respect, and is the safest model for adoption." As we understand Mr. Smith, he differs from Mr. Lawrence as to the federative form of the Government. We are not satisfied that he prefers the Swiss to the British form, but at all events he is not in favor of our Presidential system, which he deems to be subversive of true representative government.

The following is a copy of resolutions submitted to the Committee of Congress on the Revision of the Laws, relating to the election of President of the United States:

ARTICLE XVI.

SECTION 1. The executive power shall be vested in, and shall be hereafter administered by, three Presidents, constituting a Supreme Executive Council of three, to be elected by the qualified electors of each and all of the States, and each to be taken from one of the three several prominent sections of the United States, known, one as the Western States, one as the Eastern and Middle States, and the other as the Southern States, and no two of whom should be citizens of the same section, or district of the country. And the boundaries of each of the said three Presidential districts shall be defined specifically, and established by law.

SEC. 2. The stated Presidential term of office shall be six years; and no President having served a full term shall be eligible for a second term. And at the first election under this article, the President from the Western district shall be elected for a fractional term of two years, and the President from the Southern district for a fractional term of four years, and the President from the Eastern and Middle district for a full term of six years; and after the first election, one President shall be elected **from one** of the three several districts every two years.

Sec. 3. The time and place of holding the elections **for** President in the several States, and the rules and regulations for conducting the same, and the time and mode of making the returns of such elections, and of counting the votes, and declaring the results, shall be prescribed by Congress.

Sec. 4. Each one of the three composing the Presidential Council, shall have all the qualifications to make him eligible to the office heretofore required of the President of the United States; and each, before entering upon the discharge of his duties, shall take the oath of office now required of the President of the United States; and each of the three shall be subject to the liability of removal from office, on impeachment, to which the President is now subjected.

Sec. 5. In electing the members of the Supreme Executive Council, the qualified voters of each State shall vote directly for the candidates for such office; and the three candidates having the highest number of votes in any State shall be entitled to the vote of such State in such election; and the vote of each State thus ascertained shall entitle the candidates having such highest number of the votes to a vote for the Presidential office equal to the whole number of Senators and Representatives to which such State may be entitled in the Congress of the United States; and the three candidates having the highest number of votes of all the States thus counted, shall be declared elected to the Presidential Council; and in the case of a tie, in the popular vote of any State, or in the count of the votes in the several States, every such tie vote shall be determined as Congress shall provide by law.

Sec. 6. The said Presidential Council shall have full power to perform all the duties, and execute all the authority, now conferred and enjoined upon the President of the United States; and, in so doing, all questions arising in the administration of the executive authority, upon which a difference of opinion may exist, shall be decided promptly by a majority vote. And in the case of the removal of any member of the Presidential Council from office, or of the death, resignation, or inability, of either to discharge the powers and duties of the said office, such vacancy shall be filled by such other officer of the United States or in such manner as may be provided by law. And it is made the duty of the Congress of the

United States to prescribe by law the mode and authority for filling all vacancies occurring in the Presidential Council, until an election can be duly held according to law.

SEC. 7. A majority of the Presidential Council shall always be competent for the transaction of the business of the Council; and, in case of the temporary vacancy in the places of two members of the Council at any one time, the remaining member shall, for the time being, perform the duties of the Council until the vacancies can be filled.

SEC. 8. Each member of the Presidential Council shall be entitled to full information from the heads of each of the executive departments, and also to the opinions and suggestions, in writing, of any such officer, on any subject connected with the business of his department, whenever he may require the same. And the military and naval forces of the United States shall be subject to the authority and control of the Presidential Council; but no member of the Council shall take personal command of the army of the United States in actual service in the field.

SEC. 9. The Supreme Executive Council shall have a journal, regularly kept, of their proceedings, in which the votes of the several members shall be entered and recorded, upon every important subject upon which a division of opinion may arise; and each member shall, when he desires it, have a note made on the journal of his reasons for any such vote given by him. A duplicate of such journal shall be sent to the Congress of the United States at the beginning of every regular session.

SEC. 10. Instead of the Vice-President, now provided for, the Senate of the United States shall, every four years, elect a President of the Senate, who is not a member of that body, and who, as the presiding officer of the Senate, shall have; and exercise, all the authority heretofore conferred on the Vice-President.

SEC. 11. Each of the Presidents shall, at stated times, receive for his service a compensation, not exceeding thirty thousand dollars a year, and which shall neither be increased nor diminished during the period for which he shall have been elected; and neither of the Presidents shall receive, within that period, any other emolument or perquisite from the United States, or any of them, either in the way of furnishing him with his dwelling-house, or paying the expenses thereof, or otherwise ; and all subsidies, presents, or donations to either of the Presidents, from any foreign government, prince, potentate, or subject, or from any resident of the United States, shall inure to the benefit of the United States, and be at once delivered over to the Treasurer for that purpose.

On the 25th day of May, 1878, the author of these resolutions, Mr. T. W. Bartley, urged their adoption, and presented certain arguments in their support. He claimed that "no one man as the Executive, whatever may be his capacity, can fully comprehend, and give proper attention to, the vast and diversified interests of this immense scope of country. The Cabinet officers, who are subordinates, and the President's little *coterie* of personal and political friends, are never selected as representatives of the distinct sections and interests of this vast country. * * * There cannot be anything, therefore, in the nature of the Executive authority of a republican form of government essentially repugnant to a plural Executive. In a monarchy, which is a government of one man, there cannot be a plural Executive in the nature of things, for the unity in the head or single Executive, is the monarch himself. But in a republic, which is a government of the people by means of representation, there is no such repugnancy ; on the contrary, the more perfect the popular representation the more perfect is the government, so far as representation is practicable and consistent with the public interests. * * * Prior to the adoption of the Constitution of the United States, such a thing as a republic, with the Supreme Executive power vested in the hands of a single person, was at least rare, and no such government had ever acquired any great distinction for stability and permanency. Subsequently, however, the example of the United States, in this regard, was followed by the people of Mexico, and also by some of the South American States, as well as by the people of France, in numerous attempts to maintain republican government with a single Executive. But, it must be conceded, that these various experiments, as to stability and permanency, at least, have not been successful, but to a great extent failures. With a plural Executive, these countries might have had, and probably would have had, different results. * * * "In the Convention which framed the Constitution of the United States, it was not even claimed by Alexander Hamilton, who was the most strenuous advocate for a single Executive, that it was republican in form. * * * For the organization of the Executive, however, three several plans were submitted to the Convention. One was for an Executive of three members, to be taken from the different parts of the country; another was for a single Executive, in connection with an Executive Council of five, on the plan of the Grecian Ephori; and the third was for a single Executive unrestricted. * * * * * The fixed genius of the people of America requires a different form of government. He could not see why the great requisites for the Executive department—vigor, despatch and responsibility, could not be found in three men as well as in one man. The Executive ought to be independent. It ought, therefore, in order to support its independence, to consist of more than one."

Dr. Franklin said, 'I am apprehensive, therefore, perhaps too apprehensive, that the government of these States may in future times end in a monarchy.' * * * It will only furnish a fœtus of a king, as the honorable gentleman from Virginia very aptly expressed it, and a king will the sooner be set over us.'*

"Mr. Williamson said,† 'He did not like the unity in the Executive. He had wished the Executive power to be lodged in three men, taken from three districts, into which

---

* Madison's Papers, Vol. ii, 763-4, 771 and 773.
† Ibid., 1189.

the States should be divided.' The Presidency of the United States has, by the enlargement of the country, and the exaltation of its powers, become in reality and in fact a fully developed elective monarchy by whatever other name it may be called. Invested with the Supreme Executive power over the whole country, the President collects and disburses an annual revenue exceeding $300,000,000, and exercises the power of appointment and removal over at least two hundred thousand officers and agents of the United States, together with an influence over more than twice that number of applicants and expectants of the offices, honors and emoluments of the Government. With the qualified, but primary power of making treaties with foreign nations, the President has the sole power of executing the treaties, and is the sole representative of the United States in their intercourse with foreign nations. By his financial policy and executive measures, the President exercises a daily influence on the money market and exchanges of the country, domestic and foreign, and consequently more or less upon the prices of commodities, and wages of labor. Clothed with all these high powers, and made 'the Commander-in-Chief of the army and navy of the United States, and of the militia of the several States, when called into the actual service of the United States,' who can deny that the President has become a monarch, wielding more power than any one of four-fifths of the monarchs of Europe? Wielding the powers above mentioned, a president elected as a political partisan, is placed at the head of his party, which, if in the majority in both branches of Congress, and on the bench of the Supreme Court, gives him a controlling influence with both the legislature and the judicial branches of the Government. The whole country has recently seen how completely the political majorities in both branches of Congress, and on the bench of the Supreme Court, are under the control of the political party in power. So that the President, as the head of the political party in power, wielding his vast powers and extensive patronage, would exercise a controlling influence over the legislative and judicial, as well as the Executive departments, and therefore, would exercise the powers of an absolute monarch. And the history of the world has shown that the most corrupt and debasing of all monarchies is the elective monarchy. It debases and corrupts the foundations of society, and places the control of the country in the hands of men governed by ambition, cupidity, and self-aggrandizement, crushing out all elevated patriotism and magnanimous regard for advancement and improvement in man's condition. Far better for the country to have a hereditary and absolute monarchy at once."

While the extracts herein quoted contain many expressions which we fully endorse, still, we desire to state, that we arrive at an entirely different conclusion. We do not believe in the plan proposed in the resolutions. It retains all the objectionable power now conferred on the President. The very pith of our argument is against the regal powers of our Executive. These resolutions substantially present one of the plans submitted to the Convention. That fact enlists our attention and respect. But let it be said, in a word, that history, and all events subsequent to the formation of our Government, teach us that a plural Executive, representing different sections, is radically defective and subversive of all good administration of law. These Presidents, for they would soon be regarded as such, although nominally but members of an Executive Council, would be influenced by the interests of their own particular section, and there would be a tendency to divide the army among them. The people of each section would naturally adhere to their immediate representative in the Council; and thus the masses would be arrayed against each other. The proposed system of a plural and sectional Executive would soon cause disintegration and disunion.

CHAPTER XXIII.

VIEWS OF THE FOUNDERS.

The presidential system, when first proposed, encountered the most strenuous opposition, not only in the Convention which framed the Constitution and in the different State Conventions which ratified it, but also at the hands of the press of the country. Not solely did the plan, as a whole, meet with objections, but each particular part of it was severely criticised. Prominent patriots resisted the establishment of any government which even savored of a limited monarchy. There seemed to be no division of opinion as to the absolute perniciousness of the elective form of monarchy.

It was contended, on the other hand, that there were many plausible arguments in favor of the hereditary system. Education, culture, refinement, permanent interest in the people was universal, and an absence of popular elections, were among the characteristics of hereditary government. Hamilton had early a dread of republicanism; a dread of the "fierce democratie" who, in his opinion, were intent upon creating a condition of license and ultimate anarchy. He desired the autonomy of the States, free from any political association with the mother country; but, at the same time, he insisted that the traditions and laws of the English, together with the monarchical features of their Constitution, should be retained. In 1775, he wrote : "What can actuate those men who labor to delude any of us into the opinion that * * * * the commotions in America originate in a plan, formed by some turbulent men, to erect it into a republican government?" In the same year, in reply to the "Westchester Farmer," he made use of these words: "I earnestly lament the unnatural quarrel between the parent State and the Colonies, and most ardently wish for a speedy reconciliation—a perpetual and mutually beneficial union. I am a warm advocate for limited monarchy, and an unfeigned well-wisher to the present royal family."

It is true that these sentences were written before the declaration of independence, when Hamilton was about twenty years of age, and that his sentiments were somewhat modified in after life; but these early writings indicate the bent of his mind. In fact, he never thoroughly abandoned the position which the words quoted would indicate his holding. He continued to write against the principles of pure republicanism and to advocate the system of a life president endowed with monarchical power. This was the pervading and controlling idea of the Federal party, at whose head Hamilton stood, and to him and his *confreres* must attach the shame or glory of these characteristics of our law. In the sixty-eighth number of the *Federalist*, General Hamilton sought to disprove the parallel that had been drawn between the President of the United States and the king of Great Britain. He pointed out "the principal circumstances of dissimilitude" in the following manner: "The President of the United States would be an officer elected by the people for four years; the King of Great Britain is a perpetual and hereditary Prince. The one would be amenable to personal punishment and disgrace; the person of the other is sacred and inviolable. The one would have a qualified negative upon the acts of the Legislative body; the other has an absolute negative. The one would have a right to command the military and naval forces of the nation; the other, in addition to this right, possesses that of declaring war, and of raising and regulating fleets and armies by his own authority. The one would have a concurrent power with a branch of the Legislature in the formation of treaties; the other is the sole possessor of the power of making treaties. The one would have a like concurrent authority in appointing to offices; the other is the sole author of all appointments. The one can confer no privileges whatever; the other can make denizens of aliens, noblemen of commoners; can erect corporations with all the rights incident to corporate bodies. The one can prescribe no rules concerning the commerce or currency of the nation; the other is, in several respects, the arbiter of commerce, and in this capacity can establish markets and fairs, can regulate weights and measures, can lay embargoes for a limited time, can coin money, can authorize or prohibit the circulation of foreign coin."

General Hamilton, the reader will hardly need to be reminded, was writing in 1787-8, and of course without any knowledge of the many important changes that were to take place in the British Constitution in the following one hundred years; but he should have known, or knowing, should have stated, the law correctly and as it existed at the time he was constructing the above synopsis. The point we wish to make is, that the English Constitution had long ceased to be a monarchy in any true sense, and that the powers which General Hamilton ascribed to the sovereign, belong to the ancient, and, even at that early day, effete, theories of the English law. He overrated the prerogatives of the king, and underrated the powers which he was advocating for the President. The correctness of this statement can be proved by reference to English history. The leading principles of the British Constitution were interpreted as early as 1688, as consisting of "the personal irresponsibility of the king, the responsibility of ministers, and the inquisitorial power of Parliament." "Prior to that epoch, the Government of England was mainly carried on by virtue of the royal prerogative," and by ministers appointed by him and only responsible to him, except for "direct abuse of their functions."* The fact is, that the grouping by this eminent writer in the *Federalist* is not true, as has been conclusively shown in the preceding pages of this work. Although the king's person might, by a fiction of the law, be considered inviolable, still, it was not meant that he was " above the law," for his acts were controlled by law, and he could do no wrong to the people for which the Constitution did not provide a remedy.† General Hamilton admits, in the following number of the *Federalist*, that " there is an idea, which is not without its advocates, that a vigorous Executive is inconsistent with the genius of Republican Government." He then proceeds to state what are undoubtedly his peculiar ideas on the subject. He says that " energy in the Executive is a leading character in the definition of good government." * * * * " A feeble Executive implies a feeble execution of the government " * * * * " Let one Executive be appointed who dare execute his powers " There is no doubt there were many leading men, at the close of the American Revolution, who were in favor of adopting the British Constitution, as they understood it. In no other way can the fact be accounted for, that the framers embodied the present form of the presidency in the Constitution. Whence did these extraordinary powers, come? What principles actuated then? Certainly not any that could be deduced from the theories of representative government—a government of the people. General Hamilton was the leader of this class of political thinkers. In the Federal Convention he makes a plain admission, that he had no intention of advocating a government established

---

* " See Todd's " Parliamentary Government," vol., I. page 3. " Since the Revolution of 1688, the Crown has never attempted to govern without Parliament." *Edinburgh Review*, vol. cix, p. 275.

† See Amos' " English Constitution in the reign of Charles II," pp. 11, 19. Cox. Eng. Gov., p. 416.

on "Republican principles."* He says: "Their House of Lords was a noble institution." He goes on to give the reasons: "As to the Executive, it seems to be admitted, that no good one could be established on republican principles." * * * * "The English model was the only good one on the subject." * * * * "The hereditary interest of the king was so interwoven with that of the nation, and the personal emolument so great, that he was placed above the danger of being corrupted." etc. † Yates' Minutes of the Federal Convention report General Hamilton as saying: "I believe the British Government forms the best model the world ever produced ; and such has been its progress in the minds of many, that the truth generally gains ground." Mr. Gouverneur Morris, in the Federal Convention, said, "we must either, then, renounce the blessings of the union, or provide an Executive with sufficient vigor to pervade every part of it. * * * * One great object of the Executive is, to control the legislature. * * * It is necessary then that the Executive Magistrate should be the guardian of the people, even of the lower classes against legislative tyranny, against the great and wealthy, who, in the course of things, will necessarily compose the legislative body." Mr. Morris seemed to admire the British Executive, who, in his opinion, had so great an interest in the royal prerogatives, and possessed such powerful means of defending them. Mr. King relied on the vigor of the Executive as a great security for the public liberties.

We desire, on the other hand, to show that the opposition to the presidential form of government is not born of to-day. Leading thinkers and writers have resisted it from the very formation of our system. If any one have the curiosity to investigate this subject, let him read the forty-sixth number of the *Federalist*, contributed by General Hamilton. It will be

* Yates in Elliot, 450.   † Yates in Elliot 1. 422.

seen that he was not in a very judicial frame of mind when he penned its contents. A strong executive power was his special hobby, and he may be excused for using rather overwrought and intemperate language in writing about it. He thus states the views of the writers against the Constitution: " Calculating upon the aversion of the people to monarchy, they have endeavored to enlist all their jealousies and apprehensions in opposition to the intended President of the United States, not merely as the embryo, but as the full grown, progeny of a detested parent. To establish the pretended affinity, they have not scrupled to draw resources, even from the regions of fiction. * * * He (the President) has been decorated with attributes superior in dignity and splendor to those of a king of Great Britain. He has been shown to us with a diadem sparkling on his brow and the imperial purple flowing in his train. He has been seated on a throne, surrounded with minions and mistresses, giving audience to the envoys of foreign potentates, in all the supercilious pomp of majesty. The images of Asiatic despotism and voluptuousness have scarcely been wanting to crown the exaggerated scene. We have been taught to tremble at the terrific visages of murdering janizaries, and to blush at the unveiled mysteries of a future seraglio." If General Hamilton's contemporaries had ever written anything that justified this extravagant picture, it only proves how earnest and sincere they were in their opposition to the form that had been given to the Executive power in the Constitution. The janizaries, of course, have not arrived, nor has the seraglio been established; but a very respectable number of the people of this country believe, to-day, that more than one President has assumed monarchical power that would have caused a revolution in Europe, if exercised by a hereditary king.

Still, there were those who spoke in the Convention against the supposed prerogatives of the King being transferred to the President. Mr. Lancaster, in the North Carolina Convention, inveighed against the presidential powers, and Mr. Miller denounced them as defects in the Constitution. Mr. Porter and Mr. Spencer both objected to certain powers being conferred upon the President. Mr. Rawlins, in the South Carolina Convention, adverting to the powers of the President, considered them as erroneous, and Mr. James Lincoln made the following pertinent remarks: "But, pray who are the United States? A President and four or five Senators. Pray, sir, what security have we for a republican form of government, when it depends on the mere will and pleasure of a few men, who, with an army and navy, and with a treasury at their backs, may change and alter it as they please?"

Mr. Butler also protested against making the executive too powerful. He thought that in all countries the executive power is in a state of constant increase. He said: "Gentlemen seem to think that we had nothing to apprehend from an abuse of the executive power. But why may not a Catiline or a Cromwell arise in this country, as well as in others?"

Col. Mason said: "We are, Mr. Chairman, going very far into this business; we are not, indeed, constituting a British Government, but a more dangerous monarchy—an elective one. * * * * Do you, gentlemen, mean to pave the way for an hereditary monarchy? * * * * The people will never consent. * * * He hoped that nothing like monarchy would ever be attempted in this country. * * * * He never would agree to give up all the rights of the people to a single magistrate." *

Mr. Luther Martin very explicitly sets forth the objections to the whole system, in an able letter on the action of the Federal Convention, and his views of its various members.

* On another occasion Col. Mason wrote (vide Elliot's Debates, vol. 1, p 494.) "This government will commence in a moderate aristocracy; it is at present impossible to foresee whether in its operation it will produce a monarchy, or a corrupt, oppressive aristocracy; it will most probably vibrate some years between the two, and then terminate in the one or the other."

He details the objections that were made to conferring on the President the power to command the army and navy; to grant reprieves and pardons; (particularly in relation to the pardon of those guilty of treason, for the President may be engaged in the treason himself,) to establish himself in regal authority; to nominate officers, civil and military. He further urges that the President, as constituted, was a King in everything but in name; that though he was to be chosen for a limited time, yet, at the expiration of the period, if he is not re-elected, it will depend upon his own moderation whether he will resign that authority with which he has been invested.

Continuing, Mr. Martin contends that the President, from having the appointment of all the various officers, in every part of the civil department, for the Union, who will be very numerous in themselves—and their connections, relations and friends and dependents, still more numerous—will have a formidable host devoted to his interests, and ready to support his ambitious views. Mr. Martin is also apprehensive that the army and navy which may be increased without restraint and commanded by the President in person, the officers of which, from the highest to the lowest, are to be appointed by him, will be dependent on his will and pleasure, and of course subservient to his wishes, and ready to execute his commands; in addition to which, the militia will also be entirely subjected to his orders; that all these circumstances, in fine, combined together, will enable him, when he pleases, to become a King, in name, as well as in substance, and establish himself in office, not only for his own life, but if he chooses even to have that authority perpetuated in his family.

Mr. Grayson, in the Virginia Convention, after saying that the powers of the different branches are perpetually varying and fluctuating, continues: "The Executive is still worse, in this respect, than the Democratic branch. He is to be elected by a number of electors in the country ; but the principle is changed when no person has a majority of the whole number of electors appointed. * * * Then the Lower House is to vote by States. It is thus changing through the whole. It seems rather founded on accident than on any principle of government I ever heard of."

Mr. Patrick Henry, in the same Convention, said : " You President may easily become a king. * * * If your American Chief be a man of ambition and abilities,. how easy it is for him to render himself absolute. The army is in his hands, and if he be a man of address, it will be attached to him, and it will be the subject of long meditation with him to seize the first auspicious moment to accomplish his design ; and, sir, will the American spirit solely relieve you when this happens ? I would rather, infinitely—and I am sure most of the Convention are of the same opinion—have a king, lords, and Commons, than a Government so replete with insupportable evils. If we make a king, we may prescribe the rules by which he shall rule his people, and interpose such checks as shall prevent him from infringing them : but the President in the field, at the head of his army, can prescribe the terms on which he shall reign master, so far that it will puzzle any American ever to get his neck from under the galling yoke. I cannot, with patience, think of this idea. If ever he violates the laws, one of two things will happen ; he will come at the head of his army, to carry everything before him ; or he will give bail, or do what the Chief Justice will order him. If he be guilty, will not the recollection of his crimes teach him to make one bold push for the American throne ? Will not the immense difference between being master of everything and being ignominiously tried and punished, powerfully excite him to make this bold push ? But, sir, where is the existing force to punish him ? Can he not, at the head of his army, beat down every opposition ? Away with your President ; we shall have a king; the army will salute him monarch ; your militia will leave you and assist in making him king, and fight against you; and what have you to oppose this force? What will then become of you and your rights? Will not absolute despotism ensue."

In April, 1796, Thomas Jefferson wrote to his friend Mazzei, then in Italy. "The aspect of our politics has wonderfully changed since you left us. In place of that noble love of Liberty and Republican Government which carried us triumphantly through the war, an Anglican, monarchical, and aristocratical party has sprung up, whose avowed object is to draw over us the substance, as they have already done the forms, of the British Government. The main body of our citizens, however, remain true to their republican principles; the whole landed interest is republican, and so is a great mass of talents. Against us, are the Executive, the Judiciary, two out of three branches of the Legislature, all the officers of the Government, all who want to be officers, all timid men who prefer the calm of despotism to the boisterous sea of liberty, British merchants and Americans trading on British capital, speculators and holders in the banks and public funds, a contrivance invented for the purposes of corruption and for assimilating us in all things to the rotten as well as the sound parts of the British model. It would give you a fever were I to name to you the apostates who have gone over to these heresies, men who were Samsons in the field, and Solomons in the Council, but who have had their heads shorn by the harlot, England." * It will be observed that Jefferson had great fears that the Executive would become endowed with too great power ; that is, he was opposed to monarchical powers being conferred upon the President. He did not be-

* While Secretary of State, Jefferson wrote: "But I cannot describe the wonder and mortification with which the table conversations fill me. Politics were the chief topic, and a preference of kingly over republican government was evidently the favorite sentiment * * "I found myself, for the most part the only advocate on the republican side of the question."—Jefferson, by Morse —114.

lieve in the Presidential form of government. He also distrusted the powers of the judiciary. His theory was, that the President could not, in any case, use the army to coerce a State, and that the States respectively had the right and power (never delegated by them to the general government,) of deciding for themselves all questions arising out of public affairs. He also fell into the common error of the day, of judging the British Government as a monarchical one, and apparently of overlooking all its tendencies toward responsible Cabinet government. Jefferson was thoroughly imbued with the idea that a king would take possession of the American Government. He habitually spoke of the English King as a despot, the adoption of the English system as the introduction of absolutism. Jefferson believed that there existed a monarchical conspiracy, at whose head stood Hamilton; and he spoke of him as an enemy of the Constitution. For years he referred continuously to "monarchists" and "monocrats." He abhorred every exercise of governmental power; he hated the military establishment; internal taxation he thought should be left to the States; and the proposition of a National Bank seemed to enrage him. He accused Hamilton, who was Secretary of the Treasury, with making money out of his office; that he was not only "a monarchist, but for a monarchy bottomed on corruption; * * * that the ultimate object of all this is to prepare the way for a change from the present republican form of government to that of a monarchy; that he was positive that corruption would prove the instrument for producing in future a king, lords, and Commons, or whatever else those who direct it (the Legislature) may choose." * He aimed this shaft at John Adams: "I have a cordial esteem, increased by long habits of concurrence in opinion in the days of his (Adams') republicanism; and even since his apostasy to hereditary monarchy

---

* Jefferson, by Morse, 121.

and nobility, though we differ, we differ as friends should do." (*) July 29th, 1791, he wrote to Thomas Paine, of a sect high in name, but small in numbers, who desired the people to be converted " to the doctrine of kings, lords, and commons," and adds that the people are confirmed in the good old faith of republicanism by the " Rights of man ;" and to Lafayette he wrote (1792) : "A sect has shown itself among us, who declare they espoused our new Constitution, not as a good and sufficient thing in itself, but only as a step to an English Constitution, the only theory good and sufficient in itself in their eye." He calls them " king-jobbers."

Upon a careful examination of Jefferson's life, prior to his becoming President, it will be observed that he sympathized with the people, and against the one-man power. He became enraged over the Alien and Sedition Acts, and under this provocation he compounded an antidote far worse than the Federal poison. He drew the " Kentucky resolutions," intending them as a protest against unconstitutional enactments ; he far out-ran the constitutional limits of the most vigorous protest, and wrote a document which was simply revolutionary." † It remains as foundation, precedent and authority for all subsequent secession doctrines of the Eastern States ; for nullification in South Carolina; and for the rebellion of 1861. Jefferson fell into treason. Madison's Virginia resolutions were scarcely less objectionable than Jefferson's. But as soon as Jefferson became President of the United States, he caught the infection of kingcraft. He removed from and appointed to office ; and in the matter of the Louisiana territory, he violated all the principles of Red Republicanism and Jacobinism that had been charged upon him. He was President. He saw an opportunity to perform an act of great importance and moment to the people. The chief difficulties in the way were his own theories. So

---

* Jefferson, by Morse, 127. † Idem. 193, 194.

far as the Constitution itself was involved, it mattered little. Was he to ignore the abstract, and honor the concrete? Subjective reasoning was strong, but objective fact was irresistible. The truth is, that Jefferson yielded to the force of the environment; and in opposition to his whole life of fine spun abstractions against centralization, he deliberately played the *role* of an absolute sovereign. He entered into the negotiation with the subtility and stratagem of a Seward, and concluded it with the despatch and force of a Stanton. He avowedly and premeditately did an extra-constitutional and monarchical act. While Secretary of State, he had familiarized the Spanish Court with the scheme. It was Jefferson who forecast that doctrine, afterward known as that of Monroe. He wrote to Gouverneur Morris, asking him to intimate to the British Ministry that the American people would contemplate a change of neighbors with extreme uneasiness. "That a due balance on our borders is not less desirable to us than a balance of power in Europe has always appeared to them." In October, 1800, Spain ceded all Louisiana to France. When Jefferson learned this, in 1802, he was deeply chagrined. He immediately told his old friends, in France, that this purchase, under the circumstances, was an unfriendly one. In April, 1802, he wrote to Robert R. Livingston, Minister at Paris: "It is impossible that France and the United States can continue long friends, when they meet in so irritable a position. It seals the Union of two nations, who, in conjunction, can maintain exclusive possession of the Ocean. From that moment we must marry ourselves to the British fleet and nation." "One almost discredits his own senses as he beholds Jefferson voluntarily proclaiming the bans for these nuptials, which, during so many years past, would have seemed to him worse than illicit." * Jefferson was now thoroughly in earnest, and

---

* Jefferson, by Morse, 238.

nominated as Minister to France Ex-Governor Monroe, of Virginia, who set out with private instructions. Upon arriving in France, he found Napoleon already exercising the power of Emperor, about to commence great military operations, and forgetful of his colonial ambitions. In a short time, Monroe and Livingston closed the bargain, purchasing Louisiana for sixty million livres. Jefferson did not intend that there should be any doubt about getting possession, so he sent orders to the Governor of the Mississippi Territory and to General Wilkinson to move down with the troops at hand to New Orleans, and receive possession from Mr. Laussat. " Thus did Jefferson accomplish a most momentous transaction in direct contravention of all those grand principles which for many years he had been eloquently preaching, as the political faith of the great party which he had formed and led."* Washington's levees and Hamilton's bank were thrown into the shade by this act of the "doctrinaire President." According to Jefferson's theory of the Constitution, a contract between independent parties, and not binding beyond the letter of the stipulation, it was within the province of any State to secede on account of the act performed by him. Jefferson purchased foreign territory. Lincoln emancipated the slave. They both set precedents that in the future may furnish pretexts to some President-King to overthrow the liberties of the people.† He was bound to have

* Jefferson, by Morse, 251.
† Jefferson writes to Senator Breckenridge, of Kentucky, August 12, 1803; " But I suppose they (both Houses of Congress) must then appeal to the nation for an additional article to the Constitution, approving and confirming an Act which the nation had not previously authorized. The Constitution has made no provision for our holding foreign territory, still less for incorporating foreign nations into our Union. The Executive in seizing the fugitive occurrence, which so much advances the good of their country, have done an Act beyond the Constitution. The Legislature in casting behind them metaphysical subtilties, and risking themselves like faithful servants must ratify and pay for it, and throw themselves on their country for doing for them, unauthorized, what we know they

this territory by diplomacy or by force. He got it. If Spain, France, or Great Britain had gotten it, we never would have heard of the Missouri Compromise, of Texas, the controversies of the Southwestern boundary, of California, of Mexico, of the mines of gold and silver of those lands, of the Indian wars, of Alaska, or of the Pacific railways, or, possibly, of Chinese immigration.

Henry Adams, in his life of Albert Gallatin, one of the most prominent men contemporary with the revolution, and opposed to our presidential system of government, has collected many interesting facts bearing upon the theory of the government as understood by the statesmen of the early days of the republic, and upon the various conflicts that existed between the republicans and federalists. The latter, represented by Hamilton, George Cabot, Fisher Ames, Gouverneur Morris, and Rufus Griswold, had exercised so great an influence that they were successful in introducing monarchical powers into the Constitution, for the purpose of crushing democracy in America by the strong arm of the Executive. They regarded Mr. Gallatin as a mere Jacobin, and he, in his turn regarded the Presidency, which these gentlemen had created, as a stupendous wrong. There is manifest, in many of the utterances of Mr. Gallatin, the great aversion which a large portion of the people had to the growing powers of the President. He would have reduced the authority of the Executive to little or nothing. Even the acts of Washington excited alarm among the republicans. The contest first arose over the treaty of Mr. Jay, which recognized the right of Great Britain to capture French property in American vessels, whilst British property was protected in a like situation. Washington, after a long hesitancy, signed the treaty. The two great leaders of that day were Jefferson and Hamilton.

would have done for themselves had they been in a situation to do it."—Jefferson's Works. iv. p. 500. Cited by Von Holst, "Constitutional History," vol. i., p. 191.

They were both in dead earnest. One intended the government should be a federative democracy and the other a federal republic, with strong central powers. But the British treaty could only be carried into effect by an Act of Congress. The House called on the President for papers. The Federalists claimed that the House had no right to refuse to legislate, and that it had "nothing to do with the treaty but provide for its execution." Mr. Gallatin attacked this doctrine, and declared that the House was a check upon the treaty-making power, and showed this to exist in the British Constitution. He held that the theory of the Federalists would place the legislative power in the President and Senate; said he: "They can, by employing an Indian tribe, pass any law under the color of treaty." Seventy years later the same subject was discussed in relation to the purchase of Alaska. Mr. Griswold asserted, in reply to Mr. Gallatin, that legislative power did reside in the President and Senate, and added: "Allowing this to be the case, what follows? That the people have clothed the President and Senate, with a very important power." This is an admission which the people of this day should seriously contemplate. The debate continued, and party passion was at its height. The Federalists called their opponents "disorganizers," "Anti-Unionists and traitors." They retorted by charging the adherents of Washington's administration, with intending to supersede the constitutional power vested in Congress. The President sent a message to the House not characterized by his usual dignity. He said: " Having been a member of the General Convention, and knowing the principles on which the Constitution was formed, I have, etc., etc." This sentence probably expresses more of the autocratic and personal will than anything Washington ever wrote. He had not been delegated to speak for the Convention, and his testimony should not have been sought more than that of many others who were in the same body and at that time in the Congress which he was addressing. Then, it must be remembered, that Washington was not a Constitutional lawyer, and, on this ground, at least, his opinion should not have had any more weight than that attached to others. The philosophy of conferring great powers upon the President, was to make him overbearing and headstrong. The principle was not long in taking actual form.* The intention and purpose of the Federal party, to confer extraordinary power on its President, could be shown by reciting the numerous bills which were passed. The two most famous were the Alien and Sedition laws; one related to alien enemies, and the other to alien friends. The President had authority to order out of the country any alien whomsoever "he shall judge dangerous," or " shall have reasonable grounds to suspect," to be dangerous to the public peace and safety. The President had power to do this without any process of law. In case the alien refused to obey the order of the President, he shall, on conviction thereof, be im-

*In 1778 a treaty was entered into between France and the United States, by which they were bound by an offensive and defensive alliance. In the early part of 1793 war was declared by France against Great Britain and Holland. There can be no doubt but the full sympathies of the people of the United States went out to the sister republic. Washington was President. Notwithstanding these facts, and the evident unpopularity of the act, he issued his Proclamation of neutrality. He was denounced as the enemy of republican institutions, " of usurping the functions of Congress in the decision and announcement of peace and war, and of setting at naught a solemn treaty, to whose observance the faith of the country was pledged." By the terms of the treaty, which Chief Justice Jay concluded with England, American seamen could still be impressed, American Commerce harassed and shut out from the West India trade; still, Washington signed it. This act provoked attacks upon his private character— " He was charged by the extreme Republicans with usurpation, with treason to his country, and hostility to her interests. The continued sufferings of American prisoners in Algiers were ascribed to his criminal indifference. He was accused of having some incapacity during the Revolution and of having embezzled the public funds while President. He was threatened with impeachment, with assassination. Even the honored epithet so long given to him was burlesqued, and Washington was for a time known to the Republicans as the "Stepfather of his Country." ["History of American Politics," by Alexander Johnson, A. M., p 36.]

prisoned for a term not exceeding three years, and "be denied the right to become a citizen." The party that was successful in conferring upon the President most of the detested authority of King George was composed of the very persons who afterwards formed the Federal party. The most unerring way of determining what these persons, who were most prominent in the creation of the Constitution, intended, is to refer to the legislation which they were instrumental in bringing about, just after the adoption of our presidential system. If we should do this, it would be discovered that, so far as the Federalists were concerned, they had established a system which, in truth, could only be termed an elective monarchy. What autocrat could have greater power than those conferred by the Alien and Sedition laws? The republicans, under the leadership of Jefferson, were destined to overthrow this party of centralized power in a single man, and to establish in its stead the sovereignty of the States. Contemplating our Government in the light of the ninety years of its existence, are we not forced to the conclusion that both of these theories of government are wrong. The one would create a despotism, the other a disintegrating force, which would ever prevent us from becoming a nation, at least one with a representative form. It may have been the duty of the President to execute these laws, from our standpoint; but we mention these facts to prove that there existed, in the minds of a large number of the people, a desire for a strong and vigorous Executive. To-day the same party exists.

CHAPTER XXIV.

SUPREME POWER UNDER THE ENGLISH CONSTITUTION, PRIOR TO 1688.

It is desired to invite attention to the system of government as it existed in England before the creation of the American Constitution. The two systems are so intimately connected that a comprehensive review cannot be taken of the one without constant reference to the other. Of course it is well understood that the English have no written Constitution in the sense that we have. Their whole fabric rests upon the traditions, customs, experiences, facts and laws of the nation. It is proposed first to speak of the English Constitution as it existed before parliamentary government was well established. Any such sketch would give but an imperfect idea of it as it exists to-day. Every new law, for instance the recent reform and disestablishing acts, brings about many changes, and at the same time develops new forces. Many of the descriptions of the ancient Constitution remain perfectly true of the present.

The theory was that the supreme power was vested in two branches, the legislative, consisting of the king, lords and commons, and the executive, consisting of the king alone. The king at times, however, usurped all authority and power, as we shall see. The origin of the British parliament is hidden in the ages of antiquity. Grand Councils existed among all of the northern nations, and in the development of government it was claimed that parliament consisted of the king, the lords spiritual and temporal sitting in one house, and the commons in the other. These taken together made up the great body politic. Upon their coming together the king met them, either in person or by representation, without which there could be no parliament, and he also had the power of dissolving them.

The Speaker of the House of Lords was the Lord Chancellor or any other person appointed by the King's commission. The Speaker of the House of Commons was elected by the house. After a bill had passed both houses, it was deposited in the house of peers to wait the royal assent. This assent could be given in two ways—in person, when the king went to the house of peers in his crown and royal robes, and sending for the commons to the bar, the titles of all the bills that had passed both houses were read and the king's answer announced by the clerk of the parliament in Norman French. If the king assented to a public bill the clerk said, "the king wills it so to be," if to a private bill, "be it as it is desired." If he refused, the words were, "the king will advise upon it." If it was a bill of supply, the words were, "the king thanks his royal subjects, accepts their benevolence, and wills it so to be." By statute of Henry VIII. the king could give his assent by letters patent. A prorogation of parliament was made by royal authority, by commission, or by proclamation.

This subject brings us naturally to consider, first, the question of the supreme executive power of England at this time. The power was centred in a single person, called the King or Queen, who was invested with all the prerogatives of sovereignty.* The crown was hereditary. King James I. had rather exalted notions of the prerogatives of the crown. He

---

* "At the head of the whole administrative system was the King himself, personally taking part not only in legislation, but in fiscal, judicial, and every other kind of executive business."—["English Constitutional History" by Thomas Pitt Taswell-Langmead, 144. See also Stubbs' "Cons. Hist." i., 337, 338.]

said, "It is atheism and blasphemy, in a creature to dispute what the deity may do, so it is presumption and sedition in a subject to dispute what a king may do." It was laid down that the king might send ambassadors, create peers, make war or peace. He was sovereign and pre-eminent. His person was sacred. There was no jurisdiction to try him in a criminal way. He could neither do wrong nor think wrong. He could not be guilty of negligence or laches. The executive part of the government was placed in the single hand of the king. The king was so far absolute, that there was no legal authority to delay or resist him. He could reject bills, make treaties, coin money, create peers, and pardon offences. The king had the sole power of raising and regulating fleets and armies. By statute, Car. II., the king alone held the supreme government and command of all militia within the realm, and of all forces by sea and land, and of all forts and places of strength, and parliament ought not to pretend to the same. The king had exclusive power to erect beacons, light-houses and sea marks. He was considered in domestic affairs as the fountain of justice and general conservator of the peace of the kingdom. He alone had the right of creating courts of judicature. In the early history of England the king often heard litigated causes in person, but at last delegated this power to the judges. He also had the right of issuing proclamations. The king was the fountain of honor, of office, and privilege. The theory was, that no government could be maintained, unless the people knew and distinguished who were set over them, in order to yield their respect and obedience; and no one could know the merits of the officers employed as well as the king himself, who employed them. From the same principle, also, arose the prerogative of erecting and disposing of offices. The king had the power of conferring privilege upon private persons, such as granting place and precedence to any of his subjects. He could create denizens and erect corporations.

The King was the arbiter of commerce. He established the public mart, markets, and fairs. He regulated weights and measures. He gave money authority and made it current. The impression and "stamping thereof, was the unquestionable prerogative of the Crown."

The king was considered by the laws of England as the head and Supreme Governor of the National Church. By statute 26., Henry VIII. c. I, the king's majesty justly and rightfully, is, and ought to be, the supreme head of the Church of England, "it is enacted that the king shall be reputed the only supreme head on earth of the Church of England," and shall have "all jurisdictions, authorities and commodities," to the said dignity of the supreme head of the Church appertaining." He convened, prorogued, restrained, regulated and dissolved all ecclesiastical synods. He had the right of nomination to vacant bishoprics and other ecclesiastical preferments, and an appeal lay to him in chancery from the sentence of every ecclesiastical judge.* These powers which

---

* We do not quote from Blackstone, for the reason that we believe that he took the correct view of the historic facts of the British Constitution, as they existed in his day, but to show the source whence our framers drew their inspiration. He was the accepted authority in America at the date of the Revolution. For over seventy years, at the time he wrote, there had been many important changes, looking to a Cabinet Government in England, which he does not fully acknowledge. The fact is, that he was an apologist for the encroachments that had been made upon the liberties of the people, since the establishment of the responsible ministry; and in the statements of the law of the executive, gave substantially the working of the government under the Tudors and Stuarts. He thought that the poor had no will of their own—he was in favor of the borough system. "Had a hackneyed court hireling written in this manner, it had been no matter of wonder, but if the most intelligent men in the nation are to endeavor to persuade the people that there is hardly room for a wish; that there is scarce anything capable of alteration for the better (the judge's four volumes are a continued panegyric) at the very time when there is hardly any thing in the condition it ought to be in; at the time when we have upon us every symptom of a declining state, * * * * the spirit of the Constitution gone, the foundations of public security shaken, and the whole fabric ready to come down to ruin about our heads, if they, who ought to be the watchmen of

were said to exist in the Executive, independent of parliament, were, for the most part, the same which the kings claimed as belonging to them, when they were at the acme of the exercise of their personal power. There has always, however, existed from the earliest history of England an ebb and flow in the power of Parliament and the Commons. At first, Parliament had its rise and growth, then the king nearly destroyed its existence, and at last, Parliament, in its turn, under the Stuarts (until the death of Charles I), sought to regain what had been lost during the period of Absolutism.

The struggle that went on was generally between the king on one side and the people on the other. The kings had wars to prosecute; they needed money. Their necessity was the people's opportunity. The people of to-day take a more sensible course. In the past they granted supplies upon conditions, although they did not approve in every instance of the course of the ruler; to-day, if he stand in their way, they expel him from power.*

The growth of parliament is inseparably connected with the history of the English people. It must be remembered that while the early Norman kings levied their revenues without consideration for those who paid them and asserted their right to legislate, the Magna Charta was an ordinance issued by the king. But in very few instances were the arbitrary acts of the monarch found to be in the interests of the people; if they were, it was because the nobles and people had wrung them from him: Richard II. de-

---

the public weal, are thus to damp all proposals for redress of grievances."—Burgh's " Political Disquisitions," vol. 1., 80, 81.

* " In his first appearance, therefore, the absolute monarch is only a leader of predatory companions ; then, the ruler in their name of a conquered people; then, the ruler of this people without regard to his comrades ; then he endeavors to rule his comrades as he does the conquered. * * * * And in this spirit, all is done for the king's will and interest; for the king's family, the king's friends, the king's paramours, the king's favorites."—[" The People and Politics," by G. W. Hosmer, 176].

clared that the laws were in the mouth and breast of the king, and that he could change the laws of the kingdom to suit his own purposes.

During the civil wars between the houses of York and Lancaster, the most powerful nobles fell in battle and on the scaffold. " The strength of the Lords was thus weakened or detroyed ; the Commons alone had not sufficient influence to resist the crown ; and the king, therefore, secure from the weakness of his subjects, was able to enforce his views of despotic government on the nation. Thus, from the accession of the house of York, a new period of English history commences. Up to that time the course of Constitutional development, though frequently interrupted, had been on the whole continuous. From that time, for a century and a half, England was the victim of despotic governments of a more or less intolerant character. From the accession of the house of York, parliament was generally assembled at irregular intervals ; the work of legislation was frequently interrupted by disturbances and civil war, and the necessity for taxation was partly superceded by the invention of benevolences, or loans, nominally granted to the sovereign by the benevolence or free will of the donor, but in reality exacted by the crown. These three innovations—the interruption of parliaments, the suspension of legislation, and the exaction of benevolences,—placed this country for a century and a half under the personal government of the crown. After 1523, there was no parliament for nearly seven years. Elizabeth was in this respect a greater offender than her father, and during the whole of her reign she continually dispensed for long periods with the services of a Parliament. The Tudor Parliaments usually acted with a subservience which might have won for them more consideration. In the reign of Henry VIII, Parliament enabled the king, after he had attained the age of twenty-four years, to repeal any statute passed since his accession to the throne. Shortly afterwards, it vested the proclamations of the kind in

Council with the force of legislation. The Constitutional historian may find room for congratulation that the power thus transferred to the king was conceded to him by the legislature. The result was in any case the same. The substance of authority was yielded to the king. The shadow of it was retained by the Parliament.

It may, perhaps, be thought that the power which was thus grasped by the crown was productive of few inconveniences. Parliament, indeed, resumed under Edward VI, the powers which it had conceded to his father; and, from that time forward, the legislative authority nominally remained with the legislature. But the privileges which one monarch obtains by regular processes, is grasped by another irregularly; and Elizabeth imitating her father's example, and neglecting even to obtain the sanctions of her Parliaments claimed what Hallam has called "a supplemental right of legislation." The Queen's proclamations dealt with the most varied subjects—the banishment of Anabaptists, the cultivation of woad, the exportation of corn, the regulation of wearing apparel, the growth of London. But wise and unwise, important and unimportant, these proclamations were all branded with the same mark. They all asserted the right of the crown to regulate matters which, in earlier times, the legislature had scrupulously reserved for its own treatment. The great Constitutional principles, which had been slowly elaborated in Plantagenet England, were forgotten and ignored in Tudor times; and, in matters of legislation, England had virtually fallen into a condition of personal government.

This result was, in itself, sufficiently formidable. It was made much more serious in consequence of the power, which the crown claimed, to dispense with the aid of Parliament in matters of taxation. Benevolences, the intolerable invention of Edward IV, had been declared illegal by a statute of Richard III. But it was supposed that the latter statute did not prohibit the grant of voluntary gifts to the crown ; and, with clever management, it became impossible to distinguish between the voluntary gift and the enforced exaction. In the reign of Henry VII, Archbishop Morton propounded the famous fork which has preserved his memory, but which compelled both rich and poor to submit to the illegal exactions of his master. In the reign of Henry VIII, Wolsey raised illegal taxation to a science, and issued commissions for levying a sixth part of each man's substance. The disturbances, which these unprecedented demands occasioned, forced Wolsey to give way ; and gave Shakespeare an excuse for assuming that the exaction was the minister's, the concession the king's,—

> " * * * * Have you a precedent
> Of this Commission ? I believe not any.
> We must not rend our subjects from our laws,
> And stick them in our will."

Yet those who are best acquainted with English history, will be the first to reject the charitable interpretation which Shakespeare has placed on Henry's conduct. In despotic periods, ministers adapt their policy to the wishes of their masters. Under Henry VII, Morton invented his fork ; under Henry VIII, Wolsey attempted his exactions ; under Mary, a duty on foreign cloth was imposed without the authority of the legislature ; under Elizabeth, a similar duty, equally unauthorized, was imposed on foreign wine."* For one hundred and twenty years the Tudors ruled over England with a despotic form of government. But during the reigns of Henry VII, Henry VIII, and Elizabeth the aristocracy and the people were gradually recovering from the disastrous effects of civil

---

* The "Electorate and the Legislature," by Spencer Walpole, 13, 16. The Constitutional history of England to the reign of Henry VII, has been written by Mr. Stubbs ; from the accession of Henry VII, to the death of George II, by Mr. Hallam ; from the accession of George III to the present time, by Sir Erskine May.

war. Thus forces were gathering which were to overthrow Tudor despotism. The abolutism of the 7th and 8th Henry was ostentatious and bold ; that of Elizabeth was covert and seductive. Under her government, literary genius gratified the cultured ; the prosperity of trade satisfied the merchant, and the general welfare of the people made them contented with their lot. Still the rule of the Virgin Queen was that of a personal government ; with her death autocracy was shaken to its foundation. As the head of Charles I. rolled from the executioner's block, the one-man power fell, never to rise again.* James had come to England with views quite as despotic as those of the Tudors, and in his eye " monarchy was the true pattern of divinity." The Stuarts, therefore, as the Tudors had done before them, ruled as much as possible without Parliament, issued unwarranted proclamations, and taxed the people without the consent of the legislature. The Parliaments of the first James, and the first Charles, were in continuous antagonism to their ruler. Endless and irrepressible conflict marked that epoch of English history.

* The slavish Parliament of Henry VIII, grew into the murmuring Parliament of Queen Elizabeth, the mutinous Parliament of James I, and the rebellious Parliament of Charles I. " Mr. Bagehot, cited in Herbert Spencer's " Political Institutions."

"Between the years 1640 and 1660 there were in England twenty years of strife, due to a conflict for supremacy between the ancient conceptions of government and the needs of a growing nation. . . . . . Charles's theories were the theories of Rome, in so far as the influence of Rome was felt at the Court; they were the theories which the Church of England, in its endeavor to keep the nation in Episcopal tutelage, had inherited from Rome ; and they were the theories of the lawyers whose declarations as to the kingly attributes and the prerogative were taken without consideration that they were part of the legal fiction which contemplated the king as the supreme judge, though it would not permit him to sit on the bench even as a police magistrate.

"Charles held 'that no man, nor body of men, had power to call him to an account, being not entrusted by man, and, therefore, accountable only to God for his actions.' And as to the theory that kings are only entrusted with power by the people for the public advantage, he said, ' I am not entrusted by the people ; they are mine by inheritance.' "—[" The People and Politics," by G. W. Hosmer, 318, 319].

These kings claimed to exercise their wills by force, and exact obedience to their commands. Then, the second Charles, and the second James, came into collision with the legislature, by attempting to enforce the idea that the crown was above the law. Although James had all English history before him, in which the struggle of the people for liberty had manifested itself, he continued to exhibit all the bigotry of unenlightened periods. He sanctioned the atrocities of Jeffreys by conferring honors upon him, and thus branded his own name by approving cruelty and injustice. Parliament, at last, found out a secret more valuable than the Magna Charta, more effective than the Petition of Right. It discovered that it could assert its own supremacy. The representatives in Parliament were the power-holders for the people; the real source of all power. They asserted this power, and in December, 1688, James privately quitted the kingdom. Thus the headsman lost, and Parliament found, its opportunity. We have thus referred specifically to the leading principles of the ancient British Constitution, in order to show the correspondence between its rights, privileges and prerogatives, and those of our own government, and hence be able to judge how many of its provisions already adopted by us should now, in the natural course of our growth as a nation, be repealed as absolutely pernicious.

The exercise of executive power by the Queen has clearly diminished, while that of the President has increased. The Queen is but the form, the President the force; one is powerless, the other powerful; one is an idea, the other is an actuality.

CHAPTER XXV.

PRESENT WORKING OF THE BRITISH CONSTITUTION.

We have shown that the powers of our Executive were patterned after kingly prerogatives which obtained in England long prior to the American Revolution. In the formation of our Constitution, the theory of the vicarious atonement of the ministry, which had already been foreshadowed, if not established, as will appear, was abandoned, and the unyielding form of the Presidency took its place. For we must remember that although the Plantagenet, Tudor, and Stuart kings claimed to be all-powerful and absolute, and able to bind the nation by their acts, still the theory that the minister, "by whose agency or advice" their acts were done, could be impeached and removed, was early insisted upon.* This tendency to create a Cabinet Government in England the framers of our Constitution ignored. They proceeded to clothe the President with many of the ancient powers of the king. It is remarkable that the fathers should have taken this course after their experience with George III., and in view of the fact that all the acts of the Crown must be presumed to be done by some minister responsible to Parliament, a theory so well understood at the present day, and which was unqualifiedly asserted in the reign of George II. It is the more remarkable, also, in face of the fact that it has always been ac-

---

* "At the Revolution, the arbitrary rule of the Stuart Kings finally gave way to Parliamentary Government with ministerial responsibility."—[" Constitutional History of England," by Sir Thomas Erskine May, vol. i., 1.]

knowledged, more or less distinctly, that the king's ministers were answerable for all acts of Government that could in any way be traced to their advocacy and co-operation.

In the year 1696, the principle of ministerial responsibility to Parliament had been assented to; but in 1782, the downfall of Lord North's administration made a complete change in the ministry necessary, upon its losing the confidence of the House of Commons. We wish to draw attention to the date, (1696), when parliamentary government is said to commence, and to the fact that the present Constitution of the United States was not formally proposed until 1785, when Washington recommended the calling of a convention, to meet at Annapolis, in the following year. In September, 1786, the representatives of five States assembled. On account of the few represented, the convention adjourned until the following May. Rhode Island alone failed to respond to this call; and on the second Monday in May, 1787, the representatives assembled in Philadelphia. Early in September, 1787, the Committee reported the Constitution of the United States. It was ratified by all of the States, except North Carolina and Rhode Island, and by them finally; the former in November, 1789, and the latter in May, 1790. In the meantime, (January, 1789), Washington was elected the first Chief Magistrate of the United States. We mention these dates to show, that, although great changes had been made in the Constitution of England, the framers, in 1786 and 1787, persisted in embodying the ancient prerogatives of the king in the Constitution of the United States, and, apparently, the great reforms, which had already been thoroughly discussed in England, were not mentioned here. It is an astounding fact that the ministry of Lord North was overthrown because the latter remained in office " to carry into effect the personal wishes of the Sovereign, which he preferred to the welfare of the State;" and, let it be remembered, that these wishes were, that the independence of the American Colonies should not be recognized.* The House of Commons was opposed to the continuance of the war. A vote of want of confidence, it is true, had been lost, but Lord Surrey renewed the motion, and the king was persuaded to forestall defeat by accepting the resignation of the ministry. This event was communicated to the House the day the debate was to commence. Lord Rockingham was authorized " to form an administration, upon the basis of the independence of America, and a curtailment of the influence of the Crown." * * * The contest in which the North administration had been overthrown was a struggle of the king's personal will against the independent portion of the House of Commons. When the result was known, Fox openly treated it as a victory of the Commons over the king, declaring in his place in Parliament, " that the new ministers must remember that they owed their situations to the House." This ministry was brought to an end by the death of Lord Rockingham. Two days later, Secretary Fox asked the king to appoint some member of the Rockingham party as Premier, but he refused, and appointed Lord Shelburne, whereupon Fox, Burke, Sheridan, and others, resigned. The new ministry was, however, Whig.† Great questions involving difference of opinion arose in relation to the independence of the colonies; and in February, 1782, on a motion of censure being carried, the new ministry resigned. Thus we find, too, that the effect of the American Revolution in England was to destroy the personal power of the king, and, strange as it may appear, to create a government here, with many of the ancient prerogatives of the monarch. There, the Revolution established parliamentary, and here, kingly government. So far as the executive power is concerned, the war of independence made Great Britain more republican, and our own govern-

---

* Bancroft, "History of the Formation of the Constitution of the United States," 59, 60.
† Almon's " Parliamentary Register," xxviii., 67, 68; Ibid., xxvi., 347, 341. Life of Romilly, i., 205.

ment, in many respects, more monarchical. And, still more strange, this very war for liberty here was the direct cause of all of those wonderful changes in the British Constitution. These alterations seem to have gone unnoticed in the debates in regard to the ratification of the Constitution. With the adoption of the ancient prerogatives of the king in the Constitution of the United States, our embracing the system of the old Privy Council was entirely natural; and to-day, in this respect, we find ourselves under a form of government abandoned in England nearly two hundred years ago.* We have a king, and an irresponsible council about him, with enough power to overthrow the liberties of the nation at any

---

* "The Royal Council, as its designation 'Continual' denotes, was always sitting for the despatch of business, and for that purpose it occupied different chambers about the palace, among which the Star Chamber (*la Chambre des Etoiles*) is specially mentioned in the records of Edward III.'s reign. Its powers were most extensive, and, indeed, most indefinite. It was the King's standing council of advice in all matters of administration; it received, discussed, and remitted to the proper courts a vast number of petitions, which were constantly being presented, praying for relief in various matters of judicial cognizance; it exercised by itself, or in conjunction with the Lords' House in Parliament, a very great jurisdiction in causes both civil and criminal; and in matters of a temporary, partial, or comparatively unimportant nature, it assumed, by issuing ordinances claiming the force of statutes, the exercise of legislative powers. . . . But the Council and the Chancellor, not content with their admitted sphere of action, unconstitutionally assumed original jurisdiction in cases cognizable at common law. In direct violation of the liberties guaranteed by the Great Charter, men were arbitrarily imprisoned without the legal process of indictment or presentment, and their lands seized into the King's hands. During the reign of Edward III. a series of statutes were passed, in answer to the repeated complaints of the Commons, restraining these illegal invasions by the Council upon the rights of property and personal liberty. . . . The term 'Privy Council' does not appear to have been used until after the reign of Henry VI. 'Secretum concilium' occurs in Hemingburgh (ii., 20); and Walsingham (ii., 48), speaking of the abrogation of Acts of Parliament by Richard II. and his Council, says, 'Rex cum privato consilio;' but the usual style was 'continual' or 'ordinary' council. A distinction was probably always made according to the nature of the business; subjects of purely political deliberation seem to have been discussed by the great officers of state, or, as we should now say, the ministers, alone, without the presence of the judges or other legal members of the *concilium*

moment he may desire to be despotic. But, it may be said, that no President has yet done this. That is even questionable; but, on the other hand, if we admit that no President has as yet overthrown our liberties, shall we refrain from asking why, in the face of history, was the power ever given him to do so? In this respect the English profited, and we lost, by the Revolution. We accepted the fictions of their government, and they embodied many of the logical effects of our Revolution in their Constitution. In support of the statement, that the Revolution was, in its inception, waged against the reigning king, attention may be drawn to the language of the Declaration. First, it promulgates those words of freedom and liberty declaratory of the self-evident truths held so dear by all true Americans; then follows this sentence: " The history of the present king of Great Britain is a history of repeated injuries and usurpations, all having in direct object the establishment of an absolute tyranny over these States." To prove this, a long series of specific acts of his are set forth, and every sentence is commenced by the words of personal impeachment: " He has," etc. Towards the close of this remarkable document occur these words: " A prince whose character is thus marked by every act which may define a tyrant, is unfit to be the ruler of a free people." A close examination of the pages of history will disclose the fact that the American Revolution was hastened, if not absolutely caused, by the obstinacy of King George the III. While the framers always spoke against him in terms of unmeasured condemnation, they uniformly ex-

---

ordinarium. They formed, therefore, an internal council of government, in some respects analagous to the modern Cabinet."

See Stubbs' Const. Hist. ii., 40-255 *seq.*

Sir H. Nicolas, Preface to Proceedings of Privy Council, p. iii.

31 Edw. III. st. 1, c. 12; Spence Eq..Juris. i, 330.

The above with notes is quoted from " English Constitutional History," by Thomas Pitt Taswell-Langmead, 170–175.

pressed their admiration of the British Constitution, and so far as its general construction is concerned, attempted to model ours after it. George III. was naturally fond of power, used his prerogative to its fullest extent, directed the course of his ministers, and distributed the patronage of the Crown. He loved to rule. He was courageous and resolute.* "The king continued personally to direct the measures of his ministers, more particularly in the disputes with the American colonies, which, in his opinion, involved the rights and honor of his crown.†" "He was resolutely opposed to the repeal of the Stamp Act, which ministers thought necessary for the conciliation of the colonies. He resisted this measure in council; but finding ministers resolved to carry it, he opposed them in Parliament by the authority of his name, and by his personal influence over a considerable body of parliamentary adherents.‡" Burke describes the friends of the king, whom he consulted, as the "double or interior Cabinet?" There can be but little doubt that George III. violated the principles of his own government, and by this violation lost the colonies.‖ The American people rebelled against him. It is true, however, that George III. was the last monarch who ventured to assert his will against the Commons.

It is not within the province of this essay to refer more than briefly to the different theories of the English Constitu-

* "The King was resolved to wrest all power from their hands and to exercise it himself."—["Constitutional History of England," by Sir Erskine May, vol 1., 12.]

† "The King said his ministers would undo his people in giving up the rights of his crown; that to do this he would never consent." ["Grenville Papers," iii., 370 371.]

‡ "Constitutional History of England," by Sir Erskine May, vol. 1., 37. Walpole Mem., ii., 259, 331. Rockingham Mem., ii., 250, 294."

‖ "The persecution of Wilkes, the straining of parliamentary privilege, and the coercion of America were the disastrous fruits of the Court policy." May, Cons. Hist., vol. I. 44, 49, 51, 54, 59. Lord Brougham's Works, iii., 127. Fox Mem., i., 211, 212.

tional law. Macaulay claims immemorial antiquity for the doctrine of the responsibility of ministers; another writer affirms that there is no period of history where the sovereign could act without advice; that the crown always had a privy council. We simply aim at a statement of historic fact, and the truth is, as we have already set forth, that, down to the Revolution, the sovereign did exercise an autocratic authority over the affairs of State; whether the theorists referred to had good grounds for their conclusions or not, we do not pretend to say, but simply direct attention to the present form of the Executive power. The work of government is "performed by a body of ministers belonging to the party which possesses a majority in the House of Commons, holding seats in Parliament, and responsible to Parliament for the way in which they perform their work. The principle of this responsibility was first formally recognized, in fact, in the year 1696, and first publicly proclaimed and assented to in Parliament in the year 1711."* "The principle is now firmly established and the control so complete, that there is no public act of the sovereign, whenever and however performed, for which there is not some minister, or ministers, responsible."†

Certainly those who admit that the ancient theories of the English Constitution were embodied in our Executive; and that the framers were students and admirers of that old

---

*Traill's "Central Government," 2. Lord Rochester, in a debate in the House of Lords on the affairs of Spain. Cobbett, Parl. Hist. VI., 972. Todd's "Parliamentary Government in England," ii., 101.

†"This is so, even in the case of the dismissal of a ministry by the sovereign, for it was laid down in 1807, after the dismissal of the Grenville administration by George III. and fully admitted by Sir Robert Peel, in the case above referred to, in 1834, that the incoming ministry assume undivided responsibility for the act of the Sovereign in dismissing their predecessors." Traill's "Central Government," 2. In the preparation of the two articles upon the British Constitution we have frequently consulted, among other works, "The Growth of the English Constitution," by Edward A. Freeman, and "The English Constitution," by Walter Bagehot.

system, should not insist that it is inconsistent and illogical for the present generation carefully to inquire into the present workings of that very form of government, in order to discover whether pace has been kept with its progress and reform. If the framers followed ancient modes, we should adopt the new, so far as they may be applicable. If we should be guided by the Constitution of other governments in the process of perfecting our own, it is proper to select that period of their history when they are most republican and representative. Although the retention of the prerogatives of the king in our Constitution has greatly retarded republicanism in this country, we may yet be benefited by an examination of the present workings of Executive power in England. There can be little question that the present form of parliamentary government in England is one of great wisdom. Of course, we do not think that it should be adopted by us in its entirety, but we do claim that many of its characteristics should be. As a system, it is, in many respects, more republican and elastic than ours.

We speak of the unwritten Constitution of Great Britain, and the written one of this country. Practically, ours is unwritten, while theirs is written. Theirs is stable and defined; ours unsettled and conflicting. Theirs is the growth of ages, with its experiences, facts and laws written in unambiguous terms; ours has been amended fifteen times, and there are as many different interpretations of it as there are parties and factions. No one disputes about the power and authority of the various branches of the British Constitution; every one differs as to the interpretation to be put upon ours. To define the exact limitations of government by written Constitutions may still be regarded an experiment. This statement may be answered by referring to the fact that this government sustained itself against one revolution arising out of the interpretation of the law, and, therefore, it can always perpetuate itself, and successfully resist any civil war, instituted for the purpose of enforcing theories of the right of secession; the power of Congress; the jurisdiction of the United States; or the prerogatives of the President. To spread laws upon the statute books is one thing; but to enforce them is another. Customs, experiences, morals and decisions, must be written upon the heart of man. No law will compel the Southerner to accord equal rights to the enfranchised negro; but the time may come when the white man himself will believe that it is for his physical and moral benefit that such protection be extended. Discussion and agitation are the great means of educating the people. The laws should express the thought and conscience of the nation. As amendment is the lawful and regular mode of changing the fundamental law, it is the duty of every true American to urge amendments to our Constitution, whenever he believes that the moral and political requirements of the age can be thereby met and advanced.*

* In this connection, it may be stated that President Arthur, in his message of the 3d of December, 1883, recommends several amendments to the Constitution and the laws. In that document he affirms that:

"For the reasons fully stated in my last annual message, I repeat my recommendation that Congress propose an amendment to that provision of the Constitution which prescribes the formalities for the enactment of laws, whereby, in respect to bills for the appropriation of public moneys, the Executive may be enabled, while giving his approval to particular items, to interpose his veto as to such others as do not commend themselves to his judgment."

It does not seem to enter the mind of the President that he should not exercise the power of veto in any case. On the contrary, he asks that the law be so amended that he shall have, not only the right of a general negative of all proposed laws, but in respect to bills appropriating public moneys, that he may be enabled to interpose his veto as to any particular item that does not commend itself to his judgment. It may have been his intention to ask for power to prevent the furtherance of private jobs by placing "riders" upon the appropriation bills, but those who look below the surface of this proposed amendment, will see that such a law will also enlarge the personal discretion of the Executive to such an extent that at any time he may clog the wheels of any branch of the Government towards which he may be prejudiced. It seems to us, that the suggestion would ensure an extension of his power, and for that reason we believe that it is unwise.

The message above referred to also contains the following:—

The ancient characteristics of the English Constitution have faded away into idle forms and symbols. Since the

"The fourteenth amendment of the Constitution confers the rights of citizenship upon all persons born or naturalized in the United States, and subject to the jurisdiction thereof. It was the special purpose of this amendment to insure the members of the colored race the full enjoyment of civil and political rights. Certain statutory provisions intended to secure the enforcement of those rights have been recently declared unconstitutional by the Supreme Court. Any legislation whereby Congress may lawfully supplement the guarantees which the Constitution affords for the equal enjoyment by all the citizens of the United States of every right, privilege, and immunity of citizenship will receive my unhesitating approval."

The amendment that is referred to, provides that no State shall make or enforce any law which shall abridge the privileges or immunities of citizens of the United States. Congress passed laws in pursuance of this provision. The Supreme Court declared them unconstitutional. It based its opinion upon the old distinctions of the limitations of the General and State Governments. Justice Harlan dissented. Any one desiring to see the uncertainty and obscurity which surrounds our fundamental law, may find instructive reading in these conflicting decisions; while those who know that the Supreme Court has often leaned toward wrong and injustice, and remember that it was guilty of promulgating the Dred Scott *dictum*, will not be surprised.

The third recommendation, to which we particularly desire to call attention, is in the following language :—

"At the time when the present Executive entered upon his office, his death, removal, resignation, or inability to discharge his duties would have left the Government without a Constitutional head. It is possible, of course, that a similar contingency may again arise, unless the wisdom of Congress shall provide against its recurrence. The Senate at its last session, after full consideration, passed an act relating to this subject, which will now, I trust, commend itself to the approval of both houses of Congress. The clause of the Constitution upon which must depend any law regulating the Presidential succession presents also for solution other questions of paramount importance. These questions relate to the proper interpretation of the phrase "inability to discharge the powers and duties of said office," our organic law providing that, when the President shall suffer from such inability, the Presidential office shall devolve upon the Vice-President, who must himself, under like circumstances, give place to such officer as Congress may by law appoint to act as President. I need not here set forth the numerous and interesting inquiries which are suggested by these words of the Constitution. They were fully stated in my first communication to Congress, and have since been the subject of frequent deliberations in that body. It is greatly to be hoped that these momentous questions will find speedy solution, prerogatives of the king have been taken from him, and he is left to the mere trappings of royalty, the English people do not want a monarch with any special genius, far less ambition ; and, to-day, probably the greatest misfortune that could happen to England, would be to have in the person of the sovereign, a powerful and energetic man. Tennyson, speaks of modern England as the " Crowned Republic." She gives protection to the most advanced thinkers on all social, scientific, and religious subjects. Hume, Bentham, Mazzini, Blanc, Mill, and Bradlaugh, have each been permitted to make their strictures upon her forms of government, and now many of their opinions have been adopted by the nation itself. England preserves the throne only in name. The Crown is so removed from the people, so retired, that it is almost an esoteric mystery. The lower classes may believe that they are governed by a queen ; the more intelligent know that this is not so. The Queen is a heraldic figure ; the President is a potential fact. The actual rulers of England remember that Louis Napoleon was elected the President of a Republic, and that President MacMahon attempted to crush the liberties of the French nation. The strange paradox presents itself of the one-man power disappearing behind the ermine of the Queen, while it reappears in the " dress coat of the President." *

lest emergencies may arise when longer delay will be impossible, and any determination, albeit the wisest, may furnish cause for anxiety and alarm."

We have already drawn attention to this subject, and shown the imperfect and rickety condition of the law that controls the question of Presidential succession. Propositions for reform have been made, but none have been adopted. The politicians, in the meantime, being infatuated with anticipation of controlling the immense patronage of the Government, stumble on in their course. No law prevents them from leading the country into disintegration and chaos.

* " The Revolution of 1688 marks at once a resting-place and a fresh point of departure in the history of the English Constitution. The Bill of Rights was the summing up, as it were, and final establishment of the legal basis of the Constitution. With Magna Charta and the Petition of Right it forms the legal Constitutional Code, to which no additions of equal importance (except the

The present House of Commons represents the English people. The House of Lords, however, has a certain negative power. It is this branch of their government that is most repugnant to Americans; but it must be borne in mind that that aristocracy is different from any which ever existed in the world's history. Most aristocracies were mere castes, without sympathy with the people. They neither entered into the enjoyments or the occupations of the other classes. They ignored letters and led the life of soldiers. Not so with the English aristocracy; the younger members make it the ambition of their lives to sit in the House of Commons. They affect politics. In all fairness, it must be admitted that sons of noble families have an undue influence at the polls. But this does not seem to have grown into any abuse of power. Another defect, which strikes the American mind, is the great influence of the landed interest; but it is an open question whether it controls legislation in England to the extent that great corporations do in this country. The House of Commons remains the great representative body. It constitutes the heart and brain of the nation. Its members think well on all subjects. They are in full sympathy with the people. They make free government an actual, existing fact.

One reason why the debates in our Congress are not more interesting and instructive, is that they often lead to no prac-

constitutional provisions of the Act of Settlement to be presently noticed) have since been made by legislative enactment. . . . The doctrines of Divine hereditary right, of absolute royal power, of the passive obedience of the subject, were negatived once and forever by the Revolution, and the rule of Parliament was definitively established; but the mode of exercising that rule has since become something wholly different to what it then was, and in its present form of Parliamentary Government through a Cabinet Ministry, forms the main characteristic of our Constitutional system. . . . . The Act of Settlement is characterized by Hallam (Cons. Hist., iii., 198) as 'the seal of our Constitutional laws, the complement of the Revolution itself and the Bill of Rights, and the last great statute which restrains the power of the Crown.'"— ["English Constitutional History," by Thomas Pitt Taswell-Langmead, 662, 663].

tical issue. Censure and exposure may rise in eloquent tones, but the Executive cannot be removed. In England a political discussion endangers the existence of the administration itself. The consequence is that the people study the political questions more than they do in countries under presidential forms. With us, the issue may occur just after the President is elected. The people know that no argument is going to depose the President, whose position is so impregnable that it would take four years to make a successful political assault upon him. Even impeachment has not been effective to depose for clear usurpation of power. Politics is a synonym for trickery and chicanery. Our young men pay little attention to the study of political, financial, or economical questions. It is the fixed period of the term of our Executive that takes away the interest in the study of the great issues before the country. There is, undoubtedly, much attention given to the question of the availability of various candidates for the presidency, but there is little actual investigation of questions from any scientific standpoint.

If the old maxims found in the books could be expunged, how much more rapid would be the progress of liberty! In almost any work on the British Constitution, one is informed that its powers are divided into the legislative, executive, and judicial. One hears much about kings, lords and commons; of checks and balances; of monarchy, aristocracy and cabinets. The fact is, these terms have lost much of their meaning. The requirements of human progress demand restless change. The old theories exist only as the ancient temple or statue exists, to impress the ignorant or superstitious—they should have little effect upon the reason of man.

The British Constitution, as it now exists, is a complete and harmonious blending of the legislative and Executive. All that remains of the Executive is enveloped in the cabinet, and that is enfolded in the legislative. The Cabinet is but the indirect creation of the legislature. The legislature nominates a committee to conduct the government, and if that committee fail to carry out its wishes it must resign.* The Crown does not in reality select the ministry. The leader in the House of Commons is the Premier. He is the actor; the queen is the lay figure. The Executive power—the Cabinet and the Premier—is chosen by a simple process of double election. It is direct, simple and expeditious. As a matter of form, the Premier selects his associates; as a matter of fact, the Commons determine who they shall be. The Prime Minister has less power than he appears to have. The fact is, the Cabinet is but the creature of the legislature. Probably the strangest thing about the English Cabinet is this, that there is little known about it. It has no statutory existence. The meetings are secret. No minutes are kept. No letters are written.† The Cabinet may dissolve the body to which it owes its existence. But it must appeal to the next Commons. It will be perceived that the English system, in one sense, is not an entire absorption of the Executive by the legislative, for the Cabinet has the power to destroy its creator. In point of fact, it has only the power to appeal to the people on

---

* "In practice these vast prerogatives have now long been exercised, not at the will of the Sovereign, but of the responsible ministers of the Crown, who represent the will of the majority in the House of Commons. 'In outer seeming,' it has been well observed, 'the Revolution of 1688 had only transferred the Sovereignty over England from James to William and Mary. In actual fact, it was transferring the Sovereignty from the King to the House of Commons,' . . . . The mode in which the Executive power of the Crown has gradually been transferred to what has been aptly termed 'a board of control, chosen by the legislature, to rule the nation,' has been already sketched in treating of the growth of the Cabinet."—["English Constitutional History," by Thomas Pitt Taswell-Langmead, 688, 689].

† "The sovereign is never present at any discussions of the Cabinet. This is said to have arisen by the accident that neither George the I. or II. could speak English. The reason, however, is because the king has no actual power, and the spirit of the law is to keep him in the background." Whatever the origin of this practice was, it is fortunate that the king is never present. The President *must* be present at our Cabinet meetings.

any important issue, and if it is not sustained, it disappears. It destroys only the existing representative body, but does no violence to the actual power, for the people soon again select new agents to express their desire and will. No conflict continues. Either the Commons vote a want of confidence against the ministry, or the ministry dissolves the Commons and goes before the people—then follows a reconstruction, upon the basis of harmony arrived at by the expression of the popular will. All questions may be tested at any stage of their development. One of the best illustrations of the true sympathy of the Parliament with the people, was in the case of the bill introduced by Mr. Plimsoll, for the protection of British seamen. Disraeli, who was then at the zenith of his power, gave the bill a passive support, and allowed the matter to drag along until the grouse-shooting season. Plimsoll made a violent—almost insulting—speech in favor of his measure. The nation read the debate. It endorsed the bill. The Commons saw this, and was ready to remain, even through the shooting season, to give attention to a measure in which the people had manifested so lively an interest. It became law. Why was this so quickly accomplished? Because the ministry saw, that if they opposed it, and the Commons passed it, it would be considered a vote of want of confidence. The issue had to be met then and there. There could be no delay. The very life of the Commons depended upon its action. Could the Congress of the United States have been compelled by one member—as Parliament really was—to pass a measure, undoubtedly popular with the people? We think not. If Congress did not want to pass the bill, it would have been argued that the representatives were elected for a fixed period; that by the time the matter could be brought to issue in a political contest, it would probably be forgotten. They would have been indifferent to the wishes of the people.

Among the reforms now advocated by the liberal party

in England are triennial Parliaments.* The Church has been disestablished in Ireland; it will soon be in England. It is the dream of the Liberals to accomplish all of these propositions.

Will the English nation ever abolish the orders of nobility? Will it ever place the House of Lords upon a representative basis? or abolish the House altogether? Whatever it may do, its course is towards a government that will ensure greater freedom and purer liberty for the people † Already

---

* "Thenceforward it (the question of Reform) was again and again brought before Parliament by Sir Francis Burdett, Lord John Russell, and others, until at length, under the Whig ministry of Lord Grey (who had advocated the cause of Reform for forty years), the Reform Bill, after defeats in both Houses of Parliament, a dissolution, the resignation and recall of the ministry, and a threatened creation of peers by the king—was passed amidst the greatest popular excitement, and became an act on the 7th of June, 1832. , . . . By the Reform Act of 1867—passed by Lord Derby's Conservative ministry, with the aid of the Liberal majority in the House of Commons—a further extension of the electoral franchise in England and Wales was introduced, scarcely less important than that conceded by the Reform Acts of 1832.

"The borough franchise was extended to all householders (subject to one year's residence and payment of poor's rates) as well as to lodgers occupying lodgings of the annual value of ten pounds. The county occupation franchise was reduced to twelve pounds; and thirty-three seats were withdrawn from English boroughs, twenty-five of which were transferred to English counties, and the remaining eight to Scotland and Ireland. . . . . By the same Act a perfectly new principle, that of the representation of minorities, was introduced in a tentative and partial manner into the representative system. This principle had been embodied in Lord John Russell's abortive Reform Bill of 1854, which proposed to assign three members to certain counties, and other large places, the electors of which were to be entitled to vote for two only out of the three. The city of Manchester, and the boroughs of Liverpool, Birmingham, and Leeds, were now each empowered to return three members to Parliament; and it was declared (secs. 8, 9), that at a contested election for any county or borough represented by three members, no person should vote for more than two candidates, nor in the city of London, which has four members, for more than three candidates." It may be added that in 1850 and 1868, acts were passed for Scotland and Ireland similar to the English act in principle. See 13 and 14 Vict., c. 69; 30 and 31 Vict., c. 102; 31 and 32 Vict., c. 48; 31 and 32 Vict., c.49.—["English Constitutional History," by Thomas Pitt Taswell-Langmead, 728, 731.

† "The development of free institutions, and the entire recognition of liberty

the workings of **the Executive are nearer to** the ideal of a representative **government than any upon the** face of the **earth.**

of opinion, have wrought an essential change in the relations of the government and the people * * * * They are in concert, instead of opposition, and share with one another the cares and responsibility **of** state affairs. If the power and in**dependence** of ministers are sometimes impaired by the necessity of admitting **the** whole people to their councils, their position is **more often** fortified by public approbation." May's " Constitutional History," **vol. ii, 419.**

CHAPTER XXVI.

REPRESENTATIVE GOVERNMENT.

There are various theories of our National existence. One regards the United States as a nation, and its Constitution as the organic and fundamental law of that nation. The collective people existed, as a political unit, prior to the Constitution, and were not, therefore, the consequence, but the antecedent. The Constitution was not the work of the States, as organized governments, nor of the people of those States in their capacity as independent sovereign aggregates, but the work of the people as a whole—not voting together, as a mass, but as a matter of convenience acting in their respective commonwealths. The powers held by the general government were not delegated to it by the States, regarding those States as governments, nor by the people, regarding those peoples as sovereign aggregates, but were delegated to it by the people of the United States as a whole, although in the process of delegation this one people did not vote together as a mass of electors. Powers were not reserved by the several States to themselves, for as the States, as such, did not grant any powers, they could not reserve any. They were reserved by the people to themselves.* Hence, the people of the

---

* "The National Constitution was, as its preamble recites, ordained and established by the people of the United States. It created, not a Confederacy of States, but a government of individuals." White v. Hart 13, Wall, 646 et seq. "As a Judge of this Court I know, and can decide, upon the knowledge, that the citizens of Georgia, when they acted upon the large scale of the Union as a part

United States, as a nation, are the ultimate source of all power.* This is substantially the view of the Constitution advanced by Jay, by Marshall, by Strong, by Webster, and by Lieber. The same theory has in recent times been advanced by O. A. Brownson in his "American Republic," and by George P. Marsh in letters to the *Nation.*

The directly opposite theory of our Government obtained at its formation, and has been advocated ever since. If it were practical and advisable, we might cite as authority for this statement the writings and speeches of the most honored names in history. Mr. Madison, who was an earnest supporter and advocate of the Constitution, says:† "Among a people consolidated into one nation, the supremacy is completely vested in the National Legislature. Among communities united for particular purposes, it is vested partly in the general, and partly in the municipal, legislatures. In the former case, all local authorities are subordinate to the supreme, and may be controlled, directed, or abolished by it at pleasure. In the latter, the local or municipal authorities form distinct and independent portions of the supremacy, no more subject, within their respective spheres, to the general authority, than the general authority is subject to them, within its own sphere. In this relation,

---

of the people of the United States, did not surrender the supreme or sovereign power to that State; but as to the purposes of the Union, retained it to themselves. As to the purposes of the Union, therefore, Georgia is not a sovereign State." Chisholm Exr *vs.* State of Georgia, 2 Dall. 453.

* "An Introduction to the Constitutional Law of the United States," by John Norton Pomeroy, 22, 23.

"The United States form not only a republic, but a confederation; nevertheless the authority of the nation is more central than it was in several of the monarchies of Europe when the American Constitution was formed. . . . He (the President) no longer governs for the interest of the State, but for that of his re-election; he does homage to the majority, and instead of checking its passions, as his duty commands him to do, he frequently courts its worst caprices." ["Democracy in America," by Alexis de Tocqueville, 95, 115.]

† In the thirty-eighth number of the *Federalist.*

then, the proposed government cannot be deemed a national one, since its jurisdiction extends to certain enumerated objects only, and leaves to the several States a residuary and inviolable sovereignty over all other objects." "Calhoun begins with a reference to the fact, seldom rightly estimated, 'that the question of the relation which the States and the general government bear to each other, is not one of recent origin;' but that 'from the commencement of our system, it has divided public sentiment.' He adopted as the basis of his argument the leading sentence in the Virginia resolutions, and said: 'The right of interposition thus solemnly asserted by the State of Virginia, be it called as it may—State right, veto, nullification, or by any other name,—I conceive to be the fundamental principle of our system, resting upon facts historically as certain as our resolution itself, and upon deductions as simple and as demonstrative as that of any political or moral truth whatever.' From both points of view, he sought, then, proof for these statements. * * * * * * * * The State governments are not, he said, the Federal governments; the States are not subject to the Union."* "Ours is not such a nation; it is sovereign to the foreign world in most things, but even then not in all. It could not cede to Great Britain, for example, a part of Maine, without Maine's consent. In our domestic world, it is sovereign only in a few things."†

These two theories of government are known as the "National theory," and the "State Sovereignty theory." In so far as the first represents the people as a mass, it is the correct form. The second creates a confederation.

The Senate, State and Presidential systems belong to both theories, and their operation forms a barrier to representative government in this country. The Constitution provides that "the Senate of the United States shall be com-

---
* Von Holst, Vol. I. 467, 468.
† David Dudley Field, in *North American Review*, May, 1881.

posed of two Senators from each State, chosen by the Legislature thereof, for six years, and each Senator shall have one vote."* As in the case of all the other provisions of the Constitution, this matter was discussed in the National Convention. Mr. Dickinson thought that the Senate should bear as strong a likeness as possible to the British House of Lords, and consist of men distinguished for their rank in life and their weight of property.† To depart from the proportional representation in the Senate, said Madison, on the other hand, " is inadmissible, being evidently unjust."‡ Charles Pinckney proposed to divide the States periodically into three classes, according to their comparative importance; the first class to have three members, the second two, and the third one member each, but the proposal received no attention. § The threats and entreaties of the smaller States at last prevailed, and this un-republican and aristocratic provision became part of the law. It is so glaring a violation of all justice, that it seems like waste of time to enter into any discussion in relation to it. No representative government can exist until the article is stricken from the law. It can only be upheld upon the ground that it was one of the compromises, made upon the adoption of the Constitution, and no matter what changes take place in the needs and requirements of the people, that all succeeding generations shall be bound by that law. In these days of advancement and reform, we hardly think that this consideration will continue to have sufficient weight to check the onward march to a purer and better form of government.

The articles of Confederation had provided but one House. All kinds of schemes, too numerous to particularize here, were advanced. David Brearly favored the complete obliteration of State lines, and the division of the whole

---

* Art. I. Sect. 3. † Gilpin, 813—Elliot, 166.
‡ Gilpin, 814.—Elliot, 167. § Gilpin, 821. Elliot, I. 185-399.

country into thirteen equal parts, based upon population. This is the remedy which should be applied to-day. A spirit of "mutual deference and concession" existed in the Convention, which produced the result of sacrificing the principle of proportional representation to that of the Federative system. Thus it is apparent that the Senate is the strongest fortress of the "residuary sovereignty" of the States. General Hamilton shows conclusively that it was not the intention of the framers to establish a pure republic; and, writing afterwards in support of the Constitution, he speaks of guarding against "an improper consolidation of the States into one simple republic." In the great issues of the future which will surely be raised, will not the people demand that the autocratic Senate shall be abolished, and a "simple republic" established?*

Numerous illustrations of the inequalities of the present senatorial system could be adduced. The State of New York, according to its population, would be entitled to about one-ninth of the representatives in this body. This State has only one-thirty-eighth part. If Delaware be entitled to two Senators, then the State of New York should have sixty-six. With the sub-division of the immense territory of the West into small States, regarded as to their population, this deformed and disproportionate representation is rapidly becoming a stupendous wrong.

* "Saint-Just was for the Republic, 'one and indivisable' and when, on the 15th of May, 1793, he spoke of that of the United States, he did so in the most disparaging terms. He did not admit that the American Republic had a republican form of government at all, or that it would last.

Anacharsis Clootz was, like Saint-Just, no admirer of the American system. Keep your unicameral legislature, said he in substance, on the 24th of April 1793, keep it, for America envies us this institution and will adopt it in turn. Frenchmen would retrograde were they to imitate the Americans, who are fast becoming disgusted with their Senate and their monarchical President. A homogeneous people like France will never admit the Anglican balance of powers, nor recognize the veto." ["America and France," by Lewis Rosenthal, 280, 281.]

Then comes another great injustice in the operation of our Senate system upon the electoral vote of the Executive. Article II. of the Constitution provides:— "Each State shall appoint, * * * * * a number of electors (of President and Vice-President) equal to the whole number of Senators and Representatives to which the State may be entitled in the Congress." Hence, large numbers of electors are now disfranchised at each Presidential election, on account of the inequalities of representation in the Senate system.* We first wrongfully confer monarchical power upon a President, in contravention of all true American and republican principles, then we augment and aggravate that injustice by taking away from the people the choice of this autocrat. The framers created a king, and were then naturally afraid to allow the people to choose him. The strongest condemnation that can be expressed in relation to this plan of government is to state what it consists of.

The Senate, during the first five years of its existence, sat behind closed doors, and little is known of its inner working. It can hardly be claimed that this procedure was democratic. But this is not the only evidence of the monarchical tendency of the Federal party in the first Senate. It was intended to reproduce the etiquette of European Courts, and to confer the title of His Highness on the citizen filling the Executive chair. William Maclay, a Senator from Pennsylvania, kept a journal of the proceedings during the first two years of the existence of this branch of the Legislature. From it we learn some curious facts.† It was proposed to put the House

---

*Another inequality is the result of our law. An elector, who votes for the successful presidential candidate in the State of New York, has ten times more political power than an elector living in the State of Delaware who votes on the same ticket. This occurs for the reason that the former has thirty-five, while the latter has but three electors.

† It has been published under the title of "Sketches of Debate in the First Senate of the United States," edited by George W. Harris.

of Representatives in the same relative position to the Senate which the Commons occupied toward the House of Lords in mediæval history. It was proposed that a Bill from the Senate to the House should be conveyed by the Secretary, but a Bill from the House to the Senate should be "carried by two members, who at the bar of the Senate should make their obeisance to the President, and thence, advancing to the Chair, make a second obeisance, and deliver the paper into the hands of the President. After having delivered the Bill, they were to make their obeisance to the President, and repeat it as they retired from the bar."

A whole day was spent in discussing the ceremonies of the inauguration of President Washington. Upon this occasion, Mr. Adams made this remarkable speech : " Gentlemen, I do not know whether the framers of the Constitution had in view the two kings of Sparta, or the two consuls of Rome when they formed it ; one to have *all* the power while he held it, and the other to be nothing. Nor do I know whether the architect who formed our room, and the wide chair in it (to hold two, I suppose), had the Constitution before him. Gentlemen, I feel great difficulty how to act. I am possessed of two separate powers—the one *in esse,* and the other *in posse.* I am *Vice-President.* In this I am nothing ; but I may be everything. But I am President also of the Senate. When the President comes into the Senate, what shall I be ? I wish, gentlemen, to think what I shall be."

At last, the day of the inauguration arrived. "This," writes Mr. Maclay, in his journal, " is a great important day. Goddess of Etiquette, assist me while I describe it ! * * * The Senate met. The President, Mr. Adams, rose in the most solemn manner. 'Gentlemen,' he said, 'I wish for the direction of the Senate. The President will, I suppose, address the Congress. How shall I behave ? How shall we receive it ? Shall it be standing or sitting ?'" A debate ensued, in which " Mr. Lee began with the House of Commons, as is usual with him, then the House of Lords, then the King, and then back again. The result of his information was that the Lords *sat*, and the Commons *stood* on the delivery of the King's speech. Mr. Izard got up and told how often he had been in the House of Parliament. He said a great deal of what he had seen there; made, however, this sagacious discovery, that the Commons stood because they had no seats to sit in on being arrived at the House of Lords. It was discovered, after some time, that the King sat too, and had his robes and crown on. The President (Adams) got up, again, and said he had been very often, indeed, at the Parliament on those occasions, but there always was such a crowd, and *ladies along*, that he could not say how it was. Mr. Carroll rose to declare that he thought it of no consequence how it was in Great Britain; they were no rule to us, and so forth." Finally, General Washington arrived. Mr. Adams was dismayed, forgot what he had to say, and stood for some time in a vacant mood. Washington, on his part, was discomposed, agitated, and embarrassed. He could scarcely read. The following day, when the minutes were read, it was discovered that the Secretary had referred to Washington's address as "His most gracious speech." These words, usually prefixed to the speech of the King, were, after debate, stricken out.

In the meanwhile, a Committee had been appointed to devise a title for the President. Mr. Maclay was informed, at one time, that "the title selected from all the potentates of the earth for our President was to have been taken from Poland, viz., Elective Majesty. What a royal escape!" The Committee, at last, reported that it would be proper to address the President as "His Highness the President of the United States of America, and Protector of their Liberties." In the debate which followed, Mr. Adams supported the monarchical view of the Constitution. "'Gentlemen,' said Mr. Adams, 'I must tell you, that it is *you* and the President that have the making of titles. Suppose,' he went on, 'the President to have the appointment of Mr. Jefferson at the Court of France. Mr. Jefferson is, by virtue of that appointment, the most illustrious, the most powerful, and what not. But the President himself must be something that includes all the dignities of the diplomatic corps and something greater still. What will the common people of foreign countries, what will the sailors and soldiers, say? George Washington, President of the United States, they will despise him.'" The whole scheme, having for its object the conferring of titles upon the President, failed. Few persons know what a strong monarchical and oligarchical element existed at the formation of our Government. Few know what a narrow escape we had from the efforts of these gentlemen who wished to confer the outward forms of royalty upon the President. The idea, however, permeates society to-day, and many ignorant persons address the President, as "His Excellency."

Mr. Conway has made a careful argument upon the subject of the United States Senate, and we desire to quote the following from his valuable work.* "It was not at all necessary, when it was determined that the States should have a distinct representation in the Congress, that they should also have a separate House. The State deputies might have sat in the same Chamber with the representatives of the people, just as the Knights of Shires do with other members in the House of Commons. The separation of them into two Houses was accepted upon the precedent of the British Parliament, and on no real grounds whatever. Of the original States, at the time of the adoption of the Constitution, two had but one Legislative Chamber each, and the Confederation had no more. When the proposition was made to divide the Congress into two branches, three States, the great State of New York among them, recorded their votes against it, and the

---

* "Republican Superstitions," by M. D. Conway.

delegation of another, Maryland, was equally divided on the subject. There seems, however, to have been very little discussion of the matter, which was quite overshadowed by the incomparable urgency of the only question—the relative power of the States and the General Government—which really was discussed in the Convention. The debates were in secret, and we have but brief notes of them; but a passage in the minutes, jotted down by one of the members, Chief Justice Yates, of New York, no doubt tells the whole story:—' May 31st, 1787. The 3rd resolve, to wit : " That the National Legislature ought to consist of two branches," was taken into consideration, and without any debate agreed to.' To this, Judge Yates adds, in brackets : ' N.B.—As a previous resolution had already been agreed to, to have a Supreme Legislature, I could not see any objection to its being in two branches.' So lightly was a step taken, which has proved to be of momentous consequence to America.

So far as any clear impression arises from the hazy annals of the earliest Parliamentary Government in England, it is that the King called upon the leading noblemen of the realm to become his guests for a time, for purposes of consultation, feasting them, meanwhile, in grand style. This was the only Parliament. To this assembly come groups of petitioners, deputations from the people; and these, in order that their requests may be presented with some kind of regularity, must needs organize their assemblies, and appoint some mouthpiece or speaker, now represented by the most silent official bearing that name. For it is in this group of deputations that we must recognize the future Commons' House, which, for a time, sat in the presence of the Parliament of Peers, until the latter thought it beneath their dignity to sit beside those of lower rank. The separation probably occurred at the time when the Commons ceased to be a mere crowd of petitioners to their lordships, and showed signs of becoming a normal element in the government. The House of Peers represented the supremacy of the aristocratic and clerical classes, of which the Crown was the head; the Commons represented the degree to which the people had managed to extort the first point, recognition of their existence, and of the simplest rights implied in that existence.

It is a notable fact that, while the founders of the American Constitution were taking up this relic of feudalism and clothing it with formidable power, the English nation was already preparing the forces which were to reduce the House of Lords to the secondary position it now occupies.

After reading the statement of the American historian, it may assist us to ponder the following from one of the ablest of recent writers on the English Constitution, Mr. Bagehot: 'The evil of two co-equal Houses of distinct natures is obvious. Each House can stop all legislation, and yet some legislation may be necessary. At this moment, we have the best instance of this which could be conceived. The Upper House of our Victorian Constitution, representing the rich wool growers, has disagreed with the Lower Assembly, and most business is suspended. But for a most curious stratagem, the machine of government would stand still. Most Constitutions have committed this blunder. The two most remarkable Republican institutions in the world commit it. In both, the American and the Swiss Constitutions, the Upper House has as much authority as the second; it could produce the maximum of impediment, the dead-lock, if it liked. If it does not do so, it is owing, not to the goodness of the legal Constitution, but to the discreetness of the members of the Chamber. In both these Constitutions, this dangerous provision is defended by a peculiar doctrine with which I have nothing to do now. It is said there must be in a Federal Government some institution, some authority, somebody possessing a veto, in which the separate States composing the Confederation are all equal. I confess this doctrine has to me no self-evidence, and it is assumed, but not proved. The State of Delaware is not equal in power or influence to the State of New York, and you cannot make it so by giving it an equal veto in an Upper Chamber. The history of such an institution is most natural. A little State will like, and must like, to see some memorial mark of its old independence preserved in the Constitution, by which that independence is extinguished. But it is one thing for an institution to be natural, another for it to be expedient. If, indeed, it be that a Federal government compels the erection of an Upper Chamber of conclusive and co-ordinate authority, it is one more in addition to the many other inherent defects of that kind of government. It may be necessary to have the blemish, but it is a blemish just as much.'

Mr. Bagehot then shows, that since the Reform Act of 1832, when the House of Lords for the last time really tried conclusions with the House of Commons, and was compelled to yield it has not even had a pretension to being an equal branch of the Government. 'The House of Lords has become a revising and suspending House. It can alter Bills; it can reject Bills, on which the House of Commons is not yet thoroughly in earnest, upon which the nation is not yet determined. Their veto is a sort of hypothetical veto. They say, We reject your Bill for this once, or these twice, or these thrice; but if you keep on sending it up, at last we won't reject it. The House has ceased to be one of latent direction, and has become one of temporary rejectors and palpable alterers.' As a revising House, the vigorous writer from whom I quote, maintains the utility of the House of Lords; but, like every other philosophical thinker of recent times, he bases this view upon certain serious defects and vices in the Constitution of the House of Commons. It is remarkable, that it is impossible to find among the political thinkers in England, a defender of the Two-House principle on theoretical grounds.

Having considered the views of the ablest defender of the

continued existence of the House of Lords, let us turn to those of one of the many distinguished advocates of the abolition of that House. I quote from Mr. Goldwin Smith, late Professor of Modern History in the University of Oxford; the article from which the extract is taken having been written while the author was visiting America and Canada, with every opportunity of studying the working of both the One-House and the Two-House forms. Professor Smith writes : 'Not by reason or theory alone, but by overwhelming experience, the House of Lords stands condemned. For three centuries, dating from the Tudor period, it was the most powerful branch of the Legislature, and for a century, at least, it had, through its nominees and dependents, the virtual control of the other branch. During the whole of that period, pressing subjects for legislation abounded, not only in the direction of political reform, but in all directions—legal, ecclesiastical, educational, sanitary, and economical. Yet, in all those centuries, who can point out a single great measure of national improvement which really emanated from the House of Lords? On the other hand, who can point out a single great reform, however urgent at the time, however signally ratified afterwards by the approbation of posterity, which the House of Lords has not thrown out, or obstructed, and, if it could do nothing more, damaged and mutilated to the utmost of its power? As a matter of course, it upheld the Rotten Boroughs, and resisted the Reform Bill, till it was overcome by the threat of a swamping creation of Peers, having first, in its wisdom, brought the nation to the verge of a civil war. As a matter of course, it resisted the progress of religious liberty, because the privileged church was an outwork of the privileged class. As a matter of course, it resisted, as a noble historian is compelled to confess, the extension of *habeas corpus*, and of personal liberty. As a matter of course, it resisted the removal of restraints on the press. As a matter of course, it resisted the introduction of the ballot. All these were measures, and movements, which threatened political privilege. But the House of Lords has also resisted common measures of humanity, such as the abolition of the Slave Trade, and the Reform of Criminal Law. Romilly's Bill for the abolition of the death punishment in cases of petty theft, was thrown out by the Lords; and among the thirty-two who voted in the majority, on this occasion, were seven bishops. On all subjects, about which popular opinion was not strongly excited, including many of the greatest importance to national progress, Reformers have abstained from moving, because they despaired of overcoming the resistance of the House of Lords. To make legislation on any important question possible, it is necessary to get a storm sufficient to terrify the Peers. *Thus, all important legislation is made violent and revolutionary, and this is your Conservative institution.*'

The most profound theoretical statement on the subject comes from Mr. John Stuart Mill, who, in his admirable 'Vindication of the French Revolution of 1848, in reply to Lord Brougham, and others,' expresses the following opinions: 'The arguments for a second Chamber, when looked at from one point of view, are of great force, being no other than the irresistible arguments for the necessity or expediency of a principle of antagonism in society; of a counterpoise somewhere to the preponderant power in the State. It seems hardly possible that there should be permanently good government, or enlightened progress, without such a counterpoise. It may, however, be maintained, with considerable appearance of reason, that the antagonism may be more beneficially placed in society itself than in the legislative organ, which gives effect to the will of society; that it should have its place in the powers which form public opinion, rather than in that whose proper function is to execute it; that, for example, in a democratic State, the desired counterbalance to the impulses and will of the comparatively uninstructed many lies in a strong and independent organization of the class, whose special business is the cultivation of knowledge, and will better embody itself in Universities than in Senates and Houses of Lords. A second Chamber, however composed, is a serious hindrance to improvement. Suppose it constituted in the manner, of all others, least calculated to render it an obstructive body. Suppose that an Assembly of (say) six hundred persons is elected by universal suffrage, and when elected divides itself, as under the French Directorial Constitution, into two bodies (say) of three hundred each. Now, whereas, if the whole body sat as one Chamber, the opposition of three hundred persons, or one-half of the representatives of the people, would be required to throw out an improvement; on the system of separate deliberation, one hundred and fifty, or one-fourth only, would suffice. Without doubt, the division into two sections, which would be a hindrance to useful changes, would be a hindrance also to hurtful ones; and the arrangement, therefore, must be regarded as beneficial by those who think a Democratic Assembly is more likely to make hurtful than useful changes. But this opinion, both historical and daily experience contradicts. There cannot be a case more in point than this very instance in France. The National Assembly was chosen in the crisis of a revolution, by suffrage, including all the laboring men of the community; the doctrines of a subversive character which were afloat were peculiarly favorable to the apparent interests of laboring men; yet the Assembly elected was essentially a Conservative body, and it is the general opinion, that the Legislature now about to be elected will be still more so. The great majority of mankind are, as a general rule, tenacious of things existing; habit and custom predominate with them, in almost all cases, over remote prospects of advantage; and, however popular may be the Constitution in the ordinary course of its working, the difficulty is not to prevent considerable changes, but to accomplish them when most essentially needful. Any systematic provision in the Constitution to render changes difficult, is therefore superfluous—it is injurious. It is true, that in the times which accompany, or immediately follow, a Revolution, this tendency of the human mind may be temporarily and partially reversed—partially, we say, for a people are as tenacious of old customs and ways of thinking, in the crisis of a revolution, as at any other time,—on all points, except those on which they had become strongly excited by a perception of evils or grievances; those, in fact, on which the revolution itself turns. On such points, indeed, there may easily arise, at those periods, an ardor of ill-considered change, and it is at such times, if ever, that the check afforded by a second, or Conservative Chamber, might be beneficial. But these are the times when the resistance of such a body is practically null. The very arguments used by the supporters of the institution to make it endurable, assume that it cannot prolong its resistance in excited times. A second Chamber which, during a revolution, should resolutely oppose itself to the branch of the Legislature more directly representing the excited state of popular feeling, would be infallibly swept away. It is the destiny of a second Chamber to become inoperative in the very cases in which its effective operation would have the best chance of producing less harm than good.'"

The above quotations from able English writers form a sufficient commentary upon the statement of the historian of the American Constitution. It will be seen that the United States has taken up, in the supposed interest of liberty, that which the best writers on political history in England, regard as an impediment to liberty.

We desire to call attention to a remarkable section of the Constitution. By Article V. the Congress, whenever two-thirds of both houses shall deem it necessary, shall propose amendments, or, on the application of the Legislature, of two-thirds of the several States, shall call a **Convention** for proposing amendments, which, in either case, shall be valid, when ratified by the legislatures of three-fourths of the several States; "and that no State, without its consent, shall be deprived of its equal suffrage in the Senate."

The ordinary provision of remedying an evil in the Constitution is attended with the greatest difficulty, but in case of any reform looking towards the establishment of proportional representation, it would, we fear, be impossible to accomplish such change in the law, for the " consent " of the State being necessary before it can be deprived of its equal suffrage in the Senate makes it requisite to obtain the consent of all the States. In speaking of the power of a great people, we should not have used the word "impossible." We must remember that it was they who created this Government, and that the creator is stronger than the creature. It may be that this people, in their onward march to a perfect nation, will devise a peaceful and lawful means of abolishing this great wrong.*

It is not within the province of this essay to do more than mention the immense reforms in the Executive that have been accomplished in most of the governments of Europe and of the world. The tendency, in all government, has been to concentrate the legislative and Executive power in the legislature, and for the legislature to execute its laws through a responsible ministry. England, whose Constitution is the model for so many of the governments of our day,

* "I know one," says Talleyrand, "who is wiser than Voltaire, and has more understanding than Napoleon himself, and all ministers whoever were, are, or will be, and this one is public opinion."—Cited by Lieber, in " Political Ethics," vol. i., 224. Again, who can prophesy when public opinion may demand the very reforms we ask for; but the day when they may be crystalized in what we call a written constitution is at a much greater distance in the future. Still, when society has actually set its heart upon the change, it will be carried out "by parliament, through parliament, or over parliament," as Mr. Macaulay said in 1832.

has brought that system to a condition nearer perfection than any of her imitators. Although France has a responsible ministry, still, the President is elected—not by the people, but by the Senate and Chamber of Deputies. The action of Gambetta, however, was the immediate cause of bringing personal government to an end in France, when he virtually said to President MacMahon: "You must either submit or resign." The ministry proposed measures to the President to which he would not subscribe. Any other ministry would have imposed the same terms. He resigned. Many of the advisers of the President urged him to seize upon the government. This course would have caused a revolution. He yielded, and personal government was at an end in the French Republic.

The controlling body in the Austro-Hungarian government is the delegations, and the ministers are responsible for the discharge of their official functions to the delegations.

According to the Belgian Constitution, no act of the king can have effect unless countersigned by one of his ministers, who thus becomes responsible for it. The law-making power is vested in the Chamber of Representatives and the Senate, the members of each being elected by the people.

In Denmark, the right of making laws is in the Diet; the ministers are individually and collectively responsible for their acts, and, in case of impeachment and being found guilty, cannot be pardoned without the consent of the Folkething or Lower House of Parliament.

The present Constitution of Greece vests the legislative power in a single chamber of Representatives, called the Boule, elections to which are by manhood suffrage; the executive is vested in a king with responsible ministers.

In Italy, the executive power belongs to the sovereign, but is exercised through responsible ministers. The Constitution of the Netherlands vests the executive authority in the sovereign, exercised by a responsible Council of ministers.

They attend meetings of both houses. In Portugal, the executive authority vests, under the sovereign, in a responsible Cabinet.

In Russia, as in the United States, there is no ministry responsible to any law-making power, except to the Emperor. The administration of the government is entrusted to four great boards centering in the private Cabinet of the Emperor.

In Spain, the law-making power is the "Cortes with the king." There is a responsible ministry. The king cannot marry except with the approval of the Cortes. In Sweden, the fountain of law is the Diet; and the Council of State is responsible for all acts of government. In Norway, there is no absolute royal veto, and the king exercises his exercises his authority through ministers.

The Republic of Switzerland vests the Supreme legislative and executive authority in a Parliament of two Chambers. The chief executive authority is deputed to a Bundesrath or Federal Council, elected for three years by the Federal Assembly. The President and Vice-President of the Federal Council are the first magistrates of the republic and hold office for one year.

Brazil is an empire with a responsible ministry, and Mexico is a federative republic.* Most of the Constitutions of the South American Governments are patterned after that of the United States. The frequent occurrence of *emeutes* and revolutions that characterizes the history of those so-called republics, does not particularly recommend their forms of government. The universal criticism passed upon the South American States is that the country is one of the finest in the world, but that the people have poor governments; implying that the laws provoke intrigue, corruption, conflict, and revolution.

The Republic of Hayti has a Constitution very much like

---

* See Martin's "Statesman's Year-book."

that of the United States. The President is elected for four years. The term of the incumbent, Boisrond Canal, was some years ago cut short by an insurrection, (July 20, 1879). * Notwithstanding the deplorable condition of the South American Republics, there have been many important reforms wrought out in European Governments, which the American people cannot in reason disregard. The prevailing form in Europe is that of the responsible ministry, which is much preferable to the presidential system. Our Constitution has substantially survived, while a complete organic change has taken place in others. It is true that we have stricken slavery from the fundamental law and established manhood suffrage; but the structure of the system remains undisturbed. The dominant sentiment with us seems to be that our government is perfect, and that we need not heed the warnings of the scientific specialists, who laboriously work out, often to little purpose, many of the vexed questions that enter into the consideration of human affairs. This is wrong. Our people ought to ask themselves, not what the system is, but what it ought to be.

We hold that the people are destined to rise to a higher plane in their system of government, above the traditions of the past into a living present, where the ancient compromises and bargains, however useful they were at the time of their adoption, will be abrogated and set aside. We believe that this people need a government in which they will be fairly and equally represented in a central and national legislature.†

Never before in the history of the world have the masses possessed such a favorable environment for the development of the highest and purest forms of citizenship, as exists at the present day. Those who advocate the rights and powers

---

* It would take up too much of our space even to sketch the revolutions that have taken place in this part of the world since the period referred to.

† This system should embody a plan of minority representation somewhat like that proposed by Mr. Mill and Mr. Hare.

of the people are no longer required to prove that the rule of the " many " is a better form of government than that of the " one " or the " few."

One of the potent forces that operates for the benefit of mankind is popular education. It is the foundation-stone upon which this whole superstructure of republican government rests. It is only through the diffusion of education that the people will be able to form correct opinions upon the financial, governmental, economical, and even ethical questions, that must necessarily be submitted to them for their decision. All grades of the people must associate in the common schools, in order to acquire common ideas and aspirations, and get rid of the heart-burnings of caste. A healthful community of political thought is then created by the dissemination of the book and the newspaper. The art of printing will thus prevent a monopoly of knowledge and remove mystery from statesmanship.

All issues will be understood and controlled by the people, who will require the temporary power-holder to respect their rights and opinions in matters of legislation, and finally to render account of his stewardship before his electors.

In addition to these considerations we must remember the application of steam to locomotion, and of electricity to the transmission of messages, which makes it possible for the poor not only to migrate from, but to communicate with, all parts of the world. Thus the reforms of one country are carried into the confines of others, and evolution in government goes on toward the realization of the dream of the internationalists—a universal brotherhood of mankind.

There is, unquestionably, a great diversity of interests, climate, race, and tradition in this country, all tending to postpone to a distant period the time when a people living together in the same geographical limits shall be possessed of common sympathies, common laws, of a similarity of sentiment, of pride, and of humiliation. Be it remembered always, that the evidence of the supreme power does not irrevocably lie in the written statute, but is manifested as well in the decisions of the courts, the acts of public officers, the pages of literature, and those of the historian. War is but force, and decides nothing. If we desire to trace the progress of events, we must look to the thoughts and acts of the masses. War is an eruption, history a growth.*

We urge a "government of the people, by the people, and for the people," that the masses shall be equally represented in one central body by the temporary power-holders or trustees, who shall pass upon the routine of legislation, and that all matters of importance shall be submitted to the will of the nation. It is true that this plan places great power in the hands of the representatives, but, at the same time, it will be perceived, that the light of the intelligence and will of the masses will "beat upon" them. They will understand that a violation of the principle that the sovereignty inheres in the collective whole is simply revolution. They will understand that upon their honest administration of government depends their continuance in power.

The next consideration will be, how this central body of power-holders shall execute the law, and, at the same time, provide for the submission of all issues to the will of the nation.

* "Let us remember, then, in the first place, that political institutions (however the proposition may at times be ignored) are the work of men—owe their origin and their whole existence to human will. Men did not wake on a summer morning and find them sprung up. . . . . In every stage of their existence they are made what they are by human voluntary agency."—[" Considerations on Representative Government," by John Stuart Mill, 12.]

CHAPTER XXVII.

CONCLUSION.

THE Government created by the Articles of Confederation consisted of one representative body. In that body were united all the powers,—executive, legislative, and judicial. The Members of Congress were annually chosen by the States, which might recall their delegates at any period of the year. The United States, in Congress assembled, had authority to appoint a committee, to sit in the recess of Congress, to be denominated "a Committee of the States," and to consist of one delegate from each State; to appoint such other committees and civil officers as might be necessary for managing the general affairs of the United States, under their direction, and to designate one of their number to preside, provided that no person be allowed to serve in the office of president* more than one year in any term of three years.† Herein do we find the germ of true representative government. "The Executive authority of Congress was exercised through departments accountable to them." We say, unhesitatingly, that in so far as the Executive authority is concerned, the Articles were far superior to the Constitution of the United States, under which we live to-day, and better calculated to ensure peace, tranquillity, liberty, and good government.‡

---

* That is, as Chairman of the Committee.
† Sec. 5, Art. IX., Articles of Confederation.
‡ Still, we must admit, that the Constitution was in most other respects an advance; even according to the State Sovereignty theory, a more perfect union was established. According to the Story theory, a nation was formed. The great weakness in the Constitution is the existence of the Presidency, Senate, and States.

There was no President or Senate provided for in our early law, and we look in vain for those monocratic forms which were afterwards adopted. But in their place we do find a simple, plain, direct, and logical provision, by which the committee departments were constituted for the enforcement of the will of Congress. The articles were an advance in the march to perfection of government. The Constitution, in many particulars, was a turning back of the wheels of progress. We have pointed out the evils and dangers of the present form of government. The living, practical question is: What system should be proposed to reform the fundamental law?

Our conclusion is, that the Presidency should be abolished, and the following amendments to the Constitution be adopted: The supreme power of legislating and executing all laws of the United States shall be vested in Congress,* which body shall be the final judge of its own powers, subject, nevertheless, to the right of the Executive Council, hereinafter provided for, at any time they shall elect, to dissolve Congress upon an issue framed and appeal to the people.† Congress shall appoint the following officers, who shall execute, under the direction and control of

---

* Consisting of one body.

† "The Virginia plan confided the choice of the Executive to the National Legislature."—[Bancroft's "History of the Formation of the Constitution of the United States," Vol. I., 165, 166.]

"'I,' replied Sherman, 'am for its appointment (the Executive) by the National Legislature, and for making it absolutely dependent on that body whose will it is to execute. An independence of the Executive of the Supreme Legislature is the very essence of tyranny.'"—[Gilpin, 763-779; Elliot, 140-149.]

"In the Philadelphia Convention, as well as in the Ratification Convention, it was strongly urged that the Executive power should be confided to a board, because the history of all times and nations taught to what dangers liberty is exposed, when too much power is placed in the hands of one man." . . . . [Von Holst, "Political History," Vol. II., 73.]

"The Congressional system, in fact, insures the business of legislation shall be done by an experienced committee, composed of the best qualified men in the country, and by men, moreover, acting under a sense of direct responsibility to

Congress, all laws of the United States. (1) Secretary of State. (2) Secretary of the Treasury. (3) Secretary of War. (4) Secretary of the Navy. (5) Secretary of the Interior. (6) Attorney-General and Postmaster-General. Each of the above officers shall be at the head of his respective department, and shall prescribe regulations not inconsistent with law. Each and all of the said officers shall be subject to removal from office at the pleasure of Congress, except as hereinafter provided. Each and all members of council may resign. The Secretary of State shall be the chairman of said council, and shall have authority to convene it, at any time he may elect; provided, however, that upon his refusal or neglect to do so, then, upon a request of a majority of said officers, it shall be the duty of the chairman, or other member named, to convene the said council for the transaction of any business that may come before it.

At all meetings of the Council for mutual instruction, counsel or advice, the proceedings shall be secret. It is provided, nevertheless, that after the council shall have been defeated in Congress, and the dissolution of that body be determined upon, then all motions, decisions, and speeches made, or proceedings had, shall be public.

The member of the Executive Council shall be entitled to seats in Congress, have the right to debate, and also power to initiate legislation. Each and all of them shall be subject to be called before Congress, at any time, to answer

the country for what they do, and under a feeling that their retention of office depends upon how they do it."—[Tibbit's " Reform in Federal Executive," 52.]

" On the one hand, it is needful that the men who have to carry out the will of the majority, as expressed through the Legislature, should be removable at pleasure, so that there may be maintained the needful subordination of their policy to public opinion. On the other hand, it is needful that displacement of them should leave intact all that part of the Executive organization required for current administrative purposes. . . . . . Such changes in the Executive agency as are needful to harmonize its actions with public opinion, will be, as at present among ourselves, changes of ministries."—[Herbert Spencer's " Political Institutions," 653-654.]

any question, or to give any information desired. Every member shall be responsible for all acts committed by him. When Congress is not in session, the Executive Council shall perform every act necessary to execute the laws of Congress, and to carry on the affairs of Government. At any time during recess of Congress, any member thereof may communicate with the Secretary of State requesting him to convene Congress, which request shall be published, and whenever the requests of one-half of said members shall be thus received, the said Secretary of State shall immediately cause proclamation to be made calling Congress together. The judicial power of the United States shall be confined and limited to defining, expounding, interpreting and explaining the laws and intent of Congress. There shall be thorough and complete laws regulating the civil service.* It is a remarkable and almost startling coincidence that while these pages were under consideration, President Garfield was stricken down and for months rendered absolutely incapable of performing an administrative act. During this time a Council—and an irresponsible one at that—conducted the Government. It seldom happens that a reform of such importance as proposed herein, should have actually gone into practical operation while it was being advocated. Inexorable necessity demanded it, and the Council established itself. In effect, we have already twice lived under a Council Government, first in the days of the Articles of Confederation, and second, during the Garfield administration. These are historical facts. The plan we have briefly sketched would concentrate the Supreme power in the people—the Legislature being the temporary trustee—and thus change that great political puzzle of three co-ordinate powers, the constitutional boundaries and limitations of which no one has ever been successful in clearly defining. The Legislature, in which the people

* A statement of the working of the Executive power in an essay of this character must necessarily be general.

are equally **represented, is the** natural depositary of political power. Finally, **it is** proposed to provide for an immediate appeal **to** the people, whenever the Government **becomes** divided upon any important measure. **If a certain policy of** the Council meets with the disapproval **of the Legislature,** then the Council must either resign or appeal to the people. **If it submit, or** be defeated, **a new Council would then be appointed.** This is the principle **of responsible Council Government.** It is the essence of the **representative plan.** In its essential properties, it **would be the same as the** English **Cabinet** system. All discussion of **party platforms** would **be** openly conducted. **The people would take** an interest in the issues, and **would** become educated to their varying forms. They would **vote** upon issues, not for men. Legislation would **be in the** interest of the people, and party trickery be deprived of **the** food it now feeds upon. The lobby, **no** longer supported **by** intrigue and corruption, would pass out of existence. **Patriotic, national statesmen,** having qualifications to **serve the best interests of the whole** people, would take **the place of the** incompetent trading politician in **the council** halls **of the nation.** Above all, we would have **a nation instead of a confederative monarchy.**

The classification of the various departments would remain substantially unchanged. At **the** same time, there would be an officer responsible for the management of his respective department; and, what **is so** much **to be desired,** responsible directly to the law-making **power.** The heads of the departments appointed by Congress **would** be eminent men, experienced in **public life—the** foremost **men** of the nation, though they might **not** be specialists in their particular departments. Thus it becomes **necessary that** the business of the Government should **rest** upon professional and skilled service, in which **even the chief of the department** should **not have the** unqualified **power of removal, which** should only be for cause and after hearing. By vesting in

Congress the **power of removal of the chiefs of** department and members **of the Executive Council, we** should have, in effect, an **Executive not appointed for any** definite period, irrespective of **the question of fitness for** office, **but** one **removable at the proper time, namely, when, for any** reason the members thereof **failed properly to perform the** duties imposed upon them by law. **It is likewise** apparent, **that any one of this council could be removed at any** time, when, personally, **he was found wanting in any of the** requirements of Congress. **In this respect the Executive** would be different **from the Cabinet system of England, which** causes the resignation **of the entire cabinet** upon **the defeat of** any of **its measures, though the measure may only affect one** of its **branches of government. What reason can be assigned** for the **removal of the whole** Executive **of the nation,** because, **for example, the Secretary of the** Interior **fails** to carry **out the will of Congress in** some particular? There seems **to be little logical connection between** the cause and the effect. **At the same time, it may be observed, that** the proposed **plan places it in the power** of the remaining members **of the** Council to refuse **to submit to the** removal of any one of its number, **and to appeal to the people.** This course would seem **both wise** and salutary.

With the adoption of **our** plan, **the Council** would, in fact, be independent of Congress, to **the extent** of being empowered **to submit any or** all issues to the people. The Council **has the power of** calling itself together; except when summoned **for the** special purpose of deliberation, the debates and proceedings **shall be** public. **It is apparent that this should** be so, **in order that** the people shall be assisted **in arriving at the** real **point in dispute.** The discussions would operate as a pleading in which the whole matter in controversy **would be set forth. The** people would be educated in the affairs of the **Government. All** would know that the arguments **meant the** overthrow or support **of the party** in power. When elections took place the result would express the thoughts and wishes of the people. This plan provides for an open and fairly conducted government, in which the will of the people would be law. Furthermore, the people would be informed as to the issues, and there would be some object and reason in the pursuit of the study of the affairs of government. In fine, it would be a government founded upon reason and right, not upon fictitious and obsolete refinements, which only a metaphysician could possibly take delight in contemplating.

Objection has been raised against any encroachments upon the Executive power of the United States. It is thought that there must be a strong Executive for the purpose of having a single will to command the army and navy. This theory is another survival of the past, which when carefully examined, is found to be erroneous. It is true that even in a republic there must be that force which is truly monarchical in its very elements, to wit: the army and navy. These organizations are the embodiment of despotism. The question has ever been raised, how this characteristic of absolutism can enter into the laws of a republican government, and not necessarily destroy it. This problem has been solved in England. The Queen no more commands the military forces of the nation than an inhabitant of China. This prerogative, like all others, is not exercised. War is made by the advice of a responsible minister. He can always be reached in the event of his not conducting or not concluding a war to the satisfaction of the representatives of the people. Of course it has been thought that the power of Congress to interfere with a war minister would render such officer inefficient. It is our judgment that the tendency is in the other direction, and that a minister, once having taken a step, would, as a matter of national pride, be sustained, at any rate until there was some flagrant mistake or blunder.

This system, to which we have referred in detail in another part of this essay, is substantially the same which we recommend for adoption here. The Secretary of War would be supreme, even in regard to the Navy Department, as soon as war was declared. The wisdom of this provision every one must acknowledge. He would be accountable only to Congress, thus subordinating the military to the civil government.

Under the present system, the liberties of our country will ever continue to be threatened by the hand of some President-King; but the suggested plan makes it impossible for the Secretary of War to operate beyond the constitutional restraint and responsibility. The mode of government which preserves the efficiency of the absolute will of a sovereign commander in declaring, conducting, and concluding war, and at the same time subordinates that will to the Legislature, should command our admiration.

In the absence of Congress, the President now virtually carries on the Government, but, as proposed, the different chiefs of departments would perform that service, acting together for mutual support, if necessary. Still they are powerless to do any despotic act, for the members of Congress can compel the convening of that body whenever they so desire.

One of the most important and vital suggestions herein made, is to limit the judicial power of the United States in such manner that the Supreme Court shall not have the sovereign power conferred on it, of finally determining the meaning of our fundamental law, hitherto so unyielding and inflexible, but shall merely expound and interpret the laws of Congress. A large portion of the time of our Courts, both National and State, is now occupied in determining whether the representatives of the people have the power to make laws. It is not necessary to enter into a long dissertation to prove that the Supreme powers conferred upon this branch of our Government are monarchical and unrepresentative. The Legislature of a nation should be a law unto itself, and no

Court should have the power of vetoing its enactments. Any Constitution that attempts to do this is but an invention for the continuance of a wrong. The workings of this sovereign judicial power have been almost universally against the liberties of the people, and an arrest of popular progress. "The doctrine that the Supreme Court has, under the Constitution, power to determine the political powers of the General Government and the States, or that it can, in other words, settle, by its opinion as a Court, the location of sovereign power, has been always more or less extensively asserted from the first establishment of the Government under the Constitution. * * * There is no question as to the finality of the judgment of the Supreme Court in each case coming within its jurisdiction, as defined in the Constitution; nor any question whether such a judgment is to be carried into execution by the whole force of the Government, civil and military, or that it can be resisted by citizens, or by a State or States only at their peril. The decisions of the Court are recognized to be the final arbitrament as to all private rights and obligations in cases at law, however dependent upon political doctrine."*

There is a class of thinkers that always meet any suggestion of progress in the laws with the assertion that the proposition is against the provisions of the Constitution. It is urged that all our thoughts must be shaped and controlled by the forms given us by our ancestors. To determine the right or wrong of a political question or issue, we must turn only

---

* "Theory of our National Existence," by J. C. Hurd, 350-351. Chisholm vs. Georgia, 2 Dallas, 470. Texas vs. White, 7 Wall. 724. Cooley "Constitutional Limitations," 5. Pomeroy "Constitutional Law," 3rd Ed., sec. 762. The Supreme Court also held legislative acts of the Confederate Government null and void. Mr. Hurd cites a long list of cases in his "Theory of our National Existence," 5. The opinions of various framers for and against the creation of the Judiciary as a co-ordinate branch of the Government, may be found set forth in Gilpin, 1322-1333. Elliot, iii. 387, 388, 428, 429. Bancroft "Formation of the Constitution," Vol. ii. 198, 199, 329.

to the pages of the established law; but agreeing as to its meaning, we are concluded and bound forever. Is this view just? Is it right? Is it American? We say no. Why should one generation have the right to bind a succeeding one? Are not the needs of society ever changing, ever developing into something higher and better? Has any one the temerity to assert that the laws and principles that control the vexed questions of capital and labor, of finance, of society, of crime, of pauperism, of commerce, of taxation, of tariff, of representation, and all the multiplicity of mooted considerations that enter into and constitute government itself, are not better understood and determined to-day than they were at the time when the framers met to compromise and patch up the then existing issues and interests?

Slavery has been abolished in most parts of the world, and aristocracy itself has now but few immunities, not to speak of privileges. The world has moved on to something better, and is still advancing in the march of amelioration in the condition of mankind. The abstract principles that come at last to be formulated by the competent, take more crystalized form in the new governments of the earth. The doctrine, that because one generation enters into compromises, by which it surrenders rights which should be regarded as inalienable, all future generations are hence concluded by that act, has, we imagine, but few supporters. To advocate the right of one generation to barter the rights of succeeding ones, would be attempting to uphold as absurd a dogma as the priestly postulate of Original Sin.* "The venerable

* " But it is not enough that a Constitution provide a mode for effecting its own amendments ; it is necessary that there should be developed a political conscience, impelling to make amendments in the written Constitution, when such as are really important have evolved themselves in the Constitution as a fact. Why embarrass the Courts and fly in the face of destiny by refusing to recognize accomplished facts ? . . . If political self-abnegation cannot, under written constitutions, be developed to the extent indicated, it may be laid down as certain that no commonwealth governed by such a Constitution can long survive."—[" The Constitutional Convention," by Jameson, sec. 83.]

founders believed, or rather imagined they believed, that they had got rid of the relation of sovereign and subject for themselves and for us; that abstract justice was quite enough to serve all their political uses and ours, and that the eternal antagonisms, law and consent, were thereafter to form a state to be like a perpetual motion machine, going on forever, without expenditure of force, without the effort of personal will supported by force; and that writing, fairly engrossed on parchment, tagged with a lump of seal-wax, and called 'The Constitution,' would govern, in spite of their wills, those by whose wills it was to continue as law. * * * * * * *
If we recognize this utter ignorance on the part of the people then living, as to the persons from whom the Constitution could derive its authority, and yet hold that there is *now* a theory which had become so true before 1861, that it required only a huge civil war to manifest it, by ending in favor of the Government, we must attribute to the written Constitution itself the faculty of determining who were its progenitors, the faculty of making a nation or people, and compelling States to be States by its own inherent, though long-hidden force—the fetish Constitution. * * *
As a fact, they left it (the Constitution), for us, whether we may wish it should have been otherwise or not, for, as Mr. Lincoln once said, 'We cannot escape history.' They left it, however, for us only as far as they could. They lived and had their day; and we live and have our day, as those who come after us will have theirs." * Finally, let not the people of this country lose sight of the fact, that the Constitution provides for its amendment. Can there be any doubt that we may so amend, that the original provisions of

---

* See, for illustration, the opinions of the several justices of the Supreme Court. Chief Justice Jay, Justices Iredell, Wilson, Blair, and Cushing in Chisholm *vs.* Georgia, 2 Dallas, 419 (1793), especially those of Judge Wilson and the Chief Justice, as a specimen of what was then, at least, held eloquence and sound political philosophy."—[Hurd's Note, 298. Hurd's Theory, 298, 299. Hurd's Theory, 319.]

the instrument shall be completely abrogated? If that proposition be true, then let us look at the whole subject as men endowed with a knowledge of political science, not as mere constitutional commentators.

Let us boldly advance and advocate what we believe to be right. Since the inauguration of Andrew Jackson, there has existed a political issue, of a greater or less extent, between the people on the one hand and the Executive on the other. At times this conflict has spent its force in oratorical display; at others, the leaders of the factions appeared to be organizing civil war. Congress debated: the President acted. If the American people are successful in choosing a President, they have no practical means of guarding against his exercise of monarchical power. Had the South not been crippled by the rebellion, which had then terminated, it would have made war rather than have acknowledged President Hayes as justly and constitutionally elected.

The two salient results flowing from the practical operation of our Constitution are these: First, the elevation to the Presidential dignity of the most available man, without regard to personal fitness for office; and second, the investiture of the man with regal powers. John Quincy Adams and James A. Garfield were the only Presidents who had had any considerable experience as legislators. There were seven whose reputations were military. While such legislators and orators as Clay, Webster, Douglas, and Seward, were defeated, military men such as Washington, Jackson, Harrison, Taylor, Pierce, Grant, and Hayes, were successful in the race for Presidential honors. In fact, not one great orator has ever been elevated to the Executive chair, if we except General Garfield. The promotion of a statesman in this country practically ends with service in the legislative branch.

Notwithstanding the great powers conferred upon our Presidents, a strange manifestation of political lethargy is seen to take place under certain circumstances. The President is **forced to** abstain from action, while the good of the public service demands that it should be taken. For a considerable time prior to the official death of the President, he is entreated not to take any step lest he offend the incoming one, particularly if the Opposition have elected their candidate. In this latter event any important proceeding taken by the party in power would be considered an usurpation. This interregnum extends generally from **the time of** the election **of** a President to his **inauguration.** Grant complied with the request made of **him, not to respond to the** requisitions of States. Everything was left to Hayes. Certainly, appeals were made to the Executive in a constitutional way. To take notice of these requisitions, in the opinion of the politicians, would be to derange the plans of the newly elected President. **Very true,** Hayes was not the President, but he had been elected. He was soon to **come** into power. **All** eyes **were** centred upon him, while the actual Executive yielded **to** the **pressure** brought to bear by those who make politics a trade.

While the people of the United States have **a** *quasi* republican form of government, they are retarded in their political advancement by a senatorial **as** well as by **a** Presidential system; while they have no established church to support, church property is not taxed, religious laws deface the statute-books, and most of the State Constitutions have religious preambles **in direct** violation of the spirit of the **United States Constitution;** while they have no nobility, there **is a** strong tendency **towards** moneyed aristocracy; while **they** have laws the working of which distributes **the** title of land, and induces landowners to **cultivate and** improve their possessions, there are immense **grants of** land made to the subsidized corporations of the country; while **they have** universal suffrage, the closed or **secret** ballot opens **the door** to stupendous frauds, and, in many instances, places the political trickster in **a position to defeat the** voice of the people, **as in** the South, where four millions of blacks are virtually denied the right to exercise the privilege of voting at all. The various defects in our general system of laws must be remedied without delay, or they will multiply and develop as the population and wealth of the country increase. For example, the greater the number of small States that are created, the more extensive will be the disfranchisement of the people on the basis of representation, and the greater will be the inequalities growing out of the mode of choosing the President.

The grand process of evolution in government has always been going on, and will continue, until we reach that perfection so devoutly to be wished. Regard the United States from the point of view of its early provincial, charter, and colonial governments; State governments; the government of the confederation, and the final settlement under the present Constitution, and you have proof of this statement. The continuity in this development was only twice disturbed; first, by the revolution against Great Britain, and second, by our civil war. In these various transformations, the changes were almost imperceptible, if we except the emancipation of the slaves, and the establishment of political equality,—results which were hastened by the appeal of the South to arms. Still, we are far distant from any condition of perfection. The States should be stripped of their power to legislate upon the domestic relations, which are so entangled by the multiplicity of the laws of divorce that there exists no particular certainty either as to legitimacy of birth or legality of titles to land.*

The States pass their own laws on all subjects of commercial law, and their separate Courts interpret the same. The Courts are continually called upon to decide numerous

---

* "By these operations," Jefferson said, "new channels of communication will be opened between the States; the lines of separation will disappear; their interests will be identified, and their union cemented by new and indissoluble ties."—[Jefferson, by Morse, 294.]

issues, arising out of our complicated inter-State relations. The following are a few of the mooted questions: The correlation of government; citizenship and allegiance; suability of States; inter-State right of suit, equity jurisdiction and practice; law of contracts; proof of records; insolvent discharge by State Courts; legal status of persons; commerce; marriage and divorce, and inter-State validity thereof. The confusion which follows the natural conflict of these laws and authorities acts as a tax on the people. The separate State governments, existing under the General Government, have been the prolific source of sectional strife, dissension, and civil war.

The dangers and evils of personal government exist. The law fosters and protects a disguised monarchy. The question is, whether the common sense of the masses will give timely recognition to these facts. The reform that we recommend should be initiated and perfected by the people. Universal suffrage empowers the people to make the needful changes. For the reasons specifically stated in the preceding pages, the nation should demand that the Executive shall be responsive to the will of the people, that it shall be vigorous enough to submit political issues to the popular voice, and, at the same time, sufficiently yielding to conform to the direction and authority of Congress; not so strong as to have it in its power to overthrow liberty, nor too weak to enforce the law; efficient to preserve peace and able to promote reform.

THE END.

INDEX.

A.

Absolutism, approached, **147**.
Adams, John, 26, 75, 11, (*note*). Administration of, 64. Number of removals by, 74. Speech of, 285, 287. Jefferson's opinion of, 244, 245.
Adams, John Quincy, 312. His opinion of Tyler, 149, (*note*). Memoirs of, 39. Number of removals by, 74.
Adolphus, **Gustavus, the Diet drilled by**, 190.
Alaska, purchase of, 249.
Alexander of Russia, 213.
Alien and Sedition Acts, the, **245, 250**, 251.
Almon, Register of, 264, (*note*.)
America, effete ideas in, 15.
American and English systems compared, 37. Archives, 11. Colonies, independence of, 263. Liberty, impending danger to, 102. People, decision **of**, 96. Revolution, 266. Revolution in England, effect of, 264. System, present working of, 136.
Americans, pay too **much attention to** names, 39.
Ames, Fisher, 248.
Amos, Sheldon, (*note*), **237**.
Anabaptists, 258.
Anderson, Major, **surrender** of, 164.
Anglo-Saxon, spirit **of. 11**.
Anne, Queen, as to veto power, 84.
Appleton, William, 156.
Appointment and removal, power **of**, 150.

Aristocracy, moneyed, tendency toward, 313.
Army and Navy, 307.
Army Appropriation Bill, 92.
Arthur, C. A., 32, 37, (*note*) 40, 41. Absence from Washington of, 219. Forbearance to act, 215. Message to Congress of, 217, 218, 270, 272, (*note*). Position of predecessor abandoned by, 218.
Augustus, Empire of, 86.
Austro-Hungarian, government of, 296.

B.

Bagehot, Walter, 268 ,(*note*), 113, 260, (*note*). Two houses discussed by, 289, 290.
Baker, of Indiana, 98.
Ballot, views of, 225.
Bancroft, 310, 264, 302, (*note*), 64, 35, 195.
Banks, Nathaniel P., Speaker of House, 156. Arrest of Board of Police by, 166.
Bartley, **T. W**., resolutions submitted to Congress by, 227, **230**.
Bates, Attorney-General, cases quoted by, (*note*), 173. Opinion upon writ of *habeas corpus* by, 169, 170.
Bathurst, war directed by, 58.
Bayard, Senator, 40. Remarks upon impeachment by, 107. Supports Edmund's bill, 32.
Beck, Senator, urges that secretaries report in person to Congress, 115.

318   INDEX.

Bedford, Gunning, 36. As to term of office of President, 34. Triennial elections advocated by, 194.
Belgium, government of, 296.
Bentham, 272.
Bill of Rights, provisions of, 56.
Binney, Horace, work on Habeas Corpus by, 173.
Black, Judge, opinion of President Grant by, (*note*), 188, 193.
Black, Chauncey F., essay by, 212.
Blackburn, remarks upon President Hayes, 95.
Blackstone, Sir William, as to English Constitution, 111. Opinions of, 255.
Blaine, James G., 40.
Blair, Justice, 311, (*note*).
Blanc, 272.
Blount, William, impeachment of, 140.
Bollman and Swartwout, 169.
Bourbon, house of, 13.
Bracton, H., 18.
Bradlaugh, 272.
Brazil, government of, 297.
Brearly, David, as to electors, 25. Obliteration of State lines urged by, 282.
Breckenridge, Jefferson's letter to, 247.
British Constitution, present workings of, 37, 262. Ancient theories of embodied in U S. Constitution, 84.
Brittish Ministry, 37.
Brown, John, invasion of Virginia by, 158, 159.
Brownson, O. A., 11 (*note*), 280.
Brougham, Lord, (*note*), 267.
Brutus, 162.
Buchanan, James, 39, 101. Acted on side of slavery, 151. Administration of, 156, 161, 155. Allowed property of United States to be seized, 160. Elected President, 156. Extraordinary acts of, 156. Numbers of vetoes by, 85.
Buena Vista, 154.
Burdell, Sir Francis, reform bills of, 277.
Burgh, Disquisitions of, 256 (*note*).
Burk, 264, 267.
Burlingame, Anson, 156.
Burnside, Senator, 175. Army bill of, 54.
Burr, Aaron, 65, (*note*). Charges against, 166. Conspiracy of, 167, 168. Contested election of, 26.

Butler, Benj. F., 40, 41. As to impeachment, 108. Protest against executive power by, 240.

C.

Cabinet, an official household, 20, Government of, 262. has no separate entity, 110. Irresponsibility in United States of, 113, 110. Legislature creates, 274.
Cabot, George, 248.
Cadwallader, General, refusal to obey writ of *Habeas Corpus*, by, 166.
Cæsar, fate of, 213. President Grant, compared with, 188, 190.
Calhoun, J. C., debate of, 155. Proposal of dual executive by, 226. Speech upon presidents protest, 143, 144. Theory of government by, 281. Works of, (*note*), 74.
Canal, Boisrond, 298.
Capital and Labor questions of, 310.
Carlisle, 47.
Carroll, speech of, 286.
Castlereagh, war directed by, 58.
Catiline, 240.
Caucus, a body of irresponsible men, 125. National, 37, 41. Speech on by Sumner, 121, 128.
Chamberlain, Gov., 199, not protected, 123.
Chamberlin, J. E., 125, (*note*). Opinion of Harrison by, 148, (*note*). Remarks of upon caucus, 128 (*note*).
Chapultepec, 154.
Charles I., 256.
Charles II., 237, (*note*). Guards of anti-constitutional, 56. Reign of, 254.
Charles X., 39
Chase, Samuel, impeachment of, 104.
Chattam, Lord, guided war operations, 58.
Chili and Peru, 218.
Chisholm, Exr. V. State of Georgia, 280.
Church, disestablishment of, 277.
Church of England, 260.
Cicero, 162.
Civil War threatened, 28.
Civil Service, of the old governments, 76.
Clay, Henry, 38, 39, 312. Author of Missouri Compromise, 155. As to

INDEX. 319

treaty making power, 68, 69, 70, (*note*). Claimed that Congress should continue the departments, 115. Hope for presidency lost, 150. Letters of condolence to, 129. Opinion of President Jackson, 77, 137- Private (*note*) correspondence of. 74. Resolution as to dismissal of Duane, 138.
Clingman, Thos. L., evidence of the treason of Buchanan, 156, 158.
Clootz, Anacharsis, 283, (*note*.)
Coahula, Province of, 151.
Coke, Lord, his opinion as to pardons, 63.
Commander-in-Chief, kingly powers of, 44.
Commission, Electoral, 23.
Commissions, Military, 181.
Commons, House of, 37. Has control of army, 60.
Confederate soldiers claiming seats in Congress, 80.
Confederate States, constitution of, 132, 133. Remarks upon, 131.
Confederation, Articles of, 301, 282.
Confiscation Acts, 208.
Conger, 98.
Congress, Convening of, 304. Debate in as to powers of President, 46. Denunciation by President Johnson of, 185. Dissolution of, 302. In conflict with Tyler, 149. Powers of, 101, 102. Refusal by President to convene, 181.
Conkling, Alfred, recital of President Johnson's conduct by, (*note*) 185, 187, (*note*) 182.
Connor, Commodore, instructions given to, by President, 152.
Constantine, Reign of, 86.
Constitution, Antagonisms of, 102. As to electors of President, 25. As to succession defeat of, 214. Amendment of, 294, 295, 270. Compromises of, 282. Co-ordinate powers of, 11. Different interpretations of, 269. Does not provide for Cabinet, 110. Formally proposed, 263. Impeachment, 106, 107. Interpretation of, by Southern people, 132. Its plan to elect president fallen into disuse, 126. Overleaping barriers of, 205, 206. Provides that no person holding office shall be member of Congress,

117. Provides that President shall give information, 119. As to electoral vote, 284. As to militia, 49, 50. Relics of feudalism in, 284. To be supported as President understands it, 139. Theories concerning the, 311. Upper House, 289.
Consuls of Rome, 15, 16.
Convention, Federal, 30. National Republican, of 1881, 209.
Conway, M. D., 12, 31, 68, 287, (*note*). Recital of President Johnson's usurpation by, 185. Remarks of upon one-man power, 131.
Cooley, Thomas W., 31, 309, (*note*).
Council, Executive rights of members of, 303. Members of, 303. Responsibility of, 305. Responsibility of members of, 304.
Cox, S. S., Question to President Garfield by, 205, 206.
Crimean campaign, badly managed, 57.
Cromwell, 240.
Crown, Personal government of, 257. Powers of, exercised through ministers, 57.
Curtis, G. T., 22. Life of President Buchanan, by, 161.
Cushing, Justice, (*note*), 311. Opinion of, 47.

D.

Davis, Jefferson, 41. Great power conferred upon, 134. Opinion of the United States Government, 132.
Davis, of North Carolina debates the powers of the President, 47, 48.
Davis, Garrett, on subject of Mexican war, 152.
Declaration of Independence, language of, 86, 87, 16, 266.
Delaware, State of, 25, 283.
De Lolme, as to English Constitution, 111.
Democratic party reactionary, 97.
Denmark, government of, 296.
Departments created by Congress, 111
Deposits, removal of by Jackson, 138.
Derby, Lord, 277.
Dickinson opinions of, 282.
Diplomacy, ancient rules of, 68.
Douglas, Stephen H., 312. Introduced bill as to slaves in territories, 155.

INDEX.

Dogmas, political. 22.
Duane, dismissed by President **Johnson**, 138.

E.

Edmunds, Senator 40. Bill to regulate count. of 31.
Education, popular, 299.
Edward IV., 258.
Edward VI., reign of, 258.
Election, national, plan of, **32**. System of a lottery, 38.
Elective Majesty, title for **President**, 286.
Electoral **Colleges**, 21. Manner of counting vote, **126**. President represents the, 100.
Electoral Commission, **23**, **197**.
Electoral system, history of, **23, 24, 25**. Inequalities of, 284.
Electoral vote, effect of Senate upon, 284.
Electors, registering machines, 28.
Elizabeth, Parliaments dispensed with, by, **257, 258, 259, 260**.
Elliot, (*note*), 14, 26, 35, 64, 282.
Ellis, Gov., reply to proclamation, **164**.
Emancipation of Slaves, 208.
Emory, General, instructions to from President 105
England, Cabinet government in, 262. Constitution of 252, Conveyance to Pope Innocent of, **210**. Executive power of 253. Government of grown republican, 131. Laws of, compared with those of the United States, 99. Ministry of, 13. Treaty with, 250.
English Constitution, 12. As to prerogative of declaring war, 55. Prior to 1688, 252.
English Parliament, remarks upon 92.
Ephori, Grecian, 231.
Evarts, William M., words of, **199**.
Everett, Edward, 156.
Executive Council, members of, 303. Working of, **220**.
Executive and Congress, struggle between, **91, 149**.
Executive, assumption of powers of, 149. Patronage of, 77. Plural, 231. Policy, **119**. Power and organized conflict, 12. Qualifications of, 315. Removability of, 306. Sectional, 233.
Union of purse and sword in the, 149. Vigorous powers urged for, 112.
Expunging resolution, 141.

F

Farragut, **David G.**, Admiral's flag opinion of, 220.
Federal **Convention**, 30.
Federalist, the, **15, 23, 237, 238, 249**.
Fessenden, Senator, remarks of upon English Constitution, 92.
Field, D. D., **15**, (*note*), 281, (*note*). Recital of acts of President Grant, 188.
Fillmore, **Millard**, administration of, 155. His opinion of Tyler, 149.
Flower, R. P., **40**.
Fort Sumter, fired upon, 160.
Founders, views of, **234**.
Fox, Secretary, **264**.
France, government of, 230. Ministry of, 296. Treaty with, 250.
Franklin, Benj. opposed absolute veto 83. Apprehensions of, 231.
Freeman, Edward A., 268. Criticizes Presidential government, 116, (*note*).
French Revolution, 134.
Frye, debates, powers of President, 47.
Fugitive Slave Law, 158.

G

Gallatin, Albert, Adams' life of 248, Opinion of Treaty-making power by, 249. Opinion of Presidential power by, 248. Recollection of Jackson, 137.
Gambetta, Léon, 296.
Garfield, James A., **95, 100, 101**. Administration of, 204. Aggressive policy of, 211. Assassination of, **213**. Bargain of, **210**. Conversation upon distribution of power by, 213. Debates, the powers of the President, 48. Election of, **205, 210**. Experience as legislator, 312. Interpretation of oath by, **208**. Incapacity of, 304. Opinion of Hamilton by, **211**. Personal attacks upon, 39. Performed no act after he was shot, **211**. Reply to Cox by, **205, 206**.
Geography, determines availability of candidate, **41**.

George III., 13, 18, 35, 251, 266, 262. Deposition of, 217. Derangement of, 111. Fondness for power of, 267. Obstinacy of, **190**. Wishes not followed, 56.
Gerry, 24, 25, 35.
Gibb, 11, (*note*).
Gilpin, 14, 15, 26, 35, **282**, (*notes*).
Gladstone, Cabinet form by, **194**. Compares American and English systems, 36. Describes the British Cabinet 113, 114.
Godolphin, Lord, superintended campaigns of Marlborough, 58.
Government, development of, **10**. Evolution of, **314**. General and State powers of, **12**. Of England republican in respect to the Executive, 118. Of the people, 300. Personal, 258. Personal, dangers of, 315. Presidential criticized by Freeman, 116. Without responsible head, 215.
Governor of New York, election of, 218.
Grand Councils, existence of, 252.
Grant, U. S., 40, 79, 94, 312, 313. Action of, upon inauguration of President Hayes, 52. Administration of, 188. Arbitrary acts of, 188. As to West Indies, 68. Assignment of rank to, 191. Assigned to command the army, **54**. Charged with packing the U. S. Court, 82. Concentration of army at Washington by, 188. Menace to Hayti by, 189. Number of vetoes by, 85.
Granville, Lord, as to Regency of, 1812, 60.
Grayson, objection to mode of electing President by, 241, 242.
Greece, government of, 296.
Great Britain, ancient theories of embodied in U. S. Constitution, **84**. Unwritten Constitution of, 266.
Grenville, papers, 267.
Grevy, Jules, advocated the abolition of the Presidency in France, 43.
Grey, Lord, 277. As to Regency of 1812, 60. Griswold, Rufus, 248, **249**.

H

Habeas Corpus, 118, **165**, **178**.
Hale, point of order of, **197**.

Hallam, 158, (*note*) **219**.
Hamilton, Alexander, **248**. A report to Congress by, 115. As to appointment and removal, 72. As to electors, 24. As to electing Chief Magistrate, 26, 29. **Attacked, 244.** Discusses the powers of the President, as Commander, **49**. Dread of democracy by, 234. Early writings of, **235**. Etiquette arranged by, **212**. Favors strong executive, 35, **36**. Favored veto power, 83, 84. Model executive of, **15**, 16, His opinion as to pardoning power, 64. Opposition to consolidation of States by, 283. Theories of English law by, 236, 238. Theory of executive power by, 237, 239. Views in Federalist as to Commander-in-Chief, 44, 45.
Hampton, Wade, 190.
Hare, minority representation of, **298**.
Harris, George W., 284, (*note*).
Harrison, W. H., 312. Election of, 148. Selected by compromise, 148.
Haskell, debates the powers of the President.
Hawley, Senator, **100**.
Hayes, R. B., 31, 312, 313. Administration of, 196. As to power of veto, **94**. Inauguration of, 52. **Number** of vetoes by, 85. Policy of, 123. Refusal to protect States, **201**. Regal Acts of, 122. Voyage of argument by, 202.
Hayti, government of, **297**.
Henry III., **18**, VII., **259**, **260**. VIII., head of Church, 253, **255**, **259**, **260**.
Henry of Navarre, 213.
Henry, Patrick, 141. Opinion of Presidential power, 242.
Hero worship, extent of, 192.
Hewitt, A. S., 41.
Hoar, Senator, 113.
Hobbes, 191.
Hodges, Colonel, letter from President Lincoln to, 205.
Holden William H., appointed Governor, 183.
Holt, Judge Advocate, opinion upon writ of *habeas corpus*, 178.
Hosmer, G. W., 192, 256, 260, (*notes*).
House of Commons, a representative body, **273**. Power of, 290. Vote of want of confidence by, 276.
House of Lords, compelled to yield,

290. Formalities in, 286. Hamilton's views of, 238. Speaker of, 253. Has trial of impeachment, 103. Majority vote sufficient to impeach, 104. Negative power of, 273. Opposition to abolition of Slave Trade by, 292. Opposition to reform by, 292. Position of, 289. House of Representatives declare Acts of Polk unconstitutional, 151. Proposes the impeachment, 103, Powers of, 93, 100.
Hume, 272.
Hurd, of Ohio, as to threats of President, 95.
Hurd, J. C., 22, 311, (*notes*). Theory of our National Existence by, 309. Opinton of fetish worship by, 207.

I

Independent Treasury Bill, 148, 149.
Impeachment, English authorities for, 107, 108. Inefficiency of provisions of Constitution, 109. Ineffectualness of, 274. Provisions for, 103. What acts are required for, 106, 107, 108. Washington threatened with, 250.
Iredel, Justice, 311, (*note*).
Issues, discussion of, 274.
Italy, government of, 296.
Izard, speech of, 286.

J.

Jackson, Andrew, 39, 75, 101, 104, 148, 312. Administration of, that of personal government, 146, 147. Administration of, 136. Arrest of lawyer and judge by, 176. As to veto power, 85. Assumption to make laws by, 184. Character of, 136, 137. Claimed right to exercise powers as he understood them, 142. Distributes spoils of office, 76. His course referred to, 48. Stronger than Congress, 139. Wished to preserve the morals of the people, 142.
Jackson, Gov., reply to proclamation, 164.
Jacobinism, 245.
James I., notions of, 253. II., his

army a violation of law, 56. Honors conferred on Jeffreys by, 261.
Jay, John, 11, 13, 250, 311, (*notes*). 26, as to provisional President, 27. Treaty of, 248. Views of, 280.
Jefferson, Thomas, 11, 27, 65, (*notes*). 287, 314. Contested election of, 26, 27. Congress asked to suspend *habeas corpus* by, 166. Letter to Mazzei, 243. Letter to Senator Breckenridge by, 247. Made political removals, 137. Manner of exercising pardoning power, 64. Number of removals by, 74. Objection to Presidential power by, 243, 244, (*notes*). Purchase of Louisiana by, 246. Removal from office by, 245. Removed marshals and attorneys, 76. Sympathy with people by, 245. The initiator of the system of removals, 75.
Jeffreys, honors conferred on, 261.
Johnson, Andrew, 37, 81, 104, 105, 109, 120, 121, 185, 186, 191. Acts committed as Commander-in-Chief by, 183. Administration of, 181. Advised to march troops into Mexico, 45, 46. Amnesty and pardon proclaimed by, 182, 184. Articles of impeachment against, 105, 106. Assumption of power by, 14. Conflict with the people, 37. Conflict with Congress, 54, 104. Conduct of, 79, 80. Exercise of pardoning power by, 63. Number of vetoes by, 85. Power exercised by, 181. Usurped powers of Congress; called Confederate soldiers into Congress, 106.
Johnson, Alexander, 250, (*note*).
Judiciary, limitation of power of, 304.

K

Kansas Constitution, 155.
Kent, Chancellor, 150. Upholds power of executive, 74.
Kentucky resolutions, 245.
King, personal will of, 264. Ancient prerogative of, 12, 13. As to electors, 25, 35, (*note*). Colonies rebelled against reigning king, 11. Coronation oath of, 17, 18. Opinion of 81. Executive power by, 238. Power centred in, 253, 254,

INDEX. 323

255, 256. Prerogative of command of army restrained in 1688, 61. Tendency to abridge powers of in England, 113.
King John, act of, 210.
Knights of Shires, 287.

L

Lancaster, Presidential power by, 239, 240.
Lane, of Oregon, motion for recess by, 196.
Lafayette, Jefferson's letter to, 245.
Lawrence, W. B., 13, 21, 53, 217, (notes). Compares English and American Cabinet systems, 114, (note). Opinion of patronage of President, 82, (note). Theory of, 225, 226.
Laws, conflict of, 315.
Leavitt, Judge, writ of *habeas corpus* by, 174.
Lecompton Constitution, 155.
Lee, Richard H., speech of, 285.
Lee, Robert E., 79.
Legislation, law unto itself, 308. Special, 224.
Lexington, battle of, 11.
Lieber, 30, 280, 295, (note). Opinion of Jackson, by, 138. School of, 208.
Lincoln, Abraham, 37, 38, 80, 94. Assassination of, 163, 214. Blow at Representative Government by, 180. Call for troops by, 164. Congress summoned by, 164. Election of, 30. Emancipation by, 247. Escort of, 213. Extraordinary acts of,, 162. Increase of regular army by, 181. Interpretation of oath by, 208. Message of, 163. Nominated for Presidency, 159. Not ambitious, 13. Number of vetoes by, 85. Opinion as to constitutional limits by, (note), 205. Opinion on writ of *habeas corpus* by, 175. Opinion of his own acts, 164. Orders increase of regular army, 164. Proclamation of emancipation by, 178, 180. Re-election of, 194, suspension of *habeas corpus* by, 165. Vallandigham sent beyond military lines by, 175.
Lincoln, James, remarks upon Presidency by, 240.
Lincoln, Robert, 40.
Livingston, Robert R., Jefferson letter to, 246. Purchase of Louisiana by, 246, 247.
Logan, J. A., 40.
Louis XIV., 152, XVI. ridiculed, 86.
Louisiana Purchase, 208, 246.

M

Macaulay, 166, 268, 295, (note.)
MacMahon, 272. Resignation-of, 296.
Maclay William, journal of, 284.
Madison, James, 280. As to electors 25. As to impeachment, 107, 108. Number of vetoes, 85. Opinion as to pardoning power, 64. Opinion as to power of removal by, 74. Opinion as to Senate by, 282. Resolutions, 245. Urges a Council of States, 112.
Magna Charta, 18, 118, 256, 261.
Marlborough, campaigns of, 58.
Marsh, George P., letters of, 280.
Marshall, Chief Justice 75. 169 (note), 280. Opinion on *habeas corpus* by, 166.
Martin, Luther, (note), 65. As to impeachment, 109. Objection to Presidential system by, 240, 241. Opposed President during good behavior, 36. Opposed the veto power, 83.
Martin *vs.* Mott, 171, (note). Upholds power of President to call for troops, 51.
Mason, George, 14, 15, 30. (note). Against powers of the President, 46, 240. As to treaties, (note), 70. Opinion of pardoning power, 64.
May, Sir Erskine, 262, 267, 278, (note).
Mazzini, 272.
McCulloch *vs.* State of Maryland, (note), 139.
McClurg, 35.
McDonald, 41.
McPherson, History of Rebellion by, 169, (note).
Merryman, John, arrest of, 166.
Mexico, boundary line of, 151.
Mexico, government of, 297. Texas separated from, 151. War of, 208.
Military administration subordinate to civil government, 60.
Mill, John Stuart, 300, (note), 272. Argument against two Houses by, 292, 293, 294. Minority representation of, 298.
Miller, objection to Presidential power by, 240.

Ministers, powers of prior to 1688, 111. Responsibility of, 263.
Missouri Compromise advocated, by Clay, 155, 248.
Monarch, arbitrary acts of, 256. Power of exercised, 136.
Monarchy, elective, 21, 42 232. Absolute, 34. Disguised, 315.
Monroe, James, as to impeachment, 109. Number of vetoes, 85. Number of removals. 74. Purchase of Louisiana by, 247.
Morris, Gouverneur, 246, 248. As to electors, 241. Opinion of executive power by, 238. President for life advocated by, 194.
Morrill, Senator, against the Pendleton bill, 117.
Morton, Archbishop, 259.
Mutiny Act, provisions of, 56.

N

Napoleon I., 13, 295, (*note*). War against, 58.
Napoleon III., 117, (*note*), 272.
Nation, whether the Union constitutes a, 155.
National, theory, 281. **Church, 255.**
Nepotism, 189.
Netherlands, government of, 296.
New, of Indiana, 98.
New York, State of, 283. **Opposition to two** Houses by, 288.
Nichols, 199.
Nicolas, Sir H., 266, (*note*).
Niles Register, 67, 150, (*note*).
North and South, views of Slavery by, 225.
North Carolina, governor appointed for, 183.
North, Lord, administration of, 263
Norway, government of, 297.
Nueces, River of, 151.

O

O'Conor, **Charles, theories of, 221,** 224.
Office, removal from, **72. Term of,** 34. Tenure of, 74.
Oregon Boundary, 208.

P

Packard, **Gov.**, not protected, 123, 190.
Paine, Thomas, Jefferson's letter to, 245.
Paley, as to English Constitution, 111.
Palmerston, Lord, as to war with Russia, 57.
Palo Alto, 154.
Panmure, Lord, as to directions of military affairs, 58,
Parliament, early history of, 288. English, 92. Power of, 256. Triennial, 277.
Parsons, Theophilus, opinion on *habeas corpus* by, 174.
Party, demands of, 66.
Patronage bribery, a science, 129.
Patterson, spoke against powers of President, 46.
Peace President in time of war, 38.
Peck, James L., impeachment of, 104.
Pendleton, Judge E., opposed the form of impeachment, 109.
Pendleton, Senator, G. H., bill of, to admit Secretaries to floor of Congress, 116, 117. Remarks in support of his bill, 118
People, address to the, 91. Duty of power-holders of, 208. Questions to be submitted to, 67, 306. Appeal to, 97, 305.
Personal Liberty bills, 158.
Petition of Rights, 118, 261.
Pickering, John, impeachment of, 104.
Pierce, F., 92, 101, 312. No sympathy with liberty, 93, 155. Number of vetos by, 85.
Pierpont, Francis H., appointed Governor of Virginia, 182.
Pinckney, Charles, 15, 26. Opinion as to Senate by, 282.
Pitt, Wm , memoirs of, 217. As to war with Russia, 56.
Plantagenet, England, 258. Kings, 262. Prerogatives of, 166.
Plimsoll, bill of, 276.
Polignac, Duke of, 39.
Polk, J. K., 104. Action upon question of boundary line of Texas, 151, 152, 153, 154. Administration of, 148. Arraigned, 153. Claimed to be the government, 152. Course toward England and Mexico, 152. Declared war against Mexico, 151,

INDEX. 325

152. Election of, 150. Number of vetoes by, 85.
Pomeroy, J. N., 11, 18, 71, 280, (*notes*).
Porter, objection to presidential power by, 240.
Portugal, government of, 297.
Power, one-man, 68.
President, a check against Congress, 94. A ruler, 113. Acts of unconstitutional, 151. Amnesty proclaimed by, 182. Ancient power of, 253. Assumption of power by, 21, 136. Authority to call forth the militia, by, 198. Bargains made by, 202. Beyond reach of the people, 125, (*note*). Contests in the election of, 196. Danger from the power exercised by the, 141. Difficulty in the removal of, 274. Despotic acts of, 103, 154. Duty of, 280. Elected by colleges, 160. Election of, demoralizing, 130. Election of, forced when there is no issue, 39. Election in 1876 of, 29. Eligibility for re-election, 38. Empowered to bribe his judges, 109. Exercises unconstitutional powers, 96. Family of, 220. Flag of, 219. For life, advocated, 36. Head of co-ordinate department, 18, 119. Increase of powers of, 261. Influence and power of, 232, 233. King of Great Britain, compared with, 235, 236. Legislative power of, 101. Manner of conducting treaties, 67. May use unfair means to re-elect himself, 38. Monarchical powers of, 10, 20, 197. Oath of, 17. Of Confederate States, extraordinary powers of, 134. Office of treated as captured fortress, 137. Pardoning powers of, 64, 65, 66. Power as commander-in-chief, 154. Powers and duties of, 17, 18, 19, 20. Power of appointment and removal, 72. Power of veto conferred upon, 83, 94. Power over army, navy, and militia, 61. Power to appoint Judges of Supreme Court, 81. Power to grant reprieves, pardons, and make treaties, 63. Power to make Treaties, 66. Power to involve nation in foreign war, 70. Salary of, 218. Succession of 23. System of choosing the, 23, Title for, 286, 287. Unrepublican manner of making speeches, 120.
Unyielding powers of, 262. Usurpations of, 109, 139, 142, 152. Vetoes by the, 186. War declared by, 62. When he should be removed, 156. Will of rules, 110.
Presidency, abolition of, 16, 302. Availability for, 312. Interregnum in, 313. Newspapers, nominate for, 41.
Press, of the South, indications of, 135.
Prime Minister, powers of, 275.
Prince of Wales, 217.
Privy Council, belonged to person of King, 113. Old form of, 295.

Q.

Queen, a figure head, 14, 113. Executive power of, 261, 307.

R.

Randolph, Edmund, electoral system by, 24.
Randolph, John, opinion of Jefferson by, 195. His opinion of pardoning power, 64.
Rawlins, objections to Presidential power by, 240.
Raymond, H. L., his opinion of stretch of power by Tyler, 150.
Reform Acts, 277.
Representative Government, 279.
Reprieves, Presidents' power to grant, 63.
Republican Aristocracy, 127.
Returns, duplicate set of, 31. Two sets of, 196.
Rice, Isaac L., conveyance of England described by, 210.
Richard II., powers claimed by, 256, 257. III., 258.
Rifle Clubs, 98.
Rights of man, 243.
Rio Grande, claimed as boundary line of Texas, 151.
Rives, N. C., 39.
Robeson, debates the powers of the President, 46, 48.
Rockingham, Lord, administration of, 264.
Romilly, life of, 264, (*note*).
Rosenthal, Lewis, 283, (*note*).

Rotten Boroughs, **House of Lords in** favor of, 291.
Royal prerogative prior to 1688, **111**.
Ruler, acme of **power of,** 9.
Russell, Lord **John, as to** Oregon boundary, 67. Reform bill of, 277. As to powers of Secretary of State for War, 57, 58.
Russia, government of, 297. War against, 57.
Rutledge, recommends Privy Council for President, **112**.

S.

Sacheverell, Doctrine, impeachment of, 108.
Saint-Just, views of, (*note*), 283.
Schools, common, 299.
Secession, doctrine of, 245. Ordinances passed, 160.
Secretaries, face to face with Congress, 118. Report to Congress in person by, 115.
Secretary of State for War to control the Admiralty in time of war, 59.
Secretary of War, powers of, 308.
Senate, abolition of, 224. A Privy Council to President, 109. Argument against, 287. Constitution in relation to, 281, 282. Effect upon electoral vote by, 284. Formalities of, 285, 286. Inequalities in, 283. Not Republican, 93. Should be consulted by President, 69. To choose Vice-President, 26. Trial of impeachment by, 103. Two-thirds vote required for impeachment by, 104.
Seward, W. H., 246, 312. As to powers of House, 92.
Sherman, Roger, powers of Executive by, 24, 186, 302.
Sheridan, 264.
Silver and Chinese Bills, vetoes of, 85.
Slave, a personal chattel, 156.
Slavery, agitation of, 155. Protected by Confederate States, 133.
Slaves, emancipation of, 105.
Sloat, Commodore, **commands given** to by President, 152.
Smith, Goldwin, arguments against two-house system by, 291. Opinion of President Buchanan, 161, (*notes*). Opinion of Elective Presidency, (*note*), 159. Theory of, 226, 227.
South Carolina, Governor imprisoned in, 199. Nullification in, 245.
South American Governments, 230, 297.
Spain, government of, 297.
Spencer, Herbert, 260, 303, (*notes*).
Spencer, Joseph, objection to Presidential power by, 240.
Sparks, 13, 98.
Springer, 98.
Spoils to the victors, 14.
Stamp Act, 267.
Stanton, Edwin **M.,** 246. Removal of, 104.
Star of the West, 160.
State Governments, sectional strife result of, 315.
State Department **of,** created **by an** Act of Congress, 110.
State Lines, obliteration of, 282, 283.
States, multiplicity of laws of, 314.
State Sovereignty, **12.** A heresy, 97. Theory of, 281.
Stern, S., 20, (*note*).
Stevens, Alex. H., remarks of upon constitution of Confederate States, 132.
Stickney, Albert, 66, (*note*). Work of, 157.
Story, Mr. Justice, opinion of, as to power of President to command the militia, 53. Opinion of power of removal, 72.
Story, school of, 208.
Stoughton, E. **W., as** member of cabinet, (*note*), **110.**
Strong, Caleb, 24, (*note*).
Stuart kings, 260, **262.**
Stubbs, 259, 266, (*notes*).
Succession, subject of, 217, 218.
Sumner, Charles, arraignment of President Grant by, 189, 191. Assaulted, 156. Speech of on caucus, 127, 128.
Sumner, W. S., 37, 42, (*notes*). On the subject of presidential intrigues, 158.
Supreme Court, location of sovereignty by, 309.
Surrey, Lord, 264.
Sweden, Government of, 297.
Switzerland, Constitution of, 226. Government of, 297. Upper House in, 289.

INDEX.

Talleyrand, 295, (*note*).
Taney, chief Justice appointed by Jackson, 138, decisions of, 156, opinion upon writ *habeas corpus* by, 166, 169.
Tariff, for revenue only, 39.
Taswell-Langmead, T. G., 253, 266, 273, 275, 277, (*notes*).
Taylor, Zachary, 312, administration of, 155.
Tennyson, 272.
Territories, bill of Douglas in relation to, 155.
Texas V. White, (*note*), 309.
Texas, annexation of, 150, boundary line of, 151, independence of Mexico, 151.
Theories, O'Conor, Lawrence, Smith, and Bartley, their, 221.
Third Term, discussion of, 194, 195.
Thomas, President Johnson conspired with, 105.
Thompson, his opinion of power of veto, appointment and removal, 150.
Tibbitts, 22, 29, 303 (*note*), members of the Cabinet to be interpellated, 114, 115, (*notes*).
Tilden, Samuel, 23, 41, claims he was defrauded, 137.
Times, New York, circular letter of, 38, 39.
Tocqueville, Alexis de, Democracy in America by, 280.
Todd, Alpheus, work on Parliamentary Government, 56, 237 (*note*).
Traill, 268, (*note*).
Treaties, president's power to make, 66.
Treaty, power of making, 249.
Trent, affair, 71.
Trollope's Life of Cicero, 162.
Tudor kings, 71, 257, 260, 262.
Tucker, of Virginia, 99, 100.
Tyler, John, 104, vetoes by, 85, 149, action upon question of boundary line of Texas, 150, administration of, 148, his cabinet resigned, 149, hostile to Congress, 149.

U.

United States Bank, 149. Troops of, ordered by President into Mexico, 152.
Upshur, 20, (*note*),

V.

Vallandigham, Clement L., arrest of 174.
Van Buren, Martin, 39, 66, (*note*). Administration of, 148.
Vessels, Naval, uses of, 218.
Veto, Clay's speech upon, 87, 61. Power conferred upon the President, 83. Power of, exercised by Pierce, 155. Power of, exercised, 139, 150.
Vice-President, assumption of office of President not contemplated in selection of, 216. Election of, 26. Perfunctory life of, 216. Right of judgment of inability of President of, 216. Unexpired term of, 37.
Virginia Resolution, 281.
Virginia, State of, proclamation in regard to, 182.
Voltaire, 295, (*note*).
Von Holst, 11, 55, 126, 129, 139, 151, 152, 248, 281, 302, (*notes*). Cites many cases upholding powers of President, 51.

W.

Wade, upon rights of the House, 93.
Walpole, Spencer, 259, (*note*).
War, declaration of, vests with responsible ministers, 55, 56.
War Department, property of, seized, 105.
War Minister, under British Constitution responsible, 45.
War Power, Government subjugated by, 191.
War Powers, 162.
War President, in time of peace, 38.
Warren, 73, (*notes*).
Washington, George, 11, 13, 15, 248, 250, 312. Administration of, 249, 250. As to veto power, 85. Attacked, 250. Character of, 73. Election of, 263. Inauguration of, 285, 286. Opinion of third term, 193. Recommendation for Convention by, 263. Threatened Assassination of, 250. Title for, 287.
Washington, Mr. Justice, opinion as to powers of President, 52.
Watterson, 41.

Webster, D., 11, 38, 31, 73, 129, 280, 312, (*notes*). Approved of power of removal, 75. Debate of, 155. School of, 208. Speech against power of veto, (*note*), 140, 141. Speech against the President determining law, 143, 144, (*notes*). Subject of obedience to executive will, 87.
Wellington, Lord, as to powers of Commander-in-Chief, 60.
Whelpley, Samuel, (*note*), 125.
White *v.* Hart, 279.
White House, appropriations for, 219.
White League, 99.
Wilkes, persecution of, (*note*) 267.
Wilkinson, General, movement of troops by, 247.

William and Mary, reigns of, 56.
William the Silent, 213.
Williams, of Wisconsin, claims powers for the President, 47.
Williamson, as to electors, 24. Plan of executive by, 231. Prediction of, 14.
Wilson, James, 24, 25. Favored the veto power, 84.
Wilson, Henry, 156.
Wilson, Thomas W., opinion of Cabinet Government, 113, (*note*).
Wolsey, taxation by, 259.
Wright, Silas, 39.

Y.

Yates, Chief Justice, 288.
York and Lancaster, houses of, 257.

WORKS OF REFERENCE.

Works, decisions, statutes, and magazine articles, which, among others, have been consulted, quoted, or referred to in the preparation of this book.

Works of John Adams.
American Archives.
American Republic, by Brownson.
Administrations of Washington and J. Adams.
Webster's Speeches and Arguments, Boston, 1843.
Jefferson, by Morse.
An Introduction to the Constitutional Law of the United States, by John Norton Pomeroy.
Republican Superstitions, by M. D. Conway.
Writings of William B. Lawrence in *North American Review.*
The Papers of James Madison, Elliot and Gilpin's editions.
The Debates in the several State Conventions on the adoption of the Federal Constitution, by Jonathan Elliot.
The Constitution of the United States, by Simon Sterne.
The Nature and Character of the Federal Government, by Upshur.
Reform in Federal Executive, by George Mortimer Tibbits.
The Theory of Our National Existence, by J. C. Hurd.
Civil Government, by Lieber.
Method of Electing the President, by Thomas W. Cooley.
History of the Formation of the Constitution of the United States, by George Bancroft.
Writings of Prof. William G. Sumner in *Princeton Review.*
Memoirs of J. Q. Adams.
Various Reports of the Decisions of the Supreme Court.
Statutes at Large.

Kent's Commentaries.
Story's Commentaries.
Constitution of the United States, by Paschal.
Constitutional and Political History of the United States, by Von Holst.
True Republic, by Stickney.
Nile's Register.
Private Correspondence of H. Clay.
Civil Liberty, by Lieber.
Sketches of Debate in the First Senate of the United States, by George W. Harris.
Writings of E. W. Stoughton in *North American Review.*
Writings of Thomas W. Wilson in *International Review.*
Historical Essay on Presidential Government, by Freeman.
Compend of History, by Samuel Whelpley.
Writings of J. E. Chamberlin in *International Review.*
Rise and Fall of the Confederate Government, by Jefferson Davis.
Life and Times of H. Clay, by Colton.
Life of Jackson, by Sumner.
The Great Speeches and Orations of Daniel Webster, by Edwin P. Whipple.
Writings of Prof. Goldwin Smith in *Bystander* and *Contemporary Review.*
Life of Cicero, by Anthony Trollope.
History of England, by Lord Macaulay.
History of the Rebellion, by M'Pherson.
The Powers of the Executive Department of the Government of the United States, by Alfred Conkling.
Pitkin's History.
Writings of Judge Black in *North American Review.*
Writings of D. D. Field in *North American Review.*
The People and Politics, by G. W. Hosmer.
John Randolph, by Adams.
Letter of Abraham Lincoln to Col. Hodger.
A Definition of Liberty, by Isaac L. Rice, in *North American Review.*
Essay by Chauncey F. Black.
Tomline, Memoirs of William Pitt.
Parliamentary Government, by Alpheus Todd.
History of American Politics, by Alexander Johnson.
English Constitutional History, by Thomas Pitt Taswell-Langmead.
Political Disquisitions, by Burgh.
Electorate and the Legislature, by Spencer Walpole.
Constitutional History of England, by Stubbs.
Constitutional History of England from George III., by Sir Erskine May.
English Constitution, by Walter Bagehot.
Political Institutions, by Herbert Spencer.
Almon's Parliamentary Register.

Life of Romilly.
Preface to Proceedings of Privy Council, by Sir H. Nicolas.
Walpole's Memoirs.
Rockingham's Memoirs.
Fox's Memoirs.
Works of Lord Brougham.
The Growth of English Constitution, by Edward A. Freeman.
Central Government, by Traill.
Democracy in America, by Alexis de Tocqueville.
America and France, by Lewis Rosenthal.
Statesman's Year Book, by Martin.
Considerations on Representative Government, by John Stuart Mill.
The Constitutional Convention, by Jameson.
English Government in the reign of Charles II., by Sheldon Amos.
English Government, by Cox.
Encyclopædia Britannica.
History of the Civil War in America, by Draper.
Messages of the Presidents.
The Federalist.
The American Conflict, by Greeley.
Life of Alexander Hamilton, by F. C. Hamilton and Judge Shea.
Life and Letters of Gouverneur Morris, by Sparks.
Life of Aaron Burr, by Davis.
Benton's Thirty Years in the United States' Senate.
The Conduct of the War.
The Impeachment of President Johnson.
Popular Progress in England, by James Routledge.
Historic Americans, by Theodore Parker.
American Politics, by Fenton and Cooper.
Blackstone Commentaries.
Ballot Act of 1871, 31 and 32 Vict.
Fifty Years of English Constitution, by Sheldon Amos.
France since the First Empire, by James McDonell.
Life of Albert Gallatin, by Adams.
Hallam's Works.
Macaulay's Essays.
McPherson's Political Manual.
The Nation, by Mulford.
Political Recollections, by Julian.
Palgrave's Lectures on the House of Commons.
Primer of the English Constitution, by Sheldon Amos.
Reform Act of 1871, 30 and 31 Vict.
Life of Chief Justice Taney.
Fisher Ames, Works of.
Karl Heinzen, Writings of.
Le Pouvoir Exécutif aux Etats-Unis, par Adolphe de Chambrun.

www.ingramcontent.com/pod-product-compliance
Lightning Source LLC
Chambersburg PA
CBHW021200230426
43667CB00006B/488